APPLIED DECISION ANALYSIS

McGraw-Hill Series in Quantitative Methods for Management

Consulting Editor

Martin K. Starr, *Columbia University*

APPLIED DECISION ANALYSIS

Derek W. Bunn

Fellow of Worcester College
Oxford University

McGraw-Hill Book Company

New York   St. Louis   San Francisco   Auckland   Bogotá   Hamburg
Johannesburg   London   Madrid   Mexico   Montreal   New Delhi
Panama   Paris   São Paulo   Singapore   Sydney   Tokyo   Toronto

This book was set in Times Roman.
The editor was Cheryl L. Mehalik;
the production supervisor was Marietta Breitwieser.
The drawings were done by Danmark & Michaels, Inc.

APPLIED DECISION ANALYSIS

1234567890   HALHAL   8987654

ISBN 0-07-008292-8

Library of Congress Cataloging in Publication Data

Bunn, Derek W.
    Applied decision analysis.

    (McGraw-Hill series in quantitative methods for
management)
    Includes bibliographies and indexes.
    1. Decision-making—Mathematical models.
I. Title.   II. Series.
HD30.23.B86   1984   658.4′033   83-19643
ISBN 0-07-008292-8

CONTENTS

PREFACE

Applied Decision Analysis takes a practical perspective in the study of techniques to aid decision makers faced with complex problems. It emphasizes the decomposition of large problems into more manageable elements and the personal relationship of the decision maker to a decision model. Techniques for the construction of quantitative decision models are developed as devices for testing the coherence (self-consistency) of the decision maker's own reasoning, values, and opinions, not as replacements for a decision maker's own deliberations. The focus is on the development of formal procedures to aid an individual's reasoning, not on group decision making or the organization of management decisions.

This book has evolved from the author's teaching notes to students in business, engineering, and economics at the universities of Oxford, Stanford, Southern California, and London. It is particularly suitable to students in MBA programs who have had a very elementary introduction to statistics. A large number of questions have been included, and solutions to most of them can be found in the manual available from the publisher.

The comments of many students are gratefully acknowledged, but particularly those of Mike Addison, Gus Carey, and Ian Wycherley. The consulting editor, Martin Starr, the publishing editor, Don Mason, and several referees made numerous constructive comments on earlier versions. I am grateful to the Literary Executor of the late Sir Ronald A. Fisher, F.R.S., and the Longman Group Ltd., London, for permission to reprint part of Table III from their book *Statistical Tables for Biological, Agricultural and Medical Research* (6th ed., 1974), and to the delegates of Oxford University Press for permission to publish past examination questions. I am also grateful to David Davies of Fulmer Research Laboratories, Bruce Judd of Applied Decision Analysis, Daniel Owen of Strategic Decisions Group, and Syed Shariq of SRI International for their permission to include some of their works in this volume. Finally, I am very pleased to acknowledge the support of Stanford and Oxford Universities in the preparation of the manuscript.

Derek W. Bunn

APPLIED DECISION ANALYSIS

ONE

ON THE NATURE OF DECISION ANALYSIS

1.1 DECISION MAKING

Decision making is a ubiquitous activity inherent to the behavior of individuals, organizations, and society. Ackoff and Emery (1971, 1972) have described decision making as a characteristic of "purposeful" systems. A corollary of this is that the extent and importance of decision-making activities within a system will depend upon the motivation with which it is seeking to attain objectives, targets, or goals. Evidently, a system (and this includes an individual) which possesses no purpose has no decision problems.

In the managerial context, Simon (1960) has stated: "Decision-making comprises three principal phases: finding occasions for making decisions; finding possible courses of action; and choosing among courses of action."

Indeed, Simon treats the subject matter of decision making as being synonymous with the entire study of management. *Decision analysis* is now conventionally understood to be a special topic within this domain, and, accordingly, our aims in this course will be far more modest in scope. In fact, the main focus of decision analysis is upon the last of Simon's phases of decision making, namely, that of choosing among courses of action. Furthermore, its perspective is essentially normative and methodological. How should a sensible decision maker choose between several courses of action where the associated outcomes are subject to many uncertainties? How should a sensible decision maker compare ventures with high and low risks? How can outcomes be evaluated that are composed of many, possibly conflicting factors? How can the worth of potential new sources of information be assessed? These are just a few of the methodological preoccupations of decision analysts.

Ultimately, decision analysts seek basic principles to help a decision maker choose between several, possibly very complicated options. They are not primarily concerned with augmenting the body of knowledge in particular decision-making situations (e.g., finance, marketing, or production), but in developing a framework of methods generalizable, ideally, to all decision problems. The style of decision analysis is therefore often quite abstract, although its practical motivation is never forgotten nor its real applicability more than one step away. Hence, a course in decision analysis is the study of a method rather than a context.

A question that might reasonably be posed at this point is, why we should need a general methodology for analyzing decisions in practice. Academically, this may be a viable descriptive field of study, but why should we presume that its basic normative purpose of aiding decision makers in practice is necessary? Is it not the case that a manager's job is to make decisions; that through his or her personal development as a manager, the quality of the individual's intuitive decision making improves; that only good managers reach positions of authority; and that, therefore, the really important decisions, by design, receive the highest skills in decision making? Furthermore, is not decision making the principal acquired skill of a manager and, thereby, the essence of his or her professional pride? Under these postulates is it not futile, or even an affront to suggest that managers need help in their decision making? That expert advice should be solicited on technical matters is readily granted, but that help in the form of fundamental principles of reasoning, devoid of the problem context, should be necessary, may be less readily conceded.

To the above argument, even the least cynical business student would suggest that an overly idealistic view of the managerial process is being conceived. Management promotions are based upon many factors, and in particular, there does not appear to be any clear evidence that the main consideration is an objective evaluation of decision-making ability. In part this may be due to the difficulty in measuring decision-making ability in "objective" terms. However, even if it is substantially true that decision making is an acquired skill of managers, this does not denigrate the need for would-be managers to study basic principles or for experienced managers to reevaluate their techniques. Furthermore, apart from the "training" role of decision analysis in management education, there is now the professional activity of decision analysis in management consulting. Over the past 10 years, there has been an extraordinary growth in this sort of activity. In addition to large established consulting organizations setting up specific decision analysis groups, there have been many new consulting groups exclusively concerned with this work. The success of these operations apparently demonstrates a need on the part of managers for external help of a fundamental kind in their decision making. Finally, there is ample evidence that even experienced practitioners are often systematically inconsistent in their decisions—Howard (1980) gives references on this. Thus, there are several compelling arguments to support the usefulness of the type of contribution that decision analysis seeks to make to the overall managerial decision-making process. In other words, the role that it seeks to play in the decision-making process appears to be worthwhile, at least in principle.

Descriptively, the process through which decisions are made is capable of several forms of categorization. A common distinction is between procedures that are (1) intuitive, (2) programmed, and (3) analytical.

Intuitive decisions are those choices which individuals make instinctively, without conscious thought as to the alternatives and their relative evaluations. Either innately or through habit and experience, we just know what to do in certain situations. In other situations, while we may not know instinctively what to do, we may have a set of strict guidelines or instructions to follow. This would be a programmed decision, which, in principle, should be capable of being automated. Finally, there are those important decisions about which we have to think carefully. We do not know by instinct or instruction how to cope with the problem satisfactorily. We must analyze the possible actions and their consequences. Some scientists would argue that it is only when a decision-making situation requires the analytical approach that there is any real decision as such. If the analytical approach is not required, then the situation is not problematical and, ipso facto, does not constitute a decision problem. Howard (1980) is taking this view when he asserts that "decision making is what you do when you do not know what to do."

Evidently, there is a learning issue involved in this distinction. Consider a production problem concerned with manufacturing a new component. First of all, with no experience of its manufacture, production engineers have to *analyze* the decision how best to design the manufacturing process. Thereafter, having developed a process, subsequent production will be *programmed* according to specified procedures. Ultimately, after much experience, the production controller may be operating the manufacture of these components *intuitively*, with his or her mind perhaps devoted to higher, more pleasant, metaphysical thoughts (dinner, baseball, the Aegean, etc.).

Now, even within the overall analytical approach to decision making, there are grades of sophistication. In many circumstances, decision makers are content to use crude heuristics for certain types of decisions, whereas for others, a long and detailed analysis of possible events and contingencies would be considered necessary. To an extent, the sophistication of analysis depends upon the importance of the decision, its uniqueness, the need to communicate cogently a justification for the decision to others, and, ultimately, upon the managerial style of the individual. The analytical approach to be presented here will be of an ideal type, with the "perfect" analysis requiring infinite care in the deliberations of the decision maker. It will be a model of consistency to which all conscientious decision makers should aspire!

Evidently, just how far down this road any particular decision maker chooses to go in practice will again depend upon personal and circumstantial factors. Pragmatically, the analysis should proceed only up to the point at which the decision maker feels that the insights gained are a comfortable basis for action and that further time and analytical effort cannot be justified.

1.2 ELEMENTS OF DECISION ANALYSIS

The decision analysis method is truly analytical in that its basic philosophy is to break down a decision problem into component parts, thereby allowing a decision maker to focus separately upon the critical issues. A complex decision problem is not viewed holistically, but as an assemblage of individual features. Thus, a decision problem can be decomposed into components, each of which is subjected to evaluation by the decision maker. The individual components are then re-composed to give overall insights and recommendations on the original problem. In theory, decision makers who are stunned by the overwhelming complexity of the original problem should be able to articulate their astuteness effectively on the simplified components and hence, by construction, eventually face the total problem with confidence. The pattern of relationships that is devised to allow the problem to be so decomposed is often referred to as the *decision model*, or the *structure* of the problem.

Problem complexity is, therefore, the motivating force behind this desire for analysis. Most decision problems of any seriousness will be complicated by one or more of the following features:

1. *Uncertainty.* Decision making under uncertainty is the principal arena within which the methodology of decision analysis performs. Indeed, the primary function of decision analysis, as it was originally developed, was to aid a decision maker's evaluation of options whose eventual outcomes were not known for certain (Raiffa and Schlaifer, 1961). How can you choose a course of action when you do not know exactly what is going to happen?

2. *Multiple objectives.* More recently, one of the main impacts of decision analysis has been to provide useful descriptions to deal with options whose outcomes have multiple, often conflicting attributes (Keeney and Raiffa, 1976). For example, decisions on siting a new nuclear power station require evaluations of the cost, reliability, safety, health, and environmental attributes. How can you trade off different evaluations on the separate attributes?

3. *Multiple options.* The development of reliable screening procedures to eliminate "dominated" (inferior) options is an important part of the decision analysis function of simplification. But how can you obtain powerful simplifications without the risk of missing crucial points through oversimplification?

4. *Sequentiality.* Many decision problems are multiple-stage in that they envisage a sequence of future decisions contingent upon those taken previously and in response to any new information and events occurring in the process. For example, the decision to launch a new product will envisage a future set of contingency plans to be enacted according to how the market responds and evolves over the product's life cycle. Elucidation of strategic options open to the decision maker has been another one of the practical successes of the structuring aspect of decision analysis (Watson, 1982). Associated with this has been the development of powerful techniques to evaluate the worth of new information at particular moments in the sequence of decision making.

The above features, and a few others, will comprise the basic methodological preoccupations of this course. Much more will, therefore, be said of each of them in due course. However, at this stage it is still appropriate to ponder a few more moments on the impact of uncertainty on decision making. This involves a fundamental decomposition in decision analysis, namely, the separation of uncertainty and value.

Uncertainty complicates a decision problem in two ways, (1) through the difficulty of dealing with random variables and (2) through the risk that it introduces into the selection of any option. Thus, in assessing the chances of a particular outcome — for example, the revenue from the development of a new product — a whole causal sequence of uncertain variables may have to be evaluated, such as stages in the R & D program, costs, prices, volume of sales, timing, etc. (case 1). This might be quite an elaborate decomposition of many random variables. Furthermore, because each outcome must be evaluated in the face of uncertainty, the attitude of the decision maker toward risk must be modeled (case 2). For example, suppose you were offered an opportunity in which you would either gain $5 or lose $1 with equal probabilities. You might think that the odds are in your favor and that you should, therefore, accept the opportunity. Suppose now that the situation stays the same, but the payoffs are $5 million if you win or $1 million if you lose. The odds are still in your favor, just as before; only the units of the payoffs have changed. Do you still find it as attractive? Can you take a loss of $1 million just as comfortably as that of $1 before? Maybe if you are not the typical impecunious student or average businessperson, but a very large corporation or multimillionaire, you would still find the odds attractive. However, assuming only an aversion to bankruptcy on your part, it is clear that the scale of payoffs can be continually increased to deter all of you from the wager. Hence the problem of dealing with risk in decision analysis.

Decision analysis must therefore provide a consistent, general method of evaluating uncertain options, which adequately takes into account the risk attitude of the decision maker. It has achieved this through a basic separation of uncertainty and value.

Consider again our original proposition and call it option A:

Option A: −$1 with probability 0.5

or

$5 with probability 0.5

Compare this now with option B:

Option B: −$1 with probability 0.6

or

$5 with probability 0.4

Assuming you prefer more money to less, you should prefer option A to option B because the probability of winning is higher. That is, this is only an issue of relative *uncertainties*.

Consider now option C:

Option C: −$2 with probability 0.5

or

$5 with probability 0.5

Again, assuming only that you prefer more to less, you will choose A over C, because if you lose, it will not be so much. This is now just an issue of *value*.

Comparing A with B and A with C illustrates this basic separation of value and uncertainty in decision analysis. In the above examples, these notions appear quite simple. The power of decision analysis is to turn such simple notions into prescribing how a decision maker should choose between more complicated tasks. Even in the above examples it is not obvious how the decision maker should choose between B and C, if those were the only two options. Which would you prefer? Why?

To consider a less simplistic situation, recall the issues involved in evaluating candidates in the nuclear plant siting example. The candidate sites involve issues of cost, reliability, health, safety, and environmental impact, each of which will be fraught with uncertainties. More specifically, consider one like the mortality risks associated with possible radioactive leakages. There is a chance that any facility's safety systems will fail, which will lead to a number of fatalities in the surrounding neighborhoods. Such risks are unpleasant to think about and horrible to quantify, yet decision analysts do address these problems (Keeney, 1980). Although many different styles of analysis are undertaken, the traditional decomposition would be to consider several levels of fatalities (such as <10, $10-100$, $100-1000$, $1000-10,000$). For each event (level of fatalities) the decision maker would separately (1) determine the chance of it happening and (2) value the seriousness of the event if it did happen. The chance of an event happening is usually quantified by means of a probability. The value of an event is also usually measured quantitatively by some form of index. Some people may be of the opinion that human life is priceless and, therefore, cannot be placed upon a scale that compares it to monetary costs. Public policy makers evidently do not take this position, as human life trade-offs are implicit in most of their decisions. (The fact that we are allowed to drive automobiles is ample testimony to that.) Nevertheless, valuing human life is a difficult problem and normally requires further decomposition in a decision analysis. Likewise, assessing the probability of one of those levels of fatalities actually occurring will require further decomposition in the form of identifying the causal sequence of activities necessary for such an event. Ultimately, through a procedure of decomposition and recomposition, the sites will be evaluated in terms of the value of each possible event and the associated uncertainty.

Having achieved this separation of uncertainty and value for each possible outcome, the task of decision analysis then, in its recomposition phase, is to provide a suitable criterion for the decision maker to combine the assessed probabilities and evaluations in a manner in keeping with his or her attitude toward risk. It will be shown that the criterion of expected utility does just this (Chapter 3), and that it is readily generalizable to the multiple objective complications as well (Chapter 5).

Thus, the typical decision model consists of the following two characteristic features: (1) *structural specification*, which includes decision variables, outcome variables, structural relationships, and parameters; and (2) *criterial specification*, of which the criterion for comparing uncertain outcomes is an example.

The structural specification consists essentially of a description of the options open to the decision maker (decision variables), the various things that might happen contingent upon the option chosen (outcome variables), and the way in which outcomes are determined, partially or completely, by the options (structural relationships and parameters). The criterial specification embodies the decision maker's method of evaluating the outcomes. Should the outcomes be evaluated only in monetary terms, or should other factors (for example, environmental or health impacts) be considered as well? How should a decision maker trade off low-value/high-probability "safe" outcomes against high-value/low-probability "risky" outcomes?

Example: Personal savings portfolio Suppose you have a sum of money X that you wish to invest for a month. Option S offers you a safe, fixed rate of interest r_s on a one-month term. Thus, the payoff Y_s on this option is

$$Y_s = X(1 + r_s)$$

Option R is slightly more risky, being a money market fund where the rate changes every week. Assuming you must commit your money for a month and that interest is compounded weekly, the payoff Y_r on this option is

$$Y_r = X(1 + r_1)(1 + r_2)(1 + r_3)(1 + r_4)$$

where r_1, r_2, r_3, and r_4 are the interest rates (uncertain) over the next four weeks. Furthermore, let us suppose you know something about diversified risk, and that your decision is not option S or R, but rather what fraction f of X you will put in R compared to S. Thus, your decision model is

$$Y(f) = X[f(1 + r_1)(1 + r_2)(1 + r_3)(1 + r_4) + (1 - f)r_s]$$

where $f =$ decision variable
$Y(f) =$ outcome variable

The above mathematical equation is the structural relationship with parameters X, r_1, r_2, r_3, r_4, and r_s. Parameters are usually predetermined, such as X (assuming this is not a decision variable in this case) and r_s, or require estimating, such as r_1, r_2, r_3, and r_4 (usually in the form of probability distributions). Thus, *parameters* are quantities within the structure that describe how decision variables translate into outcome variables. In this problem, we have now specified how the choice of a value for f gives a set of uncertain outcomes for $Y(f)$, that is, a probability distribution over $Y(f)$. We will presumably just value $Y(f)$ in monetary terms, but we do need some criterion to compare the different probability distributions on $Y(f)$ for each value of f.

Having developed such a model, we must now optimize it. In our context, *optimization* means the process of searching through all possible values of the decision variable f evaluating the outcomes pertaining to each in terms of the decision criterion to find that decision which gives the highest criterial value (the "optimum"). Thus in the above example, we search through a set of values for f (such as 0, 0.2, 0.4, 0.6, 0.8, 1), compute the probability distributions for $Y(0)$, $Y(0.2)$, etc., and find which has the highest criterial value. Any algorithm shortcuts or preliminary screening that can be done to reduce this search has obvious computational value.

To summarize, when faced with a decision problem, we first decompose the problem into decision variables, outcome variables, structural relationships, and parameters. Second, we decide upon a decision criterion to recompose the outcome probabilities and evaluations. Third, we optimize the model to find that decision (the optimum) which gives the most desirable set of outcome probabilities. This, in a very narrow sense, comprises the essence of the decision analysis method.

In practice, the final stage of optimization is often the least important. The modeling phase, through the process of introspection and interaction with the decision analyst, helps to clarify the decision maker's understanding of the structure of the problem, sometimes to such an extent that the "best" decision then becomes quite apparent. The actual identification of the optimal course of action is by no means as useful as the process through which it was obtained. This brings us now to the focal point, namely that the basic presumption of decision analysis is not at all to replace the decision maker's intuition, to relieve him or her of the obligations in facing the problem, or to be, worst of all, a competitor to the decision maker's personal style of analysis, but to complement, augment, and generally work alongside the decision maker in exemplifying the nature of the problem. Ultimately, it is of most value if the decision maker has actually learned something about the problem and his or her own decision-making attitude through the exercise.

1.3 WHAT CONSTITUTES GOOD DECISION ANALYSIS?

The above discussion leads us quite naturally to the issue of evaluating the quality of a decision analysis. What distinguishes good from bad practice in this profession? What areas of competence should the prospective student look forward to developing ultimately? If we push the final comments in the previous section to the point where the prime purpose of decision analysis is to make the decision maker feel comfortable with his or her own analysis of the problem, then this would seem to open the way for all sorts of sophistry and dubious consulting practices. Furthermore, if we examine what a "good" decision means to an executive, we may find certain personal considerations and organizational biases of a kind that we would think decision analysis should overcome. For example, the following features of a good decision might weigh heavily in an executive's evaluation:

1. That which elicits a favorable response from superiors
2. That which elicits a favorable response from colleagues
3. That for which responsibility has been nicely delegated
4. That which achieves a quick committee consensus

We note that in none of the above attributes is there an examination of the quality of the *analysis*. While they are all evidently desirable features of the decision-making process, their achievement seems to reflect mainly the decision maker's skill in organizational politics, persuasion, and implementation. We would like to think that a skillful manager first performs a careful analysis and then succeeds in getting the optimal decision supported and implemented. This is not to say that implementational considerations should not enter the analysis, nor that one of the useful aspects of decision analysis is that it provides a good way of communication and consensus formation in the decision-making process. The point is that, in assessing the worth of a decision analysis, we would like to find something more basic to the process of analysis. If the personal and organizational comfort of the decision maker were the major concern, then a decision analyst competent in nothing more than good humor and the ability to make numerous excellent gin and tonics might be all that is required!

An empirical definition of a good decision might be:

5. That which provides the ideal outcome given the eventual circumstances

This is an ex post evaluation and, again, does not really get at the analytical quality. If you had bet your total assets on the toss of a coin and won, thereby doubling your assets, then, in the above definition, that was a good decision. However, a priori most responsible individuals would suggest that your analysis is misguided in suggesting such a risky decision. Even ex post most people would describe it as a bad decision with a lucky outcome.

It is evident that what we are looking for is some measure of how well the decision model has been constructed and how effectively it has interfaced with the decision maker. This measure is extremely elusive, and a hint to the cause of this was given in the previous section. The decision model is a *personal* construct of the decision maker's perception, assessments, and value judgments. The decision analysis approach is only seeking to clarify and organize rationally the decision maker's own reasoning on the problem. As such, therefore, a decision model is not objective in the scientific sense of being testable against reality. Two separate decision makers facing the same problem may have quite different models, each of which may be quite sensible given their different circumstances and opinions. This subjectivity in decision modeling precludes any recourse to a traditional scientific method for evaluation.

Thus, the evaluation must be a personal one. Does the analysis help clarify the problem for the decision maker? It was mentioned previously that one of the main purposes of decision analysis is to facilitate greater understanding of the problem on the part of the decision maker. We could therefore elevate this to say that a good decision is:

6. That which results from a thorough understanding of the problem

Therefore, a good decision analysis is a process which promotes this learning.

While this seems to be getting closer to the purpose of decision analysis, we must be wary of exaggerating its intellectual and pedagogical role. Just how much insight is necessary for the decision to move from being mediocre to good? We do not want a manager's decision analysis to become a doctoral thesis. Who decides when the manager has learned enough from the model to be decisive and make a good decision?

Given the personal nature of the analysis, it has to be the decision maker again. In this respect, Phillips (1982) refers to decision modeling as being "requisite."

> The goal is to develop a "requisite" representation, requisite in the sense that everything required to solve the problem is either included in the model or can be simulated in it. To develop a requisite model, it is necessary to involve all those who are in some way responsible for aspects of the decision in the development of a requisite model. The process of building the model is iterative and cumulative and when no new intuitions emerge about the problem, the model is considered "requisite." [p. 304]

Thus, the decision model allows the manager to experiment and refine his or her intuition up to the point where it becomes a satisfactory basis for action. We seem now to have gone almost completely around the block, returning to the position of where good decision analysis essentially encourages the manager to face the decision in a relatively comfortable frame of mind.

This is the inevitable position that decision analysis takes. However, the key to avoiding superficiality in evaluating the quality of analysis is to look at the substance and assumptions upon which this "comfortable frame of mind" has been developed. It is these procedural assumptions that persuade managers to employ decision analysts, rather than our cheerful gin-and-tonic dispensers. Evidently, the assumption underlying the latter is that convivial doses of gin induce well-being. The assumptions that underly decision analysis must relate to compelling principles of rationality in the structuring of uncertainty and value.

This dilemma in the evaluation of decision analysis is similar to that of establishing high professional standards in psychotherapy. Fischhoff (1980) discusses this parallel, and in that context presents the following list of "criteria for analyzing analyses" (sic):

> Are the assumptions of the analysts listed?
> Are the assumptions of the clients listed (e.g., those implicit in the way the problem was formulated)?
> Are any of these assumptions tested, or is supporting evidence from other sources cited?
> Are probabilities used? If so, is any justification given for the particular procedure by which they are elicited?
> Are probabilities or utilities measured in more than one way?
> Are values elicited from more than one person?
> Are sensitivity analyses conducted, for probabilities, for utilities, with more than one factor varying at once?
> Are interactions between impacts considered?
> Is more than one problem structure used as a cross check?

Are possible alternatives given by the client or created with the client?
Are gaps in scientific knowledge noted?
Is a bottom line figure given, and if so, how is it hedged?
Is the public involved, and if so, at what stage?
Is there consideration of political feasibility or legal constraints?
Is there external criticism of the report, and if so, has the analysis been redone in its light?
Is there indication of when the analysis should be redone to consider possible changes of circumstance?
Is an attempt made to evaluate the analysis or to indicate how interested parties might do so on their own?
How much did the analysis cost? [p. 32]

The question that now remains is what constitutes the basic assumption(s) of rational choice behavior that gives decison analysis its prescriptive value. It turns out that almost the whole of decision analysis is supported by a theory of rationality based upon a few basic conditions of coherence.

1.4 THE COHERENCE PRINCIPLE

In simple terms, the *coherence principle* states that a necessary condition for rational beliefs and actions on the part of an individual is that they should all be logically consistent with each other, involving no mutual contradictions.

Lindley (1971) demonstrates the appeal of this principle using the evocative idea of a "perpetual money-making machine":

> The coherence is easily defended. Suppose we had an incoherent person who said E is less likely than F, F is less likely than G and instead of concluding that E is less likely than G, he concludes that G is less likely than E. Consider again a situation in which he is to receive a prize if E occurs, and otherwise not. Then, keeping the prize fixed throughout the discussion, he would prefer to base his receipt of the prize on F, rather than E, and indeed would pay you a sum of money (or part of the prize) if you would substitute F for E. Accept the money and replace E by F. Now the argument may be repeated and you can receive more money by replacing F and G. Having gained two sums of money, you can now offer to replace G by E and the person would want to accept since he regards G as less likely than E. So a third sum of money passes and we are back to the situation we started from where the prize depended upon E. The incoherent person is back where he started except that he has given you some money. The cycle may be repeated if he holds to his uncertainty relations, and the incoherent person is a perpetual money-making machine. This shows that incoherence is untenable. [p. 20]

A corollary of the above situation is that any belief that an individual holds must be coherent with all the other beliefs that are held, otherwise he or she can be made into a perpetual money-making machine. Rescher (1970) dicusses the philosophical basis of coherence more fully, pointing out that this condition is not *sufficient* to guarantee rationality (such a condition has not yet been found) but that it is *necessary*.

Thus, it is assumed that an ideally rational individual holds a certain world view, a set of basic facts, beliefs, and assumptions which act as a foundation to a perfectly coherent collection of other opinions, values, and justifications. This world view can, however, be wrong. It is the role of the scientific method to improve the accuracy of that. Thus, decision analysis works within the decision maker's basic perspective of facts and assumptions to attempt a coherent decomposition of a complex problem. Furthermore, through close scrutiny some of the decision maker's basic assumptions will be questioned; they may be revised, and they should be subjected to sensitivity analyses in terms of examining how the optimal decision might change if alternative assumptions were to hold. However, the basic procedure in decision analysis is that of attempting to explicate more and more of the decision maker's reasoning and, thereby, facilitate overall tests of coherence.

Thus, a good decision analysis is *that which explicates the decision maker's assumptions, values, and perspective on the problem to attain the highest practicable level of coherence.*

Total coherence is an unattainable ideal, requiring infinite introspection of all the beliefs and facts held by an individual. Nevertheless, it is the direction of good analysis. Just how far the analysis will proceed in this direction depends upon many factors. The importance of the decision, its uniqueness, the need to communicate cogently the analysis to others, and the managerial style of the decision maker have already been noted in this context. The fact that it stops short of the ideal evidently motivated Phillips (1982) to describe decision analysis in practice as being "requisite," and Simon (1957) to call it "satisficing." Both authors deliberately avoid using the term "optimal," since this might imply the ideal (unattainable) decision following a perfect analysis. The position taken here is that the optimal decision is that action which is considered most preferable by the decision maker in the context of his or her own decision model. Another person might have a different optimal decision. Likewise, the same person, following a more thorough analysis, might change the optimal decision. Thus, there is nothing objective or ideal in its use here; it is defined only within the context of someone's personal decision model.

1.5 SUMMARY

Decision analysis seeks to provide a logical framework within which an individual can make explicit as much as possible of his or her reasoning on a decision problem. This should help the decision-making process through:

1. Breaking up a complex problem into components
2. Eliminating major inconsistencies in the individual's own reasoning
3. Facilitating communication on the decision problem

The result, it is hoped, would be a more coherent personal and organizational view of the problem and greater insights into the problem's sensitivity to assumptions. The purpose of a decision analysis is not to replace judgment, but to help organize it and to provide a model of the problem which, through experimentation, can develop greater understanding of the situation. It provides a way of articulating creativity in problem solving, not the imposition of a standard technique.

EXERCISES

1.1 *Webster's New Collegiate Dictionary* (1975) defines *scientific method* as "principles and procedures for the systematic pursuit of knowledge involving the recognition and formulation of a problem, the collection of data through observation and experiment, and the formulation and testing of hypotheses." To what extent, if any, is decision analysis part of the scientific method?

1.2 *The Bent Coin Wager.* You are approached by your decision analyst and regular drinking companion Seymour Lite with a coin-tossing gamble. Seymour produces an old British penny which you examine and observe to be clearly bent. He offers you the option of calling heads or tails before he tosses it. If you are right, you win $2 from him; if you are wrong, you pay him $1. Observing the dubious way that you have been examining the old British penny, Seymour produces a new U.S. silver dollar, which is clearly currency of the highest caliber and not at all bent. "You have a choice of playing with the British penny, the silver dollar, or not playing at all," says Seymour.

(*a*) How do you rank these three options? Explain your reasoning.

(*b*) Suppose the monetary amounts are now $2000 and $1000. Does this change your answer to (*a*)? How and why?

(*c*) Suppose the monetary amounts are now $2 million and $1 million. Does this change your answer to (*a*)? How and why?

(*d*) What are the decision variables, outcome variables, and structural parameters in this problem? What is your decision criterion?

(*e*) Suppose the monetary amounts are $200 and $100 and Seymour offers you the opportunity to purchase five trial tosses of the coin before entering the wager. What is the most you would pay for these trials? Why?

REFERENCES

Ackoff, R. C. (1971): "Towards a System of System Concepts," *Management Science*, vol. 17, pp. 661–671.

——— and F. E. Emery (1972): *On Purposeful Systems*, Aldine-Atherton, Chicago.

Byrd, J., and L. T. Moore (1982): *Decision Models for Management*, McGraw-Hill, New York.

Fischhoff, Baruch (1980): "Clinical Decision Analysis," *Operations Research*, vol. 28, no. 1, pp. 28–43.

Harrison, E. F. (1981): *The Managerial Decision-Making Process*, Houghton-Mifflin, Boston.

Howard, R. A. (1980): "An Assessment of Decision Analysis," *Operations Research*, vol. 28, no. 1, pp. 4–27.

Keeney, R. L. (1980): *Siting Energy Facilities*, Academic Press, New York.

——— and H. Raiffa (1976): *Decisions with Multiple Objectives*, Wiley, New York.

Lindley, D. V. (1971): *Making Decisions*, Wiley, London.

Phillips, L. D. (1982): "Requisite Decision Modelling," *Journal of the Operational Research Society*, vol. 33, no. 4, pp. 303–312.

Raiffa, H., and R. Schlaifer (1961): *Applied Statistical Decision Theory*, M.I.T. Press, Cambridge, Mass.

Rescher, N. (1970): *The Coherence Theory of Truth*, Oxford University Press, Oxford.

Simon, H. A. (1957): *Models of Man*, Wiley, New York.

———— (1960): *The New Science of Management Decision*, Harper and Row, New York.

Watson, S., Ed. (1982): "The Practice of Decision Analysis," *Special Issue of the Journal of the Operational Research Society*, vol. 33, no. 4 (April), Pergamon Press, Oxford.

Zeleny, M. (1982): *Multiple Criteria Decision Making*, McGraw-Hill, New York.

PROBLEMS WITH DECISION CRITERIA

2.1 THE PAYOFF MATRIX

The simplest structure for a decision model consists of a list of the possible actions that could be taken (values of a decision variable), a list of the possible outcomes that could occur (values of an outcome variable), and a straighforward evaluation (single-valued) of each decision-outcome pairing. Thus, in formal terms, let:

a_j be the decision variable, which can take m discrete values, indexed by j. Therefore, the list of possible actions is $(a_1, a_2, \ldots, a_m)$.

θ_i be the outcome variable, which can take n discrete values, indexed by i. Therefore, the list of possible outcomes is $(\theta_1, \theta_2, \ldots, \theta_n)$.

y_{ij} be the value to the decision maker of taking action a_j if θ_i then occurs.

This can be represented as a payoff matrix:

	a_1	a_2	$\cdots$	a_m
θ_1	y_{11}	y_{12}		y_{1m}
θ_2	y_{21}	y_{22}		y_{2m}
$\vdots$				
θ_n	y_{n1}	y_{n2}		y_{nm}

Example: Preptown bookstore Sally Buyback, the manager of the bookstore at Preptown College, must decide how many copies of the required text *Thoughtful Thinking* to order for the creativity class next quarter. The maximum enrollment is 70; so far 50 are enrolled, and this could eventually go up or down. The bookstore will make $15 on each *Thoughtful Thinking* finally sold. Sally will buy back at full retail price during the first two weeks of the quarter, but thereafter will not re-purchase the book at any price. The class will not be repeated at Preptown, and any books not sold for this seminar will have to be disposed of at the end of the quarter at a loss of $5 per copy. Sally's problem is to decide what constitutes an economically sensible order.

The payoff matrix for this problem is as follows (considering only orders in units of 10 copies):

	Action (copies ordered)							
	0	10	20	30	40	50	60	70
0	0	−50	−100	−150	−200	−250	−300	−350
10	0	150	100	50	0	−50	−100	−150
20	0	150	300	250	200	150	100	50
30	0	150	300	450	400	350	300	250
40	0	150	300	450	600	550	500	450
50	0	150	300	450	600	750	700	650
60	0	150	300	450	600	750	900	850
70	0	150	300	450	600	750	900	1050

The structure of the payoff matrix as a decision model is therefore very simple. The only parameters that we have considered have been the two accounting contributions ($15 for a sale, −$5 for a no sale). We did not conduct a market model of how the outcomes might be determined. Payoff matrices do not allow any explicit representation of intricate action-outcome relationships. Likewise, we we have only looked at monetary payoffs. It may be the case that this decision problem could be evaluated upon other factors besides money. Again, a single payoff matrix does not readily succeed in representing multiple evaluations. For example, the bookstore has a service obligation to the college to provide the books that students require. If there are persistent complaints of understocking, Sally's managerial performance will be criticized by the faculty council. Also, Sally is aware that by displaying copies of this book, academic visitors will gain an enhanced impression of the college's intellectual standing, which will again please the faculty council. But Sally is also aware that the alumni will consider purchases of this book as subversive, and that the trustees of the college will be anxious to avoid their displeasure. Multiple evaluations can be represented by multiple payoff matrices, but this does not make their comparison and ultimate tradeoffs any the easier.

Even with a simple payoff matrix, the problem of selecting the optimal action is usually far from straightforward. Basically, it is an issue of choosing the most preferable column. Ordering 70 copies gives the possibility of making $1050, the highest payoff in the matrix if all 70 are sold, but also the risk of losing $350 if the class gets canceled. On the other hand, ordering 0 runs no risk but makes no money. The dilemma of choosing between a safe low return and a risky high return is the central problem of this subject. In discussing some of the criteria that have been suggested to aid such deliberations, an important distinction can be made between *stochastic* and *nonstochastic* criteria. Stochastic criteria make use of a probability distribution $P(\theta)$ on the outcome variable. We have not yet considered the possibility of Sally assessing probabilities for sales of 0, 10, 20, 30, ..., 70 copies. She might be quite disposed to assessing such chances on the basis of her past experience. Alternatively, she might wish to avoid the extra subjectivity that this introduces into the analysis. It is easier if we discuss some of the nonstochastic criteria first.

2.2 NONSTOCHASTIC CRITERIA

Outcome Dominance

This is the criterion for eliminating options which are clearly inferior to others for all outcomes that could occur. Analysts should always make an initial search for dominance, as this reduces the scale of the decision problem. Suppose we have the following payoff matrix:

	a_1	a_2	a_3
θ_1	6	3	8
θ_2	5	4	2
θ_3	7	6	3

And suppose also that the decision maker prefers more to less. Then a_1 dominates a_2 for all possible outcomes. Regardless of whether θ_1, θ_2, or θ_3 occurs, the payoff will always be greater with a_1. Thus, the decision problem is between a_1 and a_3. Note that there is no outcome dominance in Sally Buyback's payoff matrix considered in the previous section. We can state more formally:

Action a_q exhibits outcome dominance over a_p if, for every θ_i

$$y_{iq} \geq y_{ip}$$

and $y_{iq} > y_{ip}$ for at least one θ_i.

Thus, in the following payoff matrix outcome a_1 still dominates outcome a_2 because you can never do worse with a_1 than with a_2 if θ_1 or θ_2 occurs and you can do better if θ_3 occurs.

	a_1	a_2	a_3
θ_1	6	6	8
θ_2	5	5	2
θ_3	7	6	3

Note that we have made no assumptions regarding the relative chances of $\theta_1, \theta_2, \theta_3$ happening.

Maximin

Only the most fortuitous decision problems can be analyzed completely using outcome dominance. Normally, such dominance testing will "prune" the scale of the model but will still leave a payoff matrix to analyze. Thus, in the above example we still have to decide between a_1 and a_3, and in Sally Buyback's problem, dominance made no inroads at all. Maximin is the most pessimistic of the criteria. Essentially, for each action the worst possible (minimum) payoff is identified. Then that action is chosen for which the worst payoff is highest. Thus, we maximize the minimum payoffs. In the following payoff matrix, if we take a_1, the worst payoff is 5 whereas if we take a_3, the worst is 2.

	a_1	a_3
θ_1	6	8
θ_2	5	2
θ_3	7	3

Thus, under the maximin criterion we take a_1. In Sally Buyback's problem, maximin would suggest ordering no copies of *Thoughtful Thinking*. In everyday terms, most of us can think of situations where decisions have been made on the basis of "well, if it comes to the worst, ..." More formally, the maximin criterion states:

> Action a_q is optimal in the maximin sense if and only if, for each a_j, there exists a y_{ij*} which is the minimum y_{ij} over all θ_i, and y_{iq} is the maximum of all y_{ij*}.

Looking just at the worst scenarios can be very shortsighted. Consider this payoff matrix:

	a_1	a_2
θ_1	31	32
θ_2	10,000	33

Here, under a_1, you recieve either \$31 or \$10,000, and under a_2, you receive either \$32 or \$33 in each case according to whether θ_1 or θ_2 occurs. Maximin tells you to take a_2.

Maximax

Extreme optimists only look at the best that can happen. In technical terms they would be using the maximax criterion. They would search through the payoff matrix to find which action gave the largest possible payoff. In the following payoff matrix it would be a_2.

	a_1	a_2
θ_1	6	8
θ_2	5	2
θ_3	7	3

If Sally Buyback were optimal in the maximax sense, she would order 70 copies of the book. In formal terms we can state:

Action a_q is optimal under the maximax criterion if and only if there exists a θ_p such that $y_{pq} \geq y_{ij}$ for all i and j.

Maximax decision makers must be able to withstand high losses. Consider this payoff matrix (in dollars):

	a_1	a_2
θ_1	9	10
θ_2	8	$-50{,}000$

Maximax would tell you to choose a_2.

Minimax Regret

The basic idea behind this criterion, which was advocated originally by Savage (1954), was to anticipate how the decision might be viewed in the future, looking back upon what might have been done. It is looking at possible lost opportunities or regrets. Consider this payoff matrix:

	a_1	a_2
θ_1	8	9
θ_2	12	10

If θ_1 occurs, then the ideal action is a_2. Likewise, if θ_2 occurs, the ideal action is a_1. But if θ_1 occurs after we have taken action a_1, then we would have some regret at not having taken a_2. In fact, we could have been \$1 better off. Similarly, if we had taken action a_2 and θ_2 had occurred we could have been \$2 better off under a_1. Let us quantify this regret by the variable r_{ij}, which can also be termed the *opportunity loss* of a particular (θ_i, a_j) pair:

$$r_{ij} = \max_j (y_{ij}) - y_{ij}$$

Thus, we first identify the maximum payoff in the row for a given θ_i (this would relate to the ideal no-regret action) and subtract from it the actual payoff a_j for each decision that could have been taken. In the above example this is the regret (opportunity loss) matrix:

	a_1	a_2
θ_1	1	0
θ_2	0	2

The criterion used to analyze this matrix is now the reverse of maximin. For each action the maximum regret possible is identified. (In the above example these are 1 for a_1 and 2 for a_2.) Then that action is chosen for which the maximum regret is smallest (i.e., minimized). At the Preptown Bookstore, Sally Buyback's regret matrix would be:

	Action (copies ordered)							
	0	10	20	30	40	50	60	70
0	0	50	100	150	200	250	300*	350*
10	150	0	50	100	150	200	250	300
20	300	150	0	50	100	150	200	250
30	450	300	150	0	50	100	150	200
40	600	450	300	150	0	50	100	150
50	750	600	450	300	150	0	50	100
60	900	750	600	450	300	150	0	50
70	1050*	900*	750*	600*	450*	300*	150	0

The maximum regrets for each action have been asterisked. Evidently the "minimum maximum regret" is 300, obtainable with either 50 or 60 copies ordered. (If Sally were not restricted to ordering in multiples of 10, the optimum could be found between 50 and 60.)

More formally, we can state:

Action a_q is optimal in the minimax regret sense if and only if

$$r_q^* \le r_j^* \qquad \text{for all } j$$

where $r_j^* = \max_i (r_{ij})$

$r_{ij} = \max_j (y_{ij}) - y_{ij}$

The minimax regret criterion often has considerable appeal, particularly wherever decision makers tend to be evaluated with hindsight. Of course, hindsight is an exact science, and our actions are sometimes unfairly compared critically with what we might have done. Many organizations seem implicitly to review and reward their employees in this way. Whether indeed it is in an organization's best interests as a whole for its employees to be minimax regret decision makers is a debatable issue. It might be better for the company if its workers were even more cautious or, alternatively, rather more disposed to take risks.

Furthermore, many decision analysts argue that minimax regret violates the coherence principle. Lindley (1971) has shown how a minimax regret decision maker can be transformed into a perpetual money-making machine.

Consider this payoff matrix for two possible decisions a_1 and a_2 and two uncertain outcomes θ_1 and θ_2:

	a_1	a_2
θ_1	8	2
θ_2	0	4

If action a_1 is taken and θ_1 occurs, then a payoff of 8 is received.

The associated opportunity loss or regret matrix can be derived in the usual way:

	a_1	a_2
θ_1	0	6
θ_2	4	0

Thus, if action a_1 were taken and θ_1 occurred, there would be no regret or lost opportunity.

Under the minimax regret criterion, a_1 would be preferred since the maximum regret obtainable is minimized. In fact if a decision maker using this criterion found himself in the situation of taking action a_2, he would pay you some money, a little less than 2, if he could be allowed to take a_1 instead. Take the money, give him the option of making decision a_1, and also let him consider an extra decision possibility a_3. The new payoff matrix is:

	a_1	a_2	a_3
θ_1	8	2	1
θ_2	0	4	7

Its associated regret matrix is:

	a_1	a_2	a_3
θ_1	0	6	7
θ_2	7	3	0

Our minimax regret decision maker now prefers a_2 to a_1 and will even pay you some money (up to 1) to avoid taking a_1 in order to be able to take action a_2. Take the money again and offer him the original decision problem without a_3. Clearly, our decision maker is going to keep paying you money to switch from a_1 to a_2 when a_3 is not considered and then back from a_2 to a_1 when a_3 is included, even though a_3 is an irrelevant decision option—it is never an optimal action. It is as if the decision maker prefers to go to the theater one evening rather than to the cinema, but if offered the additional option of going to a concert, he prefers the cinema. The decision maker's preferences are evidently incoherent, and he is a perpetual money-making machine.

The incoherence identified above depends upon an axiom that can be called the *independence of irrelevant alternatives*. Informally stated, this implies that we should require of a sensible decision criterion that its ranking of two alternative actions shall not depend upon whether a third option, which is never preferable to both, is considered. If we do not make this requirement, then we cannot make a decision between a set of actions without having established that this is indeed the total set of possible actions that can be taken. This total set may be infinite. Some theorists would say that this is what coherence requires anyway. If, however, we take the pragmatic position that while we uphold the coherence ideal, we recognize that it is unattainable and that, therefore, we require a criterion that is not only capable of ideal coherence, were infinite pains to be taken, but is also robust to all levels of degradation, then the minimax regret criterion does not degrade nicely in this respect.

We could, however, adopt a weaker interpretation of this axiom, stating that a sensible decision criterion should not change its ranking of actions according to whether or not outcome-dominated actions are considered. Notice that in the above example a_3 was not a dominated action. Had a dominated action been introduced, it would not change the regrets of the other actions (since it would not be introducing a maximum y_{ij}). If we take the position that a valid decision model should include all conceivable undominated outcomes, then we could argue that in the above example considering only a_1 and a_2 is bad practice, and that Lindley's perpetual money-making machine is too contrived. This is quite a controversial issue. The point remains, however, that in the practical use of minimax regret the decision maker should be aware that the ranking of options could change if others are to be considered. This precludes a sequential analysis of options under this criterion.

Example: Applied payoff matrix A practical example of the use of payoff matrices for decision analysis can be seen in the work of the U.S.S.R. Siberian Power Institute (Belyaev, 1976). During the early 1970s one particular capacity expansion decision for the integrated Siberian power system involved three possible options: (1) a new gas turbine station in the southern region, (2) a new hydro station in the central region, or (3) a new hydro station in the northern region.

Since this was a socialist decision problem, its objective was to meet the anticipated demand at minimum cost and not necessarily to maximize profit. A total of 23 scenarios were identified in order to reflect various possible states of demand, investment, and operating costs. The associated cost matrix is shown below. (Note that the action and outcome rows and columns have been reversed here for easier presentation.)

						Outcomes					
1	2	3	4	5	6	7	8	9	10	11	12
1	9,295	9,862	11,087	11,076	10,712	10,169	11,343	10,988	10,429	10,619	11,361	10,077
2	9,940	6,839	10,380	11,037	10,182	9,139	10,656	9,927	8,079	10,046	10,568	9,389
3	9,891	6,831	10,395	11,048	9,957	9,118	10,808	9,939	9,478	10,097	10,515	9,171

	Outcomes (continued)										
	13	14	15	16	17	18	19	20	21	22	23
1	10,913	9,807	10,391	12,406	10,406	10,416	11,226	9,402	7,937	10,361	12,381
2	10,890	7,895	9,641	11,428	7,395	9,179	10,084	7,539	7,333	10,180	11,967
3	10,897	7,912	8,913	11,436	7,480	9,152	10,137	7,554	7,434	10,040	12,179

The costs are in million roubles. The institute then went on to identify what would be the optimal actions under several criteria, including maximax, maximin, and minimax regret. The final decision was then passed on to a more political entity. The institute had really only served to form a preliminary analysis. This example is actually quite typical of the general practice where simple payoff matrices are used only as an initial stage in the decision analysis. The problem of making a decision still remains.

2.3 STOCHASTIC CRITERIA

The above criteria take no account of the relative chances of occurrence of the different outcomes. If the decision maker has any opinion on whether one outcome is more or less likely than another, the coherence principle requires that this be taken into account in the analysis. The chosen actions of an individual should be consistent with all relevant beliefs. Furthermore, with the aim of decision analysis to explicate these beliefs for further scrutiny, some method of quantifying these opinions on uncertainty is required.

Now, if the decision maker had data on θ_i from either previous experience or a sample survey, then routine statistical analyses would result in the relative chances of θ_i being quantified as a probability distribution $P(\theta)$.

Revision Note: Probability Distributions

If we have a discrete set of outcomes θ_i ($i = 1, \ldots, n$) which are mutually exclusive (if one occurs, another cannot) and collectively exhaustive (one of them must occur), then a probability distribution $P(\theta)$ is a set of numerical measures $P(\theta_i)$ such that

$$0 \leq P(\theta_i) \leq 1 \qquad \text{for all } i$$

$$1 = \sum_{i=1}^{n} P(\theta_i)$$

$$P(\theta_r \cup \theta_s) = P(\theta_r) + P(\theta_s)$$

with the loose interpretation that the higher $P(\theta_i)$, the more likely θ_i is to occur. Thus, if an experiment can be repeated a large number of times N and x_i denotes the number of times θ_i occurred, then $P(\theta_i)$ can be estimated empirically as $\hat{P}(\theta_i)$, where

$$\hat{P}(\theta_i) = \frac{x_i}{N}$$

Because the outcome variable θ is discrete, $P(\theta)$ is referred to as a *discrete probability distribution* or sometimes as a *probability mass function*. When the outcomes are measured numerically, θ is a *random variable* that takes on only discrete values (such as number of nuclear reactors operating, number of purchases of a product, etc.). In cases where θ is a continuous random variable (such as temperature, market share) which can, in theory, be measured to any level of accuracy, we describe its uncertainty by means of a continuous probability distribution, usually called a *probability density function $f(\theta)$*. Because there are an infinite number of points that a continuous random variable can take, we cannot have point probabilities $f(\theta_i)$ analogous to $P(\theta_i)$ in the discrete case. For a continuous random variable we must evaluate the probability of events in terms of intervals on θ, such as

$$P(a < \theta \le b) = \int_a^b f(\theta)\, d\theta$$

Thus, the main condition on $f(\theta)$ is that

$$1 = \int_{-\infty}^{+\infty} f(\theta)\, d\theta$$

Because of the interval nature of continuous probability distributions, the cumulative distribution function $F(\theta)$, sometimes just called *distribution function*, is often used,

$$F(\theta_i) = P(\theta \le \theta_i) = \int_{-\infty}^{\theta_i} f(\theta)\, d\theta$$

This also exists for discrete probability distributions,

$$F(\theta_i) = P(\theta \le \theta_i) = \sum_{k=1}^{i} P(\theta_k)$$

For a basic revision of probability and statistics, the reader can refer to Bowen and Starr (1982) or Gohagen (1980).

For readers interested in a more formal analysis of coherence, De Finetti (1974) shows how an individual's quantitative assessments on uncertainty *must* become effectively a probability distribution to avoid becoming a perpetual money-making machine. Thus, we take the position in decision analysis that regardless of whether information on θ is in the form of empirical evidence or personal opinion, it should be expressed as $P(\theta)$ for analytical purposes. Furthermore, even if $P(\theta)$ is an "objective" probability distribution, being derived from purely empirical analysis, the very act that a decision maker chooses to use it in his or her analysis makes it an adopted statement of his or her belief (otherwise the decision maker would be incoherent) and therefore, in a more general sense, a "subjective" probability distribution. In most practical instances, the decision maker will have some data available in addition to some personal opinions on other diagnostic factors such that his or her task will be to form a sensible composite judgment on the chances of θ. (This synthesis of data and opinion is the central issue in the subject called *bayesian inference*.) Even if the decision maker has only a personal opinion on the chances of θ occurring, decision analysis takes the position that this can be readily encoded as $P(\theta)$ in a way that allows it to be used exactly as if it were a probability distribution with an empirical basis.

Thus, the estimation of subjective probabilities is often achieved by analogy with a simple probability reference situation, which is called a *standard device*. A standard device need not be a physical instrument, but can be purely conceptual. For example, a common standard device is to conceive of an urn containing a mixture of black and white balls. Suppose that in the Preptown Bookstore example we wished to measure Sally Buyback's subjective probability that 60 copies will be sold. We could offer her the following gamble X on the one hand:

$$X \begin{cases} \text{she receives \$100 if the demand is 60} \\ \text{or} \\ \text{she receives 0 if the demand is not 60} \end{cases}$$

as opposed to Y on the other hand:

$$Y \begin{cases} \text{she receives \$100 if she draws black ball} \\ \text{or} \\ \text{she receives 0 if she draws white ball} \end{cases}$$

Here the experiment is one of drawing at random from the urn containing 50 percent black balls. If she prefers the uncertainty in Y to that in X, it means that her subjective probability of $\theta = 60$ is less than 0.5. Now reduce the proportion of black balls in the conceptual urn to the point at which Sally is indifferent between options X and Y. Let us say this is at 40 percent. We can now say that Sally behaves *as if* she attached a probability of 0.4 to the demand being 60 books.

In this way, a full probability distribution can be obtained over θ. This is now sufficient for us to incorporate $P(\theta)$ in our decision criterion. Note that there is a considerable body of psychological work on achieving a coherent $P(\theta)$ in terms of minimizing the various biases to which the assessment procedure may be susceptible. Thus, many consistency checks are usually undertaken to establish the coherence of $P(\theta)$. In particular, we must ensure that

$$1 = \sum_{i=1}^{n} P(\theta_i)$$

More will be said of this in Chapter 7. Let us now look at some criteria that make use of $P(\theta)$.

Modal Outcome

A common heuristic used in practice is to look at the most likely outcome, the *mode*, and take the decision with the highest payoff for this outcome. For example, consider this payoff matrix:

θ	$P(\theta)$	a_1	a_2	a_3
θ_1	0.2	18	15	19
θ_2	0.7	20	22	19
θ_3	0.1	40	30	20

The mode is θ_2, and a_2 would be best for this outcome.

In formal terms, we can state:

Action a_q is optimal in the modal outcome sense if and only if there exists a θ_p such that

$$P(\theta_p) \geq P(\theta_i) \qquad \text{for all } i$$

and $\qquad\qquad\qquad\qquad y_{pq} \geq y_{pj} \qquad \text{for all } j$

It is not difficult to think of counterexamples where this criterion appears misleading. Here is one:

θ	$P(\theta)$	a_1	a_2	a_3
θ_1	0.24	0	99	98
θ_2	0.25	0	98	99
θ_3	0.51	21	20	20

Outcome θ_3 is most likely, and thus a_1 is the best decision under this outcome.

In fact, Lindley (1971) argues that this criterion is incoherent, and he constructs a perpetual money-making machine to make his point. Consider this payoff matrix:

θ	$P(\theta)$	a_1	a_2
θ_1	$\frac{2}{9}$	5	3
θ_2	$\frac{3}{9}$	5	3
θ_3	$\frac{4}{9}$	8	9

A decision maker using the modal payoff criterion first of all selects the most likely outcome, θ_3. He or she then takes that decision which has the highest payoff under θ_3, which in this case is a_2. In fact, he or she would be prepared to pay some money (up to 1) in order to avoid a_1 in favor of a_2.

Note, however, that the occurrence of θ_1 or θ_2 gives rise to the same payoffs. Thus, whether or not θ_1 or θ_2 occurs, a_1 and a_2 are identical. Thus, θ_1 and θ_2 can be grouped together:

θ	$P(\theta)$	a_1	a_2
θ_1 or θ_2	$\frac{5}{9}$	5	3
θ_3	$\frac{4}{9}$	8	9

The decision maker now looks at the occurrence of either θ_1 or θ_2 (since these are the most likely) and prefers action a_1. In fact, the decision maker will now pay a small amount of money (up to 2) to avoid a_2 and take a_1. He or she is now back to the first situation and will continue to pay money to switch from a_1 to a_2 when the events θ_1 and θ_2 are considered separate and then again to switch from a_2 to a_1 if they are considered together. He or she is thus a perpetual money-making machine. The problem in using this criterion is clearly the arbitrary way in which events can be aggregated for probabilistic purposes. The consequent incoherence of the criterion is therefore not surprising.

The problem here parallels that in data analysis where it is well known that the interpretation of the mode is sensitive to the way the data have been grouped. For example, suppose you have conducted a study on the number of bottles of wine households in a particular city purchase per week. The following data might have been obtained from a sample of size 100.

Bottles per week	Households
0	20
1	10
2	15
3	16
4	12
5	8
6	5
7	9
8 or more	5
	100

The mode in this case was clearly 0. However, the analyst might have good categorical reasons for defining the following types of events:

Type	Bottles per week	Households
Nondrinkers	0	20
Moderate drinkers	1–3	41
Regular drinkers	4–6	25
Heavy drinkers	7 or more	14
		100

Now the mode is "moderate drinkers." This aggregation issue is also evident in more subjective analyses, for example, whether a threefold market scenario (high, medium, or low) or a twofold (good or bad) should be considered.

Expected Value

By far the most common decision criterion in practice is that known as *expected value*. It consists of computing the average (mean) payoff for each action and choosing that which is largest. In modern statistical literature we tend to prefer the term "expected value" to "average" because it is a more generalizable concept. Thus, the expected value EV of action a_j is

$$EV(a_j) = \sum_{i=1}^{n} y_{ij}P(\theta_i)$$

In formal terms, this criterion states:

Action a_q is optimal on expected value grounds if and only if

$$EV(a_q) \geq EV(a_j) \qquad \text{for all } j$$

For example, recalling a payoff matrix from the previous section, we have the expected values computed in the final row:

θ	$P(\theta)$	a_1	a_2	a_3
θ_1	0.2	18	15	19
θ_2	0.7	20	22	19
θ_3	0.1	40	30	20
	$EV(a_j) =$	21.6	21.4	19.1

Action a_1 is now optimal on expected value grounds. This criterion is easily justified as a policy for repetitive situations. Thus, if the above decision problem recurred many times with the same payoff matrix, then the average return per instance, if a_1 is taken each time, would approach 21.6 more and more closely as the number of instances increases. Hence, the decision maker will maximize long-term payoff through a sequence of expected value decisions. However, the decision maker has to be able to withstand runs of bad luck (low payoffs—in this case 18) in the short term. If this is not the case, or if the decision is of a once-only type, then a more explicit evaluation of the risk attitude of the decision maker should be undertaken. We will assume, for the moment, that the decision maker can take the risks involved in using the expected value criterion. This being the case, it is useful at this stage to see the relationship of the expected value to the expected regret criterion (expected opportunity loss).

Expected Regret

This criterion is essentially the expected value approach applied to the regret (opportunity loss) matrix instead of the payoff matrix. Thus, the expected regret ER from action a_j, is given by

$$ER(a_j) = \sum_{i=1}^{n} r_{ij} P(\theta_i)$$

where the r_{ij} are derived from y_{ij} exactly as in Section 2.2 under Minimax Regret. Thus, in the above example we would have this regret matrix:

	$P(\theta)$	a_1	a_2	a_3
θ_1	0.2	1	4	0
θ_2	0.7	2	0	3
θ_3	0.1	0	10	20
	$ER(a_j) =$	1.6	1.8	4.1

Evidently, we should wish to minimize the expected regret. This gives a_1 in the above example as the optimal action. Notice that this is the same optimal action as before. In fact, it is *always* the case that maximizing the expected value gives the same optimal action as minimizing the expected regret. The proof is quite simple:

$$\min_{j} \{ER(a_j)\} = \min_{j} \left\{ \sum_{i=1}^{n} r_{ij} P(\theta_i) \right\}$$

$$= \min_{j} \left\{ \sum_{i=1}^{n} [\max_{j} (y_{ij}) - y_{ij}] P(\theta_i) \right\}$$

$$= \min_{j} \left\{ \sum_{i=1}^{n} \max_{j} (y_{ij}) P(\theta_i) - \sum_{i=1}^{n} y_{ij} P(\theta_i) \right\}$$

$$= \min_{j} \{K - EV(a_j)\}$$

where

$$K = \sum_{i=1}^{n} \max_{j} (y_{ij}) P(\theta_i)$$

is a constant for the entire payoff matrix. It would represent the expected payoff for a decision maker who always managed to take the ideal action (zero regret) for whichever outcome occurred. Thus, we see that by maximizing $EV(a_j)$ we will minimize $ER(a_j)$.

Payoff Distribution Analysis

Aside from working with the *payoff matrix*, the expected value criterion can be formalized in terms of the *payoff distribution* for each course of action. Our payoff variable in general terms is y (most often, money). Thus, in payoff matrix terms y_{ij} was a particular value of y if action j was taken and outcome i occurred. We can represent the payoff probability distribution from taking action j as $p_j(y)$. Hence, in the previous problem we have three distributions:

y	18	20	40
$p_1(y)$	0.2	0.7	0.1

y	15	22	30
$p_2(y)$	0.2	0.7	0.1

y	19	20
$p_3(y)$	0.9	0.1

Our problem is how to determine which probability distribution $p_j(y)$ we prefer. The expected value criterion tells us to choose that with the highest mean:

$$EV(a_1) = E\{p_1(y)\} = \sum y_i p_1(y) \quad \text{for all } i$$
$$= 21.6$$

$$EV(a_2) = E\{p_2(y)\} = \sum y_i p_2(y_i) \quad \text{for all } i$$
$$= 21.4$$

$$EV(a_3) = E\{p_3(y)\} = \sum y_i p_3(y_i) \quad \text{for all } i$$
$$= 19.1$$

giving $p_1(y)$, as before.

If y is a continuous random variable, then for each action j we have a payoff probability density function $f_j(y)$. The problem again is to determine the most desirable $f_j(y)$. Using the expected value criterion, we compute

$$E\{f_j(y)\} = \int_{-\infty}^{+\infty} y f_j(y)\, dy$$

for each j, and then choose the largest. Recall that in data analysis we often choose to model a random variable that is theoretically discrete as a continuous variable if the number of discrete values that can be taken becomes large and unmanageable. Furthermore, when we discuss various features of probability distributions, we often do so as if the random variable were continuous. This is a more general representation and often analytically rather more tidy. Discrete probability distribution can be considered a special case of the continuous form where $f_j(y)$ is nonzero only at certain integer points. Thus, in the remaining part of this section, although most of the presentation will be in terms of $f_j(y)$, the issues should be seen as common to $p_j(y)$ models as well.

Figure 2.1 reexpresses the point made earlier that an expected value decision maker must be able to take the risks involved. Actions a_1 and a_2, giving payoff distributions $f_1(y)$ and $f_2(y)$, have the same expected value y^* and therefore should be equally preferable to the decision maker. However, the returns from a_2 are more dispersed than those from a_1, which could make it more or less attractive, depending upon the decision maker's risk attitude. Likewise, in Figure 2.2 an expected value decision maker should again be indifferent between a_1 and a_2 since both $f_1(y)$ and $f_2(y)$ have the same mean y^*. However, $f_2(y)$ is a skewed distribution, and this may make it less attractive to a risk-averse decision maker.

Notice that in Figure 2.2 the mode of $f_2(y)$ is less than that of $f_1(y)$. Thus, the most likely result from a_2 will be lower than that from a_1. A decision maker using a modal payoff criterion would therefore prefer a_1 to a_2. The distinction between

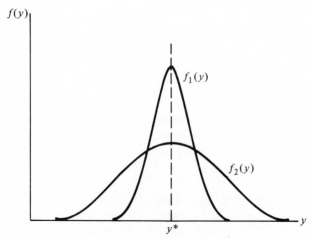

Figure 2.1 Two symmetric distributions with the same mean.

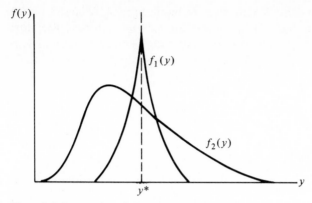

Figure 2.2 Symmetric and skewed distributions with the same mean.

modal payoff and *modal outcome* (Section 2.3) should be apparent. The latter refers to the mode of $P(\theta)$ whereas the former is dealing with the mode of $f_j(y)$ [or $p_j(y)$]. Consider, for example, this payoff matrix:

θ	$P(\theta)$	a_1	a_2
θ_1	0.3	10	20
θ_2	0.3	10	20
θ_3	0.4	15	10

The outcomes θ_1, θ_2, and θ_3 could be high, medium, and low market scenarios, the actions a_1 and a_2 could be two different production plans, and the y_{ij} could be the associated payoffs in units of \$10,000. The most likely *outcome* is θ_3 (the low scenario), and therefore under the modal outcome criterion a_1 would be preferred. However, consider two payoff distributions:

y	10	15
$p_1(y)$	0.6	0.4

y	10	20
$p_2(y)$	0.4	0.6

Clearly, a_2 now has the higher modal payoff.

    Medial payoff is sometimes also used as a criterion. Recall that the median of a probability distribution is that point which has an equal probability of being greater or less than the actual outcome, that is the y for which

$$0.5 = F(y)$$

    Government statisticians often deal in terms of median incomes, house prices, etc., for a region since that gives a more representative measure of the "typical" person's income, house price, etc., than does the mean. The mean can be influenced quite strongly by one or two extreme values.

Regardless of whether the mean, median, or mode of the payoff distribution is being used as a criterion, they are all, in a sense, measures of the "centrality" of a distribution and do not reflect dispersion. As Figures 2.1 and 2.2 have indicated, it is the dispersion of the payoff distribution which relates to risk, and risk is usually the essence of the decision problem.

2.4 RISK ANALYSIS

None of the criteria that have been discussed so far deal adequately with the issue of risk, namely, how a decision maker should compare possible low and high payoffs. Maximin and maximax avoid the comparison by focusing only on the two extremes. Minimax regret has its problems with coherence, as does modal outcome. Expected value (like other centrality measures of the payoff distribution, such as mode or median) does not consider the dispersion of the payoffs; whether or not they are relatively highly dispersed is of no account provided they "balance" around the mean. In other words, options A and B below have the same expected value and would be equally preferable on this criterion:

Option A: You receive $5 with probability $\frac{1}{2}$.
You lose $5 with probability $\frac{1}{2}$.

Option B: You receive $5000 with probability $\frac{1}{2}$.
You lose $5000 with probability $\frac{1}{2}$.

Put rather differently, if you were obliged to participate in option A, you might be able to extricate yourself by paying some fixed penalty. Let x be the maximum you are prepared to pay. Likewise, let y be the maximum you are prepared to pay to extricate yourself from playing option B. The expected value criterion says $x = y = 0$. A prospective gain and a loss of $5 in option A balance out with equal probabilities, in the same way that $\pm$$5000 does in option B. Most of us, however, view option B as more risky, and if necessary would pay proportionally more to get out of this situation than in the case of option A.

This is where the issue of risk comes in for more analysis. *Risk analysis* is now a major field of inquiry alongside decision analysis. Its wide development is in recognition of the fact that it is the riskiness of various proposals that decision makers often wish to analyze at considerable depth. Unfortunately "risk" means different things in a variety of contexts.

In colloquial terms we usually understand that a more risky option involves a greater possibility of high losses. But whether it is the possibility or the high losses which is crucial to the riskiness varies with the context. In other words, some risk analysts focus more upon the probability of undesirable events, others upon the degree of undesirability associated with an event that could conceivably happen. The former is typical of much *financial analysis*, where risk is often taken to be a statistical measure of the dispersion of the payoff probability distribution (e.g., variance). Another example is in the *political risk assessments* undertaken by large multinational corporations. Here the risk may be evaluated as the probability of expropriation associated with the assets of the company in a foreign country. Alternatively, risk in the *insurance* industry usually refers to the maximum amount of money that the company could lose on a particular policy. In *public policy analysis* there is usually some attempt at bringing both uncertainty and value into the evaluation of risk. Thus, risk is often defined as the expected value of the deleterious effects of a proposal. Hence, in its simplest terms the outcomes of a proposal are categorized as socially beneficial and disbeneficial, and the expected value of each category is taken. The expected value of the latter constitutes the risk.

The underlying motivation of risk analysis is to provide a second criterion, the riskiness of an option, to be evaluated alongside a first criterion, such as the expected value, which does not incorporate risk considerations. The idea is that rather than developing a more elaborate single-attribute criterion to incorporate risk, greater insights could be obtained by separating risk out as a second attribute. This is evidently in the decomposition spirit of decision analysis. However, it ultimately requires a further procedure for recombining these two attributes when it comes to comparing projects with different expected payoffs and risks.

Thus, in finance it has been common to evaluate investment proposals in terms of both their expected values and a statistical measure of risk. For option i we would have a payoff probability distribution $f_i(y)$ with mean $\bar{y}_i$ [that is, $\mathrm{EV}(a_i)$] and a risk measure. Several such risk measures have been used.

1. *Variance.* Following the usual definition, the estimated variance is

$$s_i^2 = \int_{-\infty}^{+\infty} (y - \bar{y}_i)^2 f_i(y)\, dy$$

Using this as a measure of risk, clearly the higher the variance of the payoff value, the higher the risk. This measure does not take account of the skewness of the probability distributions on y. Thus, as Figure 2.3 shows, two options can have equal mean and variance, but on examination of the full probability density function, option A would generally be preferred to B.

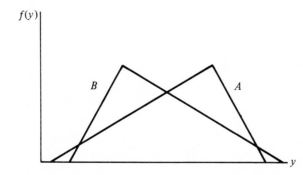

Figure 2.3 Two distributions with the same mean and variance.

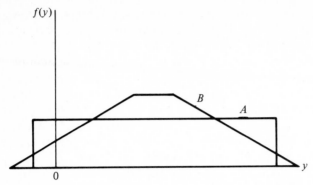

Figure 2.4 Two distributions with the same mean and equal semivariance about zero.

2. *Semivariance.* In an attempt to focus attention upon the lowest possible payoff values, the use of semivariance has been suggested from time to time. If c is some critical value, then the semivariance of an option is defined as

$$s_i^2 = \int_{-\infty}^{c} (y - c)^2 f_i(y) \, dy$$

Whilst semivariance does have the advantage of focusing upon the "risky domain," that is, the possibilities of low payoffs, it is far from reliable. Thus, in Figure 2.4 we see two distributions with equal mean and semivariance about the critical value of zero. On examination of these two probability distributions, option B would generally be considered the more risky.

3. *Critical probability.* This is very similar in spirit to the use of semivariance, except that the measure of risk is now the probability

$$P(y \le c) = \int_{-\infty}^{c} f_i(y) \, dy = F_i(c)$$

that is, the area of the probability density function below the critical value. This again has a more intuitively relevant interpretation of risk in terms of the

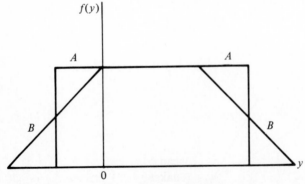

Figure 2.5 Two distributions with the same mean and equal area below zero.

probability of ruin or, less dramatically, of failure as defined by an outcome in the critical region. Again, this index is far from reliable, as Figure 2.5 demonstrates. In this example both curves have the same area below zero, although in view of option B having the possibility of greater losses, we would consider B to be the riskier option.

Fishburn (1977) has generalized the definition of semivariance and critical probability to assess risk as

$$R(a_j) = \int_{-\infty}^{c} (c - y)^\alpha f_j(y)\,dy$$

Thus when $\alpha = 2$, we have semivariance, and when $\alpha = 0$, we have the critical probability. The use of a critical value does seem to be quite natural to managers' assessment of risk. Payne et al. (1980) discuss evidence in this respect. The critical value can be a target or aspiration level, that level of performance which the manager would reasonably expect to achieve. Anything greater is a success, anything below is a failure. This, of course, makes the definition of risk a very personal matter. Kahnemann and Tversky (1979) have, in fact, developed quite a useful descriptive theory of the way that individuals assess risky options. They call it *prospect theory*. Crucial to its structure is a subjective reference point of the above kind, about which individuals assess "gains" and "losses."

The next analytical problem, assuming an acceptable evaluation of risk has been obtained, is how to compare various (expected value, risk) pairs to find the optimal decision. To develop an explicit criterion for comparing these pairs brings us back to the initial problem of finding a single-valued decision criterion to incorporate risk. Before we have to make that step, however, some progress can be made through dominance reasoning. If two options have the same expected values, but one has lower risk, then the one having the lower risk would be preferable. Alternatively, if two options have the same risk but different expected values, then the one with the higher expected value should be chosen.

For example, it is common practice in finance to screen investment opportunities according to *mean-variance dominance*. Suppose we have the following five options with payoff means and variances:

Option	$\bar{y}_i$	s_i^2
a_1	7	1
a_2	8	2
a_3	9	2
a_4	7	1.5
a_5	10	3

Evidently, a_3 dominates a_2 through its higher mean payoff and a_1 dominates a_4 by having a lower variance. Thus, the decision maker would be left with the set of options (a_1, a_3, a_5). Such a set, which cannot be further reduced by dominance reasoning, is often referred to as *efficient*. We still have to develop a way of reconciling means and variances to choose among the efficient set of options.

In some other circumstances the risk attribute can be treated as a *constraint*. Provided the level of risk is no greater than a critical level, the decision can be made on straightforward expected value grounds. Thus, for example, in the case of a multinational oil company evaluating possible overseas sites for exploration, provided the risk of expropriation does not exceed 10 percent for the next five years, the company may evaluate the sites on expected return grounds. A more common class of examples comes from decisions involving social risks. Often these are subject to government regulations which companies must meet in their operations. Thus, the Nuclear Regulatory Commission (1982) has proposed that concerning possible accidental early fatalities due to radioactive release, this risk "should not exceed 0.1 percent of the sum of early fatality risks resulting from other accidents to which members of the U.S. population are generally exposed." Early fatalities are those which occur promptly following an accident, as distinct from delayed fatalities due to induced effects (such as cancer).

Finally, we observe that there are many problems for which risk cannot be tackled by dominance reasoning or as a constraint. For these problems, risk must be explicitly treated in the overall decision criterion. In some cases there is a theory of trading off risk against expected value. For example, modern stock market theory sees risk as having a price: financial risk can be bought and sold. In other cases the tradeoff will be one of personal preference on the part of the decision maker. The task of decision analysis in the latter case is to subject the risk attitude contained in a decision criterion to as much coherence testing as possible. Utility theory has been found useful in this respect, and this will be the subject matter of the next chapter.

2.5 CLOSING PERSPECTIVE

A number of criteria have been introduced in the previous sections, and they have all come in for some quite heavy criticism. It should not be thought that the purpose of these sections was to tilt at strawmen. Decisions in practice have been, and continue to be, made through appeal to these and similar criteria. The most popular practical criterion is still the expected value, possibly associated to a greater or lesser extent with some ad hoc risk analysis. It is important to understand their limitations to be able to use them sensibly. The fact that each is inadequate in some way should not preclude the possibility of useful insight from their application. There is no criterion that is above criticism. Certainly, the expected utility criterion to be introduced next, though theoretically the most attractive, has had many critics and problems in application.

Thus, we must now appreciate the practical impact of the comments in the first session. Decision analysis will not solve a problem for us. It can provide us with the means for explicitly structuring and restructuring, analyzing and reanalyzing the problem under different assumptions and criteria. Through this we should have gained a greater understanding of the problem situation and sharper intuition, and have eliminated obvious incoherence in our reasoning. Ultimately, the choice will be one of personal preference.

Hence, we may not decide a priori that a particular criterion is appropriate. Rather, we may analyze a problem according to different criteria to see what difference they make and in this way determine which course of action is most justifiable.

EXERCISES

2.1 *Ferret's Newstand.* George Ferret buys copies of the *Sunday Clarion* for sale at his newstand every Sunday morning. He must decide now how many to order for next Sunday. He pays $0.30 a copy and sells the paper for $0.50 each. Those left would have no value. For next Sunday's sales, George estimated the following subjective probability distribution:

θ	16	17	18	19	20	21	22	23	24
$P(\theta)$	0.05	0.10	0.12	0.16	0.10	0.20	0.10	0.12	0.05

How many copies should George order under the following criteria: (*a*) maximin, (*b*) maximax, (*c*) minimax regret, (*d*) modal outcome, (*e*) modal payoff, (*f*) medial payoff, (*g*) expected value?

2.2 A specialist grocer stocks a particularly exotic melon that is flown in daily from a certain South Sea island. From past experience he has estimated the following daily demand probability distribution:

Demand	0	1	2	3	4	5	(melons)
Probability	0.1	0.2	0.4	0.1	0.1	0.1	

The grocer buys from the importer at $7 each and sells at a price of $10. The melon is perishable and cannot be sold the next day.

How many melons should the grocer stock per day using the following criteria: (*a*) maximax, (*b*) maximin, (*c*) minimax regret, (*d*) expected regret?

2.3 A decision maker is faced with the following decision problem, represented in terms of a payoff matrix:

	$P(\theta)$	a_1	a_2	a_3
θ_1	0.6	·8	10	z
θ_2	0.3	7	7	6
θ_3	0.1	7	12	11

All payoffs were relatively easy to assess except that from action a_3 if θ_1 were to occur. This has been left in the payoff matrix as an unknown z. How large must z become before a_3 could become optimal on expected value grounds?

2.4 A decision maker is faced with the following problem, represented in terms of a payoff matrix:

	a_1	a_2
θ_1	10	5
θ_2	12	15

The decision maker would like to use the expected value criterion. How large would the probability $P(\theta_1)$ have to become before a_1 would be optimal?

2.5 *Hurwicz Criteria.* In an attempt to compromise the extreme optimism of maximax with the extreme pessimism of maximin, the Hurwicz criterion uses an optimism index α ($0 \le \alpha \le 1$). Thus, the Hurwicz value for action a_j is computed as

$$H(a_j) = \alpha \max_i (y_{ij}) + (1 - \alpha) \min_i (y_{ij})$$

that is a linear combination of the best and worst payoffs for each action. The optimal a_j is then that which gives the highest $H(a_j)$. Using $\alpha = 0.4$, apply this criterion to the Preptown Bookstore in Section 2.1. How sensible or coherent do you think is this criterion?

2.6 *Laplace Criterion.* The so-called principle of insufficient reason implies that one should believe all possible outcomes to be equally likely unless there is evidence to the contrary. Thus, by appeal to this principle, the Laplace criterion computes the expected value of each option under the assumption that all $P(\theta_i)$ are equal. Apply this criterion to the Preptown Bookstore in Section 2.1. What do you think of this as a criterion?

2.7 The payoffs from eight independent investment options have the following distributions:

Option 1 is distributed normally, mean 0, variance 0
       2 is distributed normally, mean 5, variance 2
       3 is distributed normally, mean 15, variance 5
       4 is distributed normally, mean 5, variance 3
       5 is distributed normally, mean 12, variance 5
       6 is distributed normally, mean 10, variance 4
       7 is distributed normally, mean 9, variance 3
       8 is distributed normally, mean 17, variance 6

(*a*) Using mean-variance dominance, what is the efficient set of options?
(*b*) Which option offers the least chance of a payoff below 3? below 0?
(*c*) Suppose that the only two options for which the decision maker could buy a half-share are 4 and 5. Consider now this composite option as the ninth member of the above set. Does this change your answers to parts (*a*) and (*b*)?

2.8 You can undertake a venture a_1 which yields \$1 million for certain. Alternatively, you can adopt one of three more speculative ventures. Venture a_2 yields \$5 million with probability 0.1, \$1 million with probability 0.89, or \$0 with probability 0.01. Venture a_3 yields \$5 million with probability 0.1 or \$0 with probability 0.9. Venture a_4 yields \$1 million with probability 0.11 and \$0 with probability 0.89.

Comparing a_1 with a_2, which do you prefer? Why? Comparing a_3 with a_4, which do you prefer? Why?

(This problem is usually named after M. Allais who discussed it in the paper "Le Comportement de l'Homme Rational devant le Risque, Critique des Postulats et Axiomes de l'Ecole Américaine," *Econometrica*, vol. 21, 1953.)

REFERENCES

Belyaev, L. (1976): "Solutions of Complex Optimisation Problems under Uncertainty," working paper, International Institute for Applied Systems Analysis, Schloss Laxenburg, Austria.

Bowen, E. K., and M. K. Starr (1982): *Basic Statistics for Business and Economics*. McGraw-Hill, New York.

De Finetti, B. (1974): *Theory of Probability*, Wiley, London.

✓Fishburn, P. C. (1977): "Mean-Risk Analysis with Risk Associated with Below Target Returns," *American Economic Review*, vol. 67, pp. 116–126.

Gohagen, J. K. (1980): *Quantitative Analysis for Public Policy*, McGraw-Hill, New York.

Kahnemann, D., and A. Tversky (1979): "Prospect Theory: An Analysis of Decision under Risk," *Econometrica*, vol. 47, no. 2, pp. 262–291.

✓Kaplan, S., and B. J. Garrick (1981): "On the Quantitative Definition of Risk," *Risk Analysis*, vol. 1, no. 1, pp. 11–28.

Lindley, D. V. (1971): *Making Decisions*, Wiley, London.

Markowitz, H. (1959): *Portfolio Selection*, Wiley, New York.

Nuclear Regulatory Commission (1982): "NUREG-0880," Washington, D.C.

✓Payne, J. W., D. J. Laughun, and R. Crum (1980): "Translation of Gambles and Aspiration Levels in Risky Choice Behavior," *Management Science*, vol. 26, no. 10, pp. 1039–1060.

Savage, L. J. (1954): *The Foundations of Statistics*, Wiley, New York.

THREE

CERTAINTY EQUIVALENTS FROM UTILITY THEORY

3.1 CERTAINTY EQUIVALENTS

Suppose you are lucky enough to be faced with the following prospect. A fair coin will be tossed. If it comes up heads, you receive $500, and if it comes up tails, you get nothing. It costs you nothing, so you have nothing to lose by participating. However, you have been offered $200 by someone in return for not taking up the coin-tossing offer. The payoff matrix is

θ	$P(\theta)$	a_1	a_2
Heads	0.5	500	200
Tails	0.5	0	200

(assuming that you will call "heads" and that a_1 is the coin-tossing venture, etc.). In comparing a_1 with a_2, we are seeking to evaluate an uncertain prospect a_1 with a certain prospect a_2. Had you been offered $500 not to participate in the coin tossing, then you would, by dominance reasoning, take the certain option. Alternatively, had you been offered nothing, then assuming you have no moral objection to the prospect, you would, again by dominance reasoning, prefer the uncertain option. It is thus reasonable to assume that somewhere between $0 and $500 there is a value which would make you indifferent between this amount for certain and a_1. Let us assume that this is $200. In other words, a_1 and a_2 in the above payoff matrix are equally preferable. If $200 were replaced by $205, you would prefer a_2; but if it were replaced by $195, you would prefer a_1. To the nearest $5, then, we would say that $200 is your *certainty equivalent* for prospect a_1.

More formally, the certainty equivalence hypothesis states:

If we have an uncertain prospect of \$X with probability p and \$Y with probability $1 - p$ then (if $Y > X$) there should be a prospect for certain \$Z, where $X < Z < Y$, for which the decision maker is indifferent in terms of preference

between $\begin{cases} \$X \text{ with probability } p \\ \text{or} \\ \$Y \text{ with probability } 1 - p \end{cases}$

and \$Z for certain.

This is quite a powerful concept since, *in principle*, it provides a way that an individual can make coherent choices under uncertainty. For each uncertain prospect a_j a certainty equivalent $CE(a_j)$ can be assessed, and then the problem, having been transformed into a deterministic equivalent, will be quite simply reduced to selecting the highest $CE(a_j)$. For example, supposing four different payoff schedules a_1, a_2, a_3, and a_4 were offered in the previous coin-tossing example. These are shown in the following payoff matrix together with a possible set of $CE(a_j)$ which the decision maker might have assessed for each of them:

θ	$P(\theta)$	a_1	a_2	a_3	a_4
Heads	0.5	550	700	400	300
Tails	0.5	0	−100	100	150
	$CE(a_j) =$	200	150	230	220

None of options a_1 through a_4 is dominated. Option a_2 has the highest expected value but also incurs the possibility of losing money. Option a_4 would be chosen on maximin grounds, whereas under minimax regret, a_1 would be taken. These conflicting recommendations are surmounted if careful certainty equivalents are assessed for each option. In the above case, option a_3 shows up as being the most preferable. Hence, by appealing just to coherence, we have been able to devise a way of helping a decision maker choose between uncertain options.

The concept of certainty equivalence can also provide us with a coherent approach to evaluating decision criterion. We have already noticed how various criteria rank options differently and the dilemmas that can arise in evaluating which is the most appropriate. However, if we take the personal view of decision analysis, then it is apparent that *a valid decision criterion must prescribe the certainty equivalent ranking of options.*

The proof of this is very simple, following the observation:

A coherent criterion must give the same score for an uncertain prospect and its certainty equivalent.

Consider the following counterexample. Suppose that the uncertain option a_j has a certainty equivalent y^*. However, the criterial score of a_j is $C(a_j) \neq C(y^*)$. In fact, we can find a y' such that $C(a_j) = C(y')$. If such a y' could not be found, then the criterion would have serious limitations in comparing certain and uncertain options. Assume, without loss of generality, that $y' > y^*$. Thus, if our decision maker were in the position of taking option y^*, he or she would be prepared to pay a small amount of money to take y' instead. Take the money and give the decision maker y'. Now, using the decision criterion, since $C(a_j) = C(y')$, the decision maker will not mind if you substitute a_j for y'. Likewise, because y^* is the decision maker's certainty equivalent for a_j, the decision maker will again not mind if you substitute y^* for a_j. But the decision maker, using this criterion, is now where we started from, holding y^*, and has evidently the potential for being a perpetual money-making machine. Thus, such a criterion is incoherent.

It therefore follows that $y' = y^*$ and that a valid criterion is effectively providing the certainty equivalent ranking of options. Thus, in evaluating the coherence of any postulated criterion, we should subject it to this test.

Alternatively, we can analyze a decision problem by simply assessing certainty equivalents and not worrying about any other criterion. In practice this is really only feasible for relatively simple decision problems. While dichotomous outcomes (heads or tails, success or failure etc.) can be readily assessed as certainty equivalents, when the set of outcomes gets larger, this task becomes extremely difficult to conceptualize. For example, suppose an outcome has a fivefold categorization with payoffs as below from option a_1:

θ	$P(\theta)$	a_1
Excellent	0.1	10,000
Good	0.3	5,000
Average	0.3	1,000
Poor	0.2	-400
Horrid	0.1	$-3,000$

How easy is it for you to assess $CE(a_1)$? Likewise, in a decision problem involving many uncertainties, it is too much to expect a decision maker to carefully assess certainty equivalents for each random variable. It would be nice if we could make some reasonable assumptions of consistency on the part of the decision maker such that, through his or her responses to a few well-designed simple choice situations, an underlying pattern of certainty equivalents can be deduced. Hence, in more complex situations, the decision maker's certainty equivalents could then be prescribed. This is precisely what utility theory does for us.

3.2 UTILITY FUNCTIONS

The essence of utility theory is to provide a function, a *utility function*, which transforms the payoffs into a utility scale. Having thus transformed all the payoffs into utilities, it then turns out that by taking the expected value of the utilities for a particular a_j (rather than the expected value of the payoffs), we are provided with a ranking of options consistent with the decision maker's certainty equivalents. In other words, the expected utility criterion $EU(a_j)$ is coherent.

Before discussing the theory and assumptions of this, it is useful to have a practical feel for how a utility function is assessed and used in practice. Suppose we are evaluating two strategies a_1 and a_2 in a venture that can have one of three outcomes: good, satisfactory, and poor. The payoff matrix is as follows:

θ	$P(\theta)$	a_1	a_2
Good	0.3	1000	800
Satisfactory	0.4	500	600
Poor	0.3	300	400

The units are in dollars. The range of payoffs evidently goes from \$300 to \$1000. We therefore need to assess our utility function for monetary gain over this domain. It is usual to scale the utility function on the interval 0 to 1. Thus, we denote the lowest payoff in the problem as having a utility of 0 and the highest payoff as having a utility of 1, that is,

$$U(300) \; = 0$$

$$U(1000) = 1$$

by convention. We now ask ourselves what would be our certainty equivalent for a prospect that gave either \$300 or \$1000 with equal chances. Let us suppose this is \$500. Since we require certainty equivalents to be consistent with expected utilities, it follows that

$$U(500) = \tfrac{1}{2}U(300) + \tfrac{1}{2}U(1000) = \tfrac{1}{2}$$

Two further certainty equivalents can be obtained by considering (1) the prospect of \$300 or \$500 with equal chances and (2) the prospect of \$500 and \$1000 with equal chances. Let us suppose that our certainty equivalents for these are (1) \$375 and (2) \$700. Thus, from (1) we can say

$$U(375) = \tfrac{1}{2}U(300) + \tfrac{1}{2}U(500) = 0.25$$

and likewise from (2),

$$U(700) = \tfrac{1}{2}U(500) + \tfrac{1}{2}U(1000) = 0.75$$

Thus we now have five points on our utility function:

$$U(300) = 0$$

$$U(375) = 0.25$$

$$U(500) = 0.5$$

$$U(700) = 0.75$$

$$U(1000) = 1$$

These can be plotted as in Figure 3.1 and a smooth curve interpolated. Evidently, more than five points could have been obtained by continuing the above process

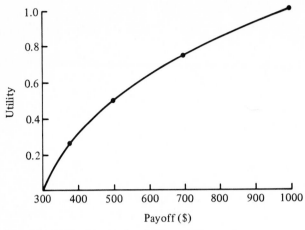

Figure 3.1 Utility function for simple payoff example.

of assessing certainty equivalents for prospects involving equal chances of out-comes with already known (i.e., previously assessed) utilities. Consistency checks should also be done to confirm or reassess some of the points. Thus, for example, the prospect of $375 or $700 with equal chances should also have a certainty equiva-lent of $500 to us. If this is not the case, we should reevaluate some of our initial assessments. Utility assessment is an iterative process which forces considerable self-evaluation in the way that uncertain prospects are valued. Notice that in the above assessment procedure, only equiprobable dichotomous outcomes were considered. This is the simplest of uncertain prospects to consider. We can now, however, use the utility function to analyze more complex decisions. Thus, in our example we can transform the payoffs into utilities, giving this utility matrix:

θ	$P(\theta)$	a_1	a_2
Good	0.3	1.00	0.85
Satisfactory	0.4	0.50	0.65
Poor	0.3	0.00	0.33
	EU =	0.5	0.61

On expected utility grounds, option a_2 would be preferred. The imputed certainty equivalents for utilities of 0.5 (a_1) and 0.61 (a_2) are $500 and $580, respectively, according to the utility function in Figure 3.1.

Thus, to recapitulate: the use of a utility function involves:

1. Deriving a utility function from certainty equivalents for very simple uncertain prospects
2. Using this utility function to transform payoffs in a more complicated decision problem
3. Applying the expected utility criterion to rank options

This method emphasizes two key principles of decision analysis, decomposition and coherence. The decomposition element is apparent in the way that individuals are only required to formulate their preferences upon greatly simplified choices abstracted from the actual, more complicated problem. Coherence enters through the theory of expected utility in that, given a utility function, the application of the expected utility criterion will prescribe the decision maker's coherent preferences for other, more complicated choices, consistent with the risk atttitude exhibited by the decision maker in assessing that function.

Example: Oil prospecting   Grayson (1960) published one of the first accounts of the application of utility functions in an entrepreneurial setting. He interviewed many oil prospectors, quantifying their preferences for hypothetical ventures in terms of utility functions. The assessment method used was slightly different from our equiprobable certainty equivalents. Each prospector was presented with a range of ventures of the sort: "If you had to invest $$X$ in a venture which could yield $$Y$ or nothing, at what probability of success p^* would you be indifferent between accepting and not accepting the venture?" Thus,

$$U(0) = p^*U(Y - X) + (1 - p^*)\, U(-X)$$

In this method, the payoffs and the certainty equivalent are fixed — the decision maker must assess some critical probability. In our equiprobable method, we fixed the payoffs and probabilities, asking the decision maker for the certainty equivalent in the belief that this is an easier task to conceptualize. Although there is some psychological evidence to support this in terms of the biases that individuals exhibit in probability assessment tasks (Tversky, 1974), research on assessment procedures is still active and has not yet yielded firm suggestions on the best method to employ.

Denoting the highest values of X and Y to be considered by X^* and Y^*, we could then, as before, make the utility scale range from 0 to 1 by fixing

$$U(-X^*) = 0$$

$$U(Y^* - X^*) = 1$$

Note that this is arbitrary and we have only adopted the interval 0 to 1 because it is becoming increasingly conventional. Whether it is scaled from 0 to 100, from -1 to 0, or from -100 to $+100$ makes no difference to the ranking of certainty equivalents. Whether we measure temperature in degrees Celsius or degrees Fahrenheit does not affect our judgment upon which of two days is warmer. All we require is consistency. Thus, in fact Grayson chose to fix

$$U(0) = 0$$

and one other point for his utility functions. Figure 3.2 has adapted (with our conventional scaling) one of Grayson's utility functions, namely, that of a William

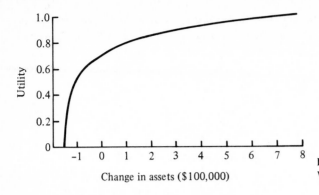

Figure 3.2 Utility function for William Beard in 1957.

Beard of the Beard Oil Company. Incidentally, it is interesting to note that a few years later, Kaufman (1963) found that a simple logarithmic expression of the form

$$U(y) = K \log (y + 150,000)$$

where $y > -150,000$, and K is a scaling constant produced an extremely good fit to William Beard's assessments.

Example: Education planning Dyer et al. (1973) assessed a utility function for a school principal concerned with evaluating a new reading program. The payoff variable is now not money, but the average reading performance of a group of school children in terms of percentile scores on standardized tests. The national median is the fiftieth percentile, and it is evidently around that point that the principal is most sensitive. Figure 3.3 shows this in terms of a change in scope of the utility function. Clearly, risk to the school principal relates to the possibility of doing worse than the national average. Just how we can interpret risk attitude from the shape of a utility function will be considered in the next section.

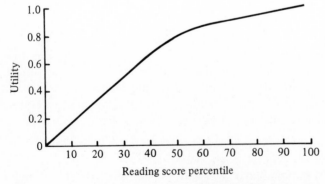

Figure 3.3 Utility function for school principal on reading performance.

For readers interested in seeing further examples of assessed utility functions, Swalm (1966), Spetzler (1968), and Keeney and Raiffa (1976) document several applied studies.

3.3 RISK ATTITUDES

Consider again the equiprobable prospect of receiving $0 or $500 (say, on the toss of a fair coin). If your certainty equivalent for this prospect really is $200, we would likely consider that your valuation of the uncertain prospect is a little conservative, that you are slightly risk-averse. You prefer the certainty of $205 to the 50:50 chances of $0 or $500. Obviously, the expected value of the prospect is $250, and compared with somebody who could afford to "play the odds," who would there-fore have a certainty equivalent of $250, you are undervaluing the prospect. Looking at it another way, the 50 percent chance of losing $200 (that is, if you give up the certainty equivalent option a_2 of $200 and if the uncertain prospect a_1 yields zero) is valued equal to the 50 percent chance of winning $300 (again with reference to passing up the certainty equivalent and a_1 yielding $500).

It is natural, therefore, to consider individual risk attitudes with reference to the expected value of options. More formally, if you are facing an uncertain prospect y (where y is a random payoff variable), then we define the risk premium RP(y) as

$$RP(y) = EV(y) - CE(y)$$

that is, the difference between your certainty equivalent and the expected value. Loosely speaking, it is the amount you are prepared to pay (forego) over the odds to avoid the uncertain prospect. In the above example, the risk premium is evidently $50. We now define the following *risk attitudes*:

1. Risk-averse if and only if RP(y) > 0
2. Risk-neutral if and only if RP(y) = 0
3. Risk-seeking if and only if RP(y) < 0

Figure 3.4 shows the typical shapes of the utility functions associated with these three risk attitudes. For an equiprobable prospect on the best and worst outcomes of y, $U(y) = 1$ and 0, respectively, the certainty equivalent of a risk-neutral person CE_{II} is equal to the expected value. That for a risk-averse person CE_{I} is less, and for a risk-seeking person the certainty equivalent CE_{III} is more.

The utility function of a risk-neutral person is a straight line. This person's certainty equivalent always equals the expected value. The risk premium is always zero. The slope of the function is constant, that is, the second derivative $U''(y) = 0$.

The utility function of a risk-averse person lies above the risk-neutral line. Because the end points are fixed, this gives a curvature to the utility function, as shown in Figure 3.4. The slope is always positive, but decreasingly so, that is, the

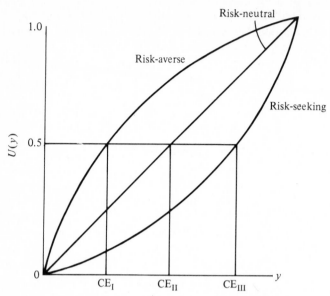

Figure 3.4 Risk-averse, risk-neutral, and risk-seeking utility functions.

second derivative $U''(y) \leq 0$. The risk premium is positive. Its curvature is technically termed concave, from the mathematical definition of a concave function,

$$u(\lambda y_1 + (1 - \lambda)y_2) \geq \lambda u(y_1) + (1 - \lambda)u(y_2)$$

where $0 \leq \lambda \leq 1$. Note that, as a function of λ,

$$Z = \lambda y_1 + (1 - \lambda)y_2$$

is a straight line between y_1 and y_2. Thus the utility of a linear combination of any two points is greater than the linear combination of the utilities of those two points.

The utility function of a risk-seeking person is always below that of the risk-neutral line. The risk premium is negative, and the curvature is such that the slope, again always positive, has the nonnegative second derivative $U''(y) \geq 0$. The curvature is convex, from the definition

$$u(\lambda y_1 + (1 - \lambda)y_2) \leq \lambda u(y_1) + (1 - \lambda)u(y_2)$$

It is evidently the opposite of risk aversion. Where the risk averse prefer to pay to avoid a gamble, the risk seeking will pay to participate.

We notice that all three of the utility functions discussed in the previous section, namely, our's (Figure 3.1), William Beard's (Figure 3.2), and the school principal's (Figure 3.3), exhibited risk aversion. This form certainly seems to have been the most common in decision analysis applications, and quite naturally so. It is reasonable to expect decision makers to be cautious (that is, risk-averse) over prospects where the payoffs are significant to their well-being. Routine, insignificant, or frivolous decisions which do not have much at stake are not usually subjected to decision analysis. Risk-neutral decision makers, moreover, do not usually discuss their analyses in terms of expected utility. If a decision maker is risk-neutral, then the expected value criterion is sufficient to prescribe coherent certainty equivalents. Thus, we see that the justification for using the expected value as a criterion in a nonrepetitive situation lies in the assumption of risk neutrality. It is often suggested that when a decision maker is dealing with payoffs that are well within the usual operating circumstances of a business, then risk neutrality should be adopted. Thus, many of the decisions faced by the average manager within a large corporation can be justified for expected value analysis. However, we observe that even the largest of corporations may be risk-averse in some of its major corporate decisions, such as new acquisitions, capital restructuring, etc. Likewise, risk neutrality is often advocated for much of public policy analysis, but major governmental decisions, such as nuclear power, defense, devaluation, etc., will usually be undertaken from a more cautious, risk-averse position.

It should, therefore, be appreciated that the designation of a risk attitude must be a well-qualified assertion. It is valid only at the time at which the utility function was assessed. At some later point in time a decision maker's utility function may be rather different, due to a change in financial or other circumstances. Thus it is conditional upon the asset level of the decision maker at the time of the analysis. You might well be risk-averse to an equiprobable prospect of $0 or $500 if your liquid assets are only $1000, but risk-neutral to the same prospect should your liquid assets rise to $20,000. Over a large range of payoffs, therefore, a utility function may change its local character. For small chances of large gains, such as the purchase of a lottery ticket, an individual may be risk-seeking. Thus, around the $0 payoff there may be a locally convex region of the utility function. Alternatively, for the chance of considerable losses the individual may be quite risk-averse (e.g., most people take out insurance against loss of their property), causing the utility function to become concave. Between these there may be a region of risk neutrality. Such a possible situation is shown in Figure 3.5 for changes in personal liquid assets in the range of −$200 to +$700. We can identify several regions of different risk attitudes within this function:

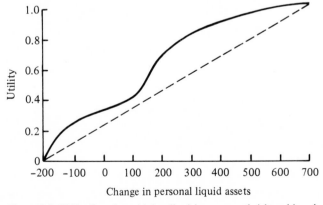

Figure 3.5 Utility function with locally risk-averse and risk-seeking characteristics.

1. *Risk neutrality*. The curve is fairly straight between about $-\$50$ and $+\$50$. Thus, for small gains or losses, the decision maker would be prepared to "play the odds." If the decision maker were offered a prospect yielding $-\$20$ or $+\$25$ with equal probabilities, he or she would take it.

2. *Risk seeking*. From about $\$50$ to $\$150$, the curve is convex, indicating a region of risk-seeking behavior. Strictly speaking, this is the only region of the function which is convex $[U''(y) > 0]$, but notice how it can "annex" risk seeking to prospects extending outside this region. For example, suppose our decision maker were offered a lottery ticket for $\$30$, which would pay $\$250$ to the winner and for which the decision maker knew that the chance of winning would be 1 in 10. On expected value grounds this is not attractive, yet our decision maker might reasonably be expected to take it. In fact, using Figure 3.5, we can compute the expected utility of the venture:

$$EU(\text{lottery}) = 0.9 \, U(-30) + 0.1 \, U(220)$$

$$\approx 0.9(0.30) + 0.1(0.68)$$

$$\approx 0.34$$

This is greater than the status quo

$$EU(\$0 \text{ change in assets}) \approx 0.32$$

3. *Risk aversion*. We notice that below $-\$50$ and above $\$150$ the curve is concave. Furthermore, we also observe that over the whole range, the utility function is predominantly concave (compare the dashed risk-neutral line), even though the middle regions are locally linear and convex. Thus, for a prospect yielding $-\$200$ or $+\$700$, the decision maker will be risk-averse. Likewise, if the decision maker has a bicycle valued at $\$200$, he or she may pay insurance of $\$10$ per year to cover its loss, even though the chance of its being stolen is only, say, 1 in 50.

Thus, we see how a utility function can demonstrate a range of risk attitudes that an individual may adopt according to the payoffs involved. It is not incompatible with utility theory that someone can be taking out insurance and buying lottery tickets at the same time. It is fair to observe, however, that if the range of payoffs in the example of Figure 3.5 had extended a lot further, such as from $-\$10,000$ to $\$50,000$, then the convex kink in the curve around $\$100$ would have paled to insignificance and the overall utility function might have followed the uniformly concave style we noted previously.

However, the important point is that there is no rational risk attitude that a decision maker should embody in his or her utility function. Utility analysis can admit, subject to coherence, various patterns of risk behavior according to the circumstances of the decision maker.

One key issue is how to describe more quantitatively how an individual's risk attitude changes over the defined range of payoffs. Suppose an individual faces the prospect of receiving y for sure and an uncertain amount ε, where ε is a random

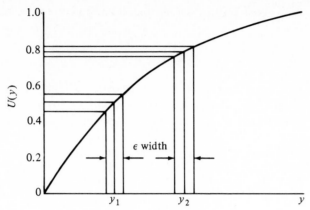

Figure 3.6 Uncertain prospect at different levels of y.

payoff variable, small in comparison to y, with zero mean and variance σ_ε^2. We can define the risk premium as

$$RP(\varepsilon + y) = EV(\varepsilon + y) - CE(\varepsilon + y)$$

$$= y - CE(\varepsilon + y)$$

Thus, we envisage the prospect ε occurring at different points within the range of values for y, and therefore the utility analyses are being undertaken across various ε-width segments throughout the range of y. This is indicated in Figure 3.6. In a sense, variation in y reflects the changing asset basis of the decision maker in facing ε.

A risk attitude is said to be:

1. Decreasing if $RP(\varepsilon + y)$ decreases with increasing y
2. Constant if $RP(\varepsilon + y)$ is constant over all y
3. Increasing if $RP(\varepsilon + y)$ increases with increasing y

These characterizations imply particular functional forms for the utility function. Thus, if an individual has a *constant* risk attitude, then the utility function will be one of the following three equations:

1. If the individual's attitude is *constantly risk-averse*, the utility function must be

$$U(y) = a - be^{-ry}$$

for $r > 0$ and a and b scaling constants.
2. If the individual's attitude is *constantly risk-neutral*, the utility function must be

$$U(y) = a + by$$

with a and b scaling constants. (This is the standard straight-line form for risk neutrality.)

3. If the individual's attitude is *constantly risk-prone*, the utility function must be

$$U(y) = a + be^{-ry}$$

for $r < 0$ and a and b scaling constants, as before.

A constant risk attitude is not so common. It is more usual to think of risk attitudes as changing over y. In particular, the idea of decreasing risk aversion is often suggested as a sensible attitude. This implies that an individual's risk premium for a prospect should decrease as his or her asset level increases relative to ε—hence, the belief that someone is more ready to "play the odds" as the risks become relatively less significant. If an individual subscribes to this attitude a priori, then the utility assessment task is that much easier as the class of admissible functions is reduced. Schlaifer (1971) uses the sumex function

$$U(y) = -e^{-ay} - be^{-cy} \qquad a > 0, bc > 0$$

in his interactive utility assessment computer package to model decreasing risk aversion.

A *proportional risk attitude* has $RP(\varepsilon + y)$ proportional to y. Thus, a constant proportional risk attitude is one that has a risk premium of the form

$$RP(\varepsilon + y) = a + by$$

Pratt (1964) provided a useful way of describing the risk attitude of a utility function in terms of the local *risk aversion function* $r(y)$,

$$r(y) = -\frac{U''(y)}{U'(y)}$$

that is, the ratio of the second derivative to the first. This is particularly useful since it can be shown that

$$RP(\varepsilon + y) \approx \tfrac{1}{2}\sigma_\varepsilon^2 \, r(y)$$

Thus, if we know the functional form of the utility function, we can evaluate the local risk premiums for small prospects.

Example Consider the quadratic utility function

$$U(y) = a + by - cy^2$$

for $b, c > 0$ and $0 \le y < b/2c$. Clearly,

$$r(y) = \frac{2c}{b - 2cy}$$

which implies that the risk premium $RP(y + \varepsilon)$ will *increase* as y increases. If a risk-averse individual were assumed to have a quadratic utility function, then that individual must have increasing risk aversion. It is interesting to speculate upon what this implies for the extensive use of least-squares (minimum-variance) estimation in statistics, with its associated implicit quadratic loss function for estimation errors.

3.4 THEORETICAL ASSUMPTIONS OF UTILITY

The preceding sections have attempted to give some idea of the style of analysis which utility theory tries to achieve. We have indicated *how* it works, but not *why* it should be the case that expected utility is a coherent criterion. In this section the basic assumptions of the method are discussed. The treatment is the traditional one in decision analysis, following quite closely that in Luce and Raiffa (1957), the origins of which are in von Neumann and Morgenstern (1947).

Notation

We have a finite set of n outcomes associated with payoffs $Y_1, Y_2, \ldots, Y_n$. Probabilities can be defined such that we can define a *prospect* A_1 to be a venture that yields Y_i ($i = 1, \ldots, n$) with probability p_{1i}. Thus we could denote A_1 by

$$(p_{11}, Y_1; p_{12}, Y_2; \ldots; p_{1n}, Y_n)$$

We can have m such prospects, indexed through j, that is A_j ($j = 1, \ldots, m$).

Furthermore, we can have a *compound prospect* C_k ($k = 1, \ldots, s$), which yields the prospect A_j with probability q_{kj}. Thus, we could denote C_k by

$$(q_{k1}, A_1; q_{k2}, A_2; \ldots; q_{km}, A_m)$$

A compound prospect is a prospect where the payoffs are further prospects. For example, the prospects A_1 and A_2 could be tosses of a fair and a bent coin, giving, respectively,

$$A_1 \equiv \begin{cases} \text{if heads } (p_{11} = 0.5) \to Y_1 = \$20 \\ \text{if tails } (p_{12} = 0.5) \to Y_2 = -\$10 \end{cases}$$

$$A_2 \equiv \begin{cases} \text{if heads } (p_{21} = 0.3) \to Y_1 = \$20 \\ \text{if tails } (p_{22} = 0.7) \to Y_2 = -\$10 \end{cases}$$

and the compound prospect C_1 could be the roll of a fair die such that if an odd number comes up, you must toss the bent coin:

$$C_1 \equiv \begin{cases} \text{if even number } (q_{11} = 0.5) \to A_1 \\ \text{if odd number } (q_{12} = 0.5) \to A_2 \end{cases}$$

Assumption 1 (Structure)

It is sufficient to describe the choices open to the decision maker in terms of payoff values and their associated probabilities.

In other words, reducing the problem to prospects or compound prospects, captures all that is essential in the decision maker's reasoning. This has been a basic assumption of our payoff matrix model. We have already noted that a decision maker may have multiple payoff variables and that therefore a more sophisticated multiple-attribute model may have to be constructed. (We shall consider multiple-attribute utility in Chapter 5.) Even within single-attribute payoffs, the decision maker can prefer one prospect to another, even though both have exactly the same payoffs and probabilities. One way that this can happen is through the *temporal resolution of uncertainty* (Kreps and Porteus, 1979). Consider two prospects A_1 and A_2, both of which will yield \$1000 or nothing on the toss of a fair coin. In both cases you will receive the prize exactly six months from now. However, A_1 consists of tossing the coin now, whereas in A_2 the coin will not be tossed for six months. Which do you prefer? Unless you are indifferent between A_1 and A_2, time will have to be modeled into the decision analysis.

Assumption 2 (Ordering)

The decision maker can express preference or indifference between any pair of payoffs.

Thus, it is assumed that we can define the relation $\gtrsim$ between payoffs, which means "is preferred or indifferent to," or equivalently, "is not preferred by." For example, $Y_1 \gtrsim Y_2$ means that the decision maker does not prefer Y_2 to Y_1; he or she either prefers Y_1 or finds them equally attractive. Assumption 2, together with coherence, implies *transitivity*, that is, if $A_1 \gtrsim A_2$ and $A_2 \gtrsim A_3$, then $A_1 \gtrsim A_3$. Hence, it is assumed that the decision maker can identify the very best Y^* and the very worst Y_* payoffs.

Assumption 3 (Reduction of Compound Prospects)

Any compound prospect should be indifferent to the equivalent simple prospect with probabilities computed according to the usual rules of probability. Thus, we have

$$
\begin{aligned}
C_k &\equiv (q_{k1}, A_1; q_{k2}, A_2; \cdots; q_{km}, A_m) \\
&\equiv [q_{k1}, (p_{11}, Y_1; p_{12}, Y_2; \ldots; p_{1n}, Y_n); \\
&\quad q_{k2}, (p_{21}, Y_1; p_{22}, Y_2; \ldots; p_{2n}, Y_n); \\
&\quad \vdots \\
&\quad q_{km}, (p_{m1}, Y_1; p_{m2}, Y_2; \ldots; p_{mn}, Y_n)] \\
&\equiv (p'_{k1}, Y_1; p'_{k2}, Y_2; \ldots; p'_{kn}, Y_n)
\end{aligned}
$$

that is, a "simple" prospect where

$$
p'_{kj} = q_{k1}p_{1j} + q_{k2}p_{2j} + \cdots + q_{km}p_{mj}
$$

This is the sort of coherence that many decision makers may wish to achieve. However, it does imply no preference on the part of the decision maker for the multiple-stage aspect of the uncertainty resolution. Any preference for the "atmosphere of the game" or the "joy of gambling" would be inconsistent with this assumption. Likewise, individuals who like a particular line of business because of the intrinsic way that the risks evolve may choose to violate this assumption.

Assumption 4 (Continuity)

Every payoff Y_i can be considered a certainty equivalent for a prospect

$$[u_i, Y^*; (1 - u_i), Y_*]$$

for $0 \leq u_i \leq 1$.

As the converse of the certainty equivalent argument which we presented initially, this seems to be a reasonable postulate of coherence. However, in practice, the worst outcome is often very unpalatable (e.g., mortality), and this assumption implies that we can find a prospect involving this very horrid outcome that we would exchange for something quite inconsequential. For example, providing you prefer $100 to nothing, we can find a nonzero probability such that you find the prospect of $100 or death attractive. Suppose we say that there is $100 in an envelope halfway across campus waiting for you tomorrow at lunchtime. Alternatively, if you choose not to go across campus for it, we will deposit $10 in your bank account. Many of you will prefer to walk across campus for the $100, even though this is not the safe option. Walking across any campus that we have known has always involved some risk to life or limb! The principle of making such choices involving unthinkable payoffs is therefore implicitly reasonable; it is the practice of thinking about it explicitly that is sometimes the problem. Fortunately most decisions do not involve such awkwardly extreme outcomes.

Assumption 5 (Substitutability)

In any prospect, Y_i can be substituted by $[u_i, Y^*; (1 - u_i), Y_*]$. In other words, Y_i and $[u_i, Y^*; (1 - u_i), Y_*]$ are indifferent not only when considered alone, but also when considered part of a more complicated prospect. This is similar to the independence of irrelevant alternatives principle discussed in Section 2.2 under Minimax Regret. The decision maker's attitude to Y_i and $[u_i, Y^*; (1 - u_i), Y_*]$ is not affected by other payoffs.

Assumption 6 (Transitivity of Prospects)

The decision maker can express preference of indifference between all pairs of prospects. This is an extension of Assumption 2 and now allows us to construct, for any prospect A_j, an equivalent that just involves payoffs Y_* and Y^*. Thus, consider A_1,

$$A_1 \equiv (p_{11}, Y_1; \ldots; p_{1n}, Y_n)$$

Assumption 4 tells us that for each Y_i there exists $[u_i, Y^*; (1 - u_i), Y_*]$, and Assumption 5 allows us to substitute this for Y_i. Thus,

$$A_1 \equiv \{p_{11}, [u_1, Y^*; (1 - u_1), Y_*]; \ldots\}$$

Assumption 3 allows us to reduce this to the simple prospect

$$A_1 \equiv [p_1, Y^*; (1 - p_1), Y_*]$$

where $\qquad p_1 = p_{11}u_1 + p_{12}u_2 + \cdots + p_{1n}u_n$

Assumption 7 (Monotonicity)

A prospect $A_r \equiv [p_r, Y^*; (1 - p_r), Y_*]$ is preferred or indifferent to

$$A_s \equiv [p_s, Y^*; (1 - p_s), Y_*]$$

if and only if $p_r \geq p_s$.

Assumption 6 allows us to apply the relation $\gtrsim$ to prospects (as well as payoffs), and we have shown that any prospect A_j can be expressed in the form

$$[p_j, Y^*; (1 - p_j), Y_*]$$

Assumption 7 now gives us a necessary and sufficient condition (a "criterion") for the relation $\gtrsim$ to exist between prospects. It is reasonable to assume that for two options with the same two alternative payoffs, we should prefer the option with the higher probability of giving the better payoff. Cases where this does not appear to be appropriate usually mean that an extra attribute has to be modeled into the decision analysis (see Assumption 1).

This now gives us our expected utility criterion. Here $A_r \gtrsim A_s$ if and only if

$$p_r \geq p_s$$

That is,

$$p_{r1}u_1 + p_{r2}u_2 + \cdots + p_{rn}u_n \geq p_{s1}u_1 + p_{s2}u_2 + \cdots + p_{sn}u_n$$

and

$$EU(A_r) \geq EU(A_s)$$

The set of numbers $(u_1, u_2, \ldots, u_n)$ are points on the utility function $U(Y)$ for particular values of Y, namely, $Y_1, \ldots, Y_n$. We note (Assumption 4) that the utility u_i [i.e., $U(Y_i)$] is essentially the *probability* of the best outcome that would make you indifferent between Y_i and the uncertain prospect of Y_* or Y^*. When $Y_i = Y^*$, this would be 1, and hence we scale $U(Y^*) = 1$. Likewise, when $Y_i = Y_*$, this probability would be zero, and hence again $U(Y_*) = 0$. Thus, our conventional utility function is scaled between 0 and 1.

3.5 SOME CAVEATS IN INTERPRETING UTILITY

We have been developing a *normative* theory. If a decision maker wishes to be coherent in the sense of adopting the above assumptions, then if he or she assesses a consistent utility function, the application of the expected utility criterion will *prescribe* the certainty equivalent ranking of more complicated options. It is not necessarily a *descriptive* theory. It suggests what people *should* do to be coherent, not what they *are* doing. Indeed, there is evidence in economics and behavioral science (e.g., Kahnemann and Tversky, 1979) that typically individuals violate expected utility in practice to a greater or lesser extent depending upon the circumstances. This is perhaps fortunate for the role of decision analysis. Otherwise there would be no scope for improved methods of decision making. We shall return to this point in the next sections. It is important to indicate now certain pitfalls in using expected utility that should be avoided.

Utilities Don't Add Up

If the ultimate payoff to a venture consists of a sequence of component payoffs, such as costs and revenues year by year, you cannot evaluate the expected utility of each component individually and then sum these expected utilities. More formally,

$$U(A + B) \neq U(A) + U(B)$$

This is the whole point of the curvature of the utility function. A given risk at one asset position will be viewed differently when the asset base changes. If the utility function is linear, that is, the decision maker is risk-neutral and thereby adopts the expected value criterion, then the expected values of the components can be summed to give the total expected value for the venture. Thus, when applying expected utility to a venture, the net total payoffs for each option should be computed before transforming to utilities.

Utility Differences Do Not Express Strength of Preferences

If $Y_1 > Y_2 > Y_3 > Y_4$ and $[U(Y_1) - U(Y_2)] > [U(Y_3) - U(Y_4)]$, in other words, going from Y_2 to Y_1 causes a larger increase in utility than going from Y_4 to Y_3, we cannot say that this greater utility difference implies a greater preference for this change. Utility theory (the von Neumann and Morgenstern version, that is) only provides a numerical scale to *order* preferences, not to measure their strengths. Like many subjective scales of value, it is an "ordinal" and not an "interval" measure. Consider another example. Students are usually asked to grade teachers on a numerical scale, often 1 through 7. This is interpreted to mean that a teacher with a score of 6 has done a better job than one with a score of 5. Nowhere in the structure of this measure is the implication that a teacher whose average rating went from 5 last semester to 6 this semester made exactly the same progress as another who went from 6 to 7 in the same period. An interval scale, however, such as weight, can allow you to say that a person who grew from 140 to 150 pounds last month put on the same weight as one who went from 155 to 165 pounds in the same period. The function of the numbers in the utility measure is just to provide a ranking of prospects.

Utilities Are Not Comparable from Person to Person

Because two people assign the same expected utilities to a venture, it does not imply that it is worth the same to each of them. A utility function is a personal statement of an individual's risk attitude and does not provide a common basis for aggregating preferences across groups of different people.

3:6 ISSUES IN THE ASSESSMENT OF UTILITY FUNCTIONS

The methodological aspirations of utility theory in the context of decision analysis are clearly valuable. However, the assessment of a utility function is not an approach that comes naturally to practical human decision making. In aiming for extensive decomposition and coherence, are we not in danger of putting the decision maker in such an awkward unnatural frame of mind that we might lose more than we gain in the process? The expected utility analysis builds everything upon the assessed utility function. If there are serious errors at the input stage, this can distort the entire subsequent analysis.

The decision analyst's position is that utility theory can be very useful in bringing the decision maker's risk attitude into the analysis, but it must be undertaken carefully. The decision maker should understand what utility analysis is trying to do and perceive it to be worthwhile. In assessing the certainty equivalents for the contrived prospects in order to obtain the utility function, any levity or minor frivolity that might come into the process because of its apparent abstraction away from the real problematic situation should be resisted. It is easy to introduce a certain lack of gravitas into the assessment when important payoffs are being evaluated by analogy to the toss of a coin. The context of the assessment process should clearly be kept as close as possible to the real seriousness of the problem.

The basic assessment situation consists, as we have seen, of confronting the decision maker with two prospects, X and Y:

$$X \equiv \text{a payoff for certain}$$

$$Y \equiv \begin{cases} \text{payoff } G \text{ with probability } p \\ \text{or} \\ \text{payoff } L \text{ with probability } 1 - p \end{cases}$$

where G(gain?) is greater than L(loss?). There are several ways of doing this, which can be discussed according to the following:

Response mode In comparing X and Y, there are four variables to consider, X, G, L, and p. Any three can be fixed and the fourth left as the assessment which the decision maker gives for indifference between X and Y. Following the terminology in Hershey et al. (1982), we therefore have four procedures:

1. *Certainty equivalence*, where G, L, and p are fixed and the decision maker assesses X (this is the way we did it earlier)
2. *Probability equivalence*, where X, G, and L are fixed and the decision maker assesses p
3. *Gain equivalence*, where X, L, and p are fixed and the decision maker assesses G
4. *Loss equivalence*, where X, G, and p are fixed and the decision maker assesses L

The relative merits of these four procedures are currently far from being completely understood. The first two procedures are the most common, and Hershey et al. (1982) report some preliminary investigations that suggest that method 1 tends to reveal more risk aversion for gains and more risk seeking for losses than the average risk attitudes exhibited by use of method 2.

Levels of probability In the utility assessment procedures that we discussed previously, the probability level was fixed at 0.5. It could, of course, have been fixed at another level (such as 0.7), and in the probability equivalence method it is a variable at the discretion of the decision maker. There is ample evidence (Hogarth, 1980) that individuals distort probability judgments. This is particularly so with small probabilities which either get over- or underperceived. Thus, we have to be prepared for the effects that probability distortions might have in utility assessments. Karmaker (1978) discusses how utility functions may vary according to the level of probabilities chosen for the assessment when the decision maker exhibits certain forms of probability distortion. Again the evidence on this topic is far from definitive. The view among decision analysts seems to be that the 50:50 assessment method is the least biased in this respect and that the burden of proof still lies upon any alternative method to replace it in practice.

Levels of payoff The utility function is defined between the extremes of G and L appropriate to the decision problem which it serves. Thus the extreme values of G and L are set by the maximum and minimum payoffs in the problem and are not an assessment issue. However, the manner in which G and L are varied within this interval to obtain the required certainty equivalents is such an issue. Previously we used a sequence of nested assessments working inward from the extremes. There is some evidence (see Kahnemann and Tversky, 1979) that this method might introduce some bias toward risk aversion if the extremes are very extreme. Since these act as initial reference points, they may be overly influential in the decision maker's perception of the problem. Kahnemann and Tversky have discussed many times the so-called adjustment bias in an individual's formulation of opinion and preference. Essentially an individual makes judgments upon a new aspect by evaluating it as an adjustment from some reference point. Typically, this adjustment is not enough and an individual's assessments are often said to be "anchored" at a reference point. This bias was originally identified in probability assessment (Tversky, 1974) and later recognized in utility assessment (Kahnemann and Tversky, 1979). All sequential assessments will exhibit adjustment bias to some degree; the practical problem is to design procedures that mitigate its effect. Farquhar (1982) reviews many useful developments in this respect. There is also some evidence (see Hershey et al., 1982) that if the assessments over the "losses" and "gains" regions of payoff are as much as possible kept separate rather than being simultaneously assessed, then a much less risk-averse utility function will result. It seems to be the case that the more widely spread G and L are in terms of gains and losses, the higher the risk premium for a prospect. The further understanding of the nature of these cognitive dysfunctions and the importance of isolating the role of an "aspiration level" (or "target payoff") from which payoffs become apparent gains or losses has been an important area of research in behavioral decision theory. Again, this research is not yet definitive, and conscientious decision analysts in practice attempt to achieve some consistency from a hybrid of various methods.

Assumption or transfer of risk The basic decision-making situation that the assessment task provides is that of the decision maker having to change his or her status quo to X or Y. Thus, the decision maker will be assuming either the certainty X or the risk Y. Now, in their well-intentioned eagerness to aid the decision maker's deliberations, decision analysts are apt to rephrase this question. This is particularly so when both G and L are losses. When confronted with assuming either a fixed loss X or a variable loss Y, the decision maker would really prefer neither. The decision maker, for the purposes of deriving the utility function, is, of course, not allowed to do this. Thus, the question is often reposed in the form of "if you are facing Y, how much would you pay to have it removed?" This is analogous to the purchase of insurance, a situation which might appear more realistic. Observe that in this case we are assessing X as an indifference point for the transfer of risk. Hershey et al. (1982) discuss the different risk attitudes that can result from such rephrasing. They have identified a so-called inertia bias—a tendency for people to stay with the current situation unless the alternative is demonstrably superior. (This has shades of anchoring attached to it.) Systematic conclusions on this effect are still underdeveloped, but such rephrasing has obvious value in checking the articulated assessments for consistency.

One form of rephrasing to be avoided is that of interchanging the buying and selling price for an uncertain prospect (see Raiffa, 1968). Thus, if you assess X as the minimum selling price for Y (the risk transfer situation above), then it is a valid certainty equivalent since you are basically choosing between receiving X for sure and the risky prospect. However, this would not usually be the same (unless you have a constant risk attitude) as saying that X is the most you would *pay* to assume Y. Here you are essentially comparing the prospects

$$A \equiv \text{status quo}$$

$$B \equiv \begin{cases} \text{payoff } G - X \text{ with probability } p \\ \text{or} \\ \text{payoff } L - X \text{ with probability } 1 - p \end{cases}$$

which is not at all the same problem.

There is now a large body of evidence concerning the heuristics and dysfunctions that individuals exhibit in their decision making. The above discussion of utility assessment has only hinted at some of the issues. Readers who are interested in seeing more of this literature may find the work by Hogarth (1980) useful. It is clear that individuals do not make judgments and decisions entirely consistent with expected utility. For this reason, psychologists and economists who are interested in *descriptive* theories of decision making have sought to modify the theory to give it more empirical validity (for example, Kahnemann and Tversky,

1979; Machina, 1982). However, as a *normative* theory, decision analysts still seek to advise the use of expected utility whenever appropriate. A careful analyst will, however, be sensitive to possible cognitive biases and situations where the utility assumptions do not appear to hold. In part, the decision analyst is a decision-making psychotherapist with the task of helping the decision maker understand his or her reasoning on a problem. Through coherence testing it may be apparent that the decision maker does not want to subscribe to the expected utility approach. That is fine, provided the decision maker now understands more about his or her preference structure and its limitations.

Consider the Allais problem (Exercise 2.8—if you have not yet looked at this problem, it may be a good idea to do it now before reading on). Recall that we have four options:

$$a_1 = \quad \text{payoff \$1 million for certain}$$

$$a_2 \equiv \begin{cases} \text{payoff \$5 million, probability 0.1} \\ \text{payoff \$1 million, probability 0.89} \\ \text{payoff \$0, probability 0.01} \end{cases}$$

$$a_3 \equiv \begin{cases} \text{payoff \$5 million, probability 0.1} \\ \text{payoff \$0, probability 0.9} \end{cases}$$

$$a_4 \equiv \begin{cases} \text{payoff \$1 million, probability 0.11} \\ \text{payoff \$0, probability 0.89} \end{cases}$$

Do you prefer a_1 to a_2, or vice versa? Alternatively, which of a_3 or a_4 do you prefer? This study has been undertaken many times, with the majority of responses being of the form $a_1 > a_2$ and $a_3 > a_4$. This is incoherent under expected utility theory. Let $U(0) = 0$ and $U(5) = 1$. Then

$$EU(a_1) = U(1)$$

$$EU(a_2) = 0.1 + 0.89\, U(1)$$

Thus, $a_1 > a_2$ if and only if

$$U(1) - 0.89U(1) - 0.1 > 0$$

that is,
$$0.11U(1) > 0.1$$

Likewise,

$$EU(a_3) = 0.1$$

$$EU(a_4) = 0.11U(1)$$

and $a_3 > a_4$ if and only if

$$0.1 > 0.11U(1)$$

Thus, either $a_1 > a_2$ and $a_4 > a_3$ or $a_1 < a_2$ and $a_4 < a_3$ is coherent. Essentially, moving from prospect a_1 to a_2 and from a_4 to a_3 consists of both reducing the probability of \$1 million payoff by 0.11 and increasing that of \$5 million and \$0 payoffs by 0.1 and 0.01, respectively. Kahnemann and Tversky (1979) attribute the common incoherence in this problem to the *certainty effect*—that individuals tend to over-weight a certain outcome compared to expected utility theory. When confronted with this, many subjects revise their opinion to be coherent. However, Moskowitz (1974) still found that, even after discussion, the majority of his subjects preferred to stay with their original nonexpected utility preferences. Thus, in this latter case, the simple application of expected utility would not be appropriate.

Thus, we should not take the applicability of expected utility for granted. Further, even where it does seem applicable, the utility assessment task should involve many consistency checks, and the final decision analysis should be checked for sensitivity to the assessed utility function. The use of an interactive computer assessment facility can help this process considerably (Farquhar, 1982, references some work on these), not only for consistency and sensitivity work, but also in recording the assessed utility function accurately.

Failure to appreciate this latter point has been the cause of many practical disappointments with utility analysis carried out by hand. Suppose a utility function is being assessed over the range −$50,000 to $300,000, not unrealistic for most medium-sized business decisions. Given the subjectivity of the task, the decision maker may quite reasonably feel that the utility function is only approximate to the extent that, for example, $U(160,000)$ could be anywhere between points A and B in Figure 3.7 and $U(180,000)$ likewise could be anywhere between points C and D. What we should not do is to plot the utility function with a blunt instrument and argue that the utility scale is only accurate to one decimal place, that is, both $U(160,000)$ and $U(180,000)$ equal 0.9. In transforming our payoffs to utilities, we would thus be asserting that payoffs of $160,000 or $180,000 are indifferent. A lot of care may have been taken at the accounting end to assess the payoffs of various proposals to three or four significant figures. This should not be destroyed in the utility analysis by working only to one or two significant figures. The actual point is that although the utility function could pass anywhere

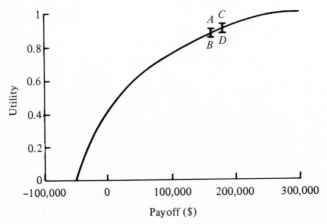

Figure 3.7 The approximate nature of a utility function.

between A and B, its increasing nature is not in question. Thus, if it goes through A, it will most likely go through a point close to C, certainly not D. Thus, having assessed a utility function, work with it accurately to the same number of significant figures as were embodied in the payoff calculations in order to preserve the ordering of payoff preferences. Afterwards do sensitivity analyses on changes in curvature. Evidently, this is not always easy to do graphically by hand.

3.7 FINAL PERSPECTIVE

A coherent decision criterion for uncertain prospects will effectively prescribe the decision maker's certainty equivalents. By making several apparently reasonable assumptions about the way that an individual makes choices, utility theory can provide a model to prescribe a decision maker's certainty equivalents in complex situations on the basis of his or her responses to several simple situations. This model is the expected utility model. All payoffs in a decision problem are transformed, via a utility function, into utilities, and the criterion is then to maximize expected utility. The utility function can exhibit varying degrees of risk aversion, risk neutrality, or risk seeking across the spectrum of payoffs. The assessment of the utility function is not a trivial task and requires considerable sensitivity to the cognitive processes of the subjects and the sorts of biases to which they may be prone. Expected utility will only be the appropriate criterion if the decision maker accepts its assumptions. It will not always be the correct way to model certainty equivalence. Nevertheless, even if it is not appropriate, the process of discovering why this is the case can provide considerable insight to the decision maker.

EXERCISES

3.1 You are lucky enough to be faced with the following prospects:

1. $3000 for certain
2. $12,000 with probability $\frac{1}{3}$ and $0 with probability $\frac{2}{3}$
3. $10,000 with probability $\frac{1}{3}$, $1000 with probability $\frac{1}{2}$, and $0 with probability $\frac{1}{6}$
4. $2000 with probability $\frac{1}{3}$, $5000 with probability $\frac{1}{2}$, and $0 with probability $\frac{1}{6}$
5. $1000 with probability $\frac{1}{5}$, $-$2000 with probability $\frac{2}{5}$, and $15,000 with probability $\frac{2}{5}$

Without doing any analysis, rank the prospects in terms of preference. Construct your utility function over the range of payoffs and then rank the prospects according to expected utility. Any surprises? How do you reconcile them?

3.2 Construct an example to demonstrate that the expected utility of both the buyer and the seller of an insurance policy can increase with the transaction.

3.3 An individual may receive two uncertain increments x_1 and x_2 to his assets. If the individual is risk-averse, show that

$$U(x_1 + x_2) < U(x_1) + U(x_2)$$

3.4 An investor has $1000 to invest. He has a choice of two ventures, each costing $500 as the minimum investment. Thus, he could invest $500 in each, or $1000 in one of them, or not invest at all. Each investment is independent and will either double or halve the sum invested with equal probability. If the investor is slightly risk-averse what will he do?

3.5 Is it incoherent for an enterprise to use the expected value criterion for new ventures and to pursue diversified holdings?

3.6 The government of the United Kingdom sells premium bonds to its residents in units of £1. No regular interest is paid on these bonds, but each month bonds are selected at random for a variety of prizes ranging from £25 to £100,000. Furthermore, the bond holder can always cash in a bond and reclaim its unit value. The total value of the prizes awarded each month (almost £6 million in 1978) depends to a certain extent on the U.K. government base lending rate. At a time in 1978 when the interest on regular savings was about 9 percent (taxable) and about 12 percent (taxable) on fixed medium-term savings, the annual prize fund amounted to about 6 percent (taxfree) of the total value of premium bonds being held. Because of the distribution in value of the prizes, each unit of £1 had, at this time, a chance of about 1 in 12,000 of being a winner in any month, with approximately 98 percent of the monthly prizes being either £50 or £25. Once a unit has won a prize, it is no longer eligible for future draws.

A person has just taken out an insurance policy for loss or damage to his gold watch valued at £200. He is now considering whether to invest £500 in premium bonds. Are these two decisions coherent?

3.7 The following offer has been made to you by an enormously wealthy individual whose integrity in paying off debts is impeccable. A fair coin will be tossed repeatedly until a head turns up. If it turns up on the first toss, you will be paid $1; if it turns up on the second toss, you will be paid $2; if it turns up on the third toss, you will be paid $4; if it turns up on the fourth toss, you will be paid $8, and so on. What is the maximum you would pay to participate in this venture? How do you justify your answer? What is the implicit "risk premium" in your answer?

[This is an adaptation of an old problem, known as the Petersburg problem—see, for example, Todhunter (1949): *A History of the Mathematical Theory of Probability*, Chelsea, New York.]

3.8 A friend of yours has been offered the choice of either the following gamble:

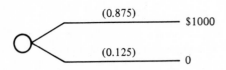

or a sure thing payment in the amount of $675. This friend had great difficulty dealing with the probability 0.875 and so came to you for help. After great effort, you obtained the five points on your friend's utility curve as shown at the top of page 65.

(*a*) Your friend is able to comprehend gambles where there are two prizes, each with probability 0.5, and is able to assess certainty equivalents for such gambles. What question would you ask your friend (using the above data) concerning such gambles, which would determine whether your friend should take the gamble or the sure thing?

(*b*) Suppose your friend understands the concept of risk aversion and is certain that he or she is risk-averse in the above range. Using the above data [but not your answer to (*a*)], can you tell whether your friend should take the sure thing or the gamble? Why or why not?

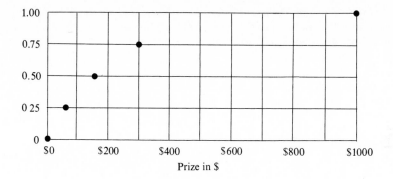

Prize in $

3.9 General Public Electric (GPE) needs to build a new power plant. However, the management is worried about the financial risk. The plant will contribute $10 million per year to net earnings if all goes well. But if something happens and the plant is shut down, the annual loss to the owner is $10 million per year. The probability of the plant being shut down is 10 percent.

GPE management approaches two neighboring power companies—Public Service, Inc. (PSI) and People's Power Company (PPC)—to discuss joint ownership of the new plant. They agreed to these terms:

1. All three companies will be part owners of the plant.
2. Each company will own at least 20 percent of the power plant.
3. Each company will share earnings or losses in proportion to their share of the ownership.

GPE is more risk-averse than either neighboring company. PSI is risk-neutral, and PPC is, in fact, risk-preferring. GPE and PPC assign the following risk premiums:

Share of ownership (percent)	0	20	40	60	80	100
GPE risk premium ($million/yr)	0	1.1	2.0	3.8	6.6	10
PPC risk premium ($million/yr)	0	−0.2	−0.4	−0.6	−0.8	−1.0

The companies have not yet decided how to divide the ownership (that is, what share each company will own).

(*a*) GPE is trying to decide whether to ask for 20, 40, or 60 percent ownership. Determine which of these three shares is best for GPE, considering their attitude toward risk. Explain your answer.

(*b*) Assume GPE owns the share determined in part (*a*). Also, assume PSI and PPC will divide the remaining shares so that they maximize the sum of their annual certain equivalent earnings. PSI will own 20, 40, or 60 percent, and PPC will own whatever is not owned by PSI and GPE. Determine the shares going to PSI and PPC.

(This problem was originally prepared by Bruce Judd.)

3.10 *Probabilistic Insurance.* You have considered insuring a particular item of property (such as a bicycle, a camera, your home contents, etc.), but after considering the risks and the insurance premium quoted, you have no clear preference of either purchasing the insurance or taking the risk. The insurance company then comes back to you with a new scheme called *probabilistic insurance.* You pay half the above premium, but have coverage only in the sense that in the case of a claim there is a probability of one-half that you will be asked to pay the other half of the premium and will be completely covered, or that you will not be covered and will have your premium returned. We assume that these probabilities will be fairly and randomly assigned. Would you purchase probabilistic insurance?

3.11 *Risk Sharing*

(a) In a day or two's time you will be offered a 50:50 chance of winning x or losing y. All that you know at the moment is that both x and y will be between $0 and $2000. Furthermore, you must give instructions to an agent who will act on your behalf when the opportunity arises. It is suggested that you plot a curve that divides all possible (x, y) combinations into an "acceptance set" and a "rejection set."

(b) Assess your own utility function for an opportunity which could give you, at best, a gain of $2000 or, at worst, a loss of $2000. How does this curve relate to the one you would construct for the purposes of (a)?

(c) Consider your individual answer to part (a) and whether *collectively* you, as a member of a group, would be prepared to accept an (x, y) proposal which is not in your acceptance set. If you can answer this question alongside a fellow student, find a joint curve which an agent can use on behalf of your "partnership." Upon what features of your partnership does this curve depend?

REFERENCES

Dyer, J., W. Farrell, and P. Bradley (1973): "Utility Functions for Test Performance," *Management Science*, vol. 20, pp. 507–519.

Farquhar, P. (1982): "Utility Assessment Methods," W. P. 81–5, University of California, Davis.

Grayson, C. J. (1960): "Decisions under Uncertainty: Drilling Decisions by Oil and Gas Operators," Harvard Business School, Boston.

Hershey, J. C., H. C. Kunreuther, and P. J. H. Shoemaker (1982): "Sources of Bias in Assessment Procedures for Utility Functions," *Management Science*, vol. 28, pp. 936–954.

Hogarth, R. M. (1980): *Judgment and Choice: The Psychology of Decision*, Wiley, New York.

Kahnemann, D., and A. Tversky (1979): "Prospect Theory: An Analysis of Decision under Risk," *Econometrica*, vol. 47, no. 2, pp. 263–291.

Karmaker, U. S. (1978): "Subjectivity Weighted Utility," *Organizational Behavior and Human Performance*, vol. 21, pp. 61–72.

Kaufman, G. (1963): *Statistical Decision and Related Techniques in Oil and Gas Exploration*, Prentice-Hall, Englewood Cliffs, N.J.

Keeney, R., and H. Raiffa (1976): *Decisions with Multiple Objectives*, Wiley, New York.

Kreps, D., and E. Porteus (1979): "Temporal Von-Neumann–Morgenstern and Induced Preferences," *Econometrica* vol. 20, pp. 81–109.

Luce, R. D., and H. Raiffa (1951): *Games and Decisions*, Wiley, New York.

Machina, M. (1982): "'Expected Utility' without the Independence Axiom," *Econometrica*, vol. 50, no. 2, pp. 277–327.

Moskowitz, H. (1974): "Effect of Problem Representation and Feedback on Rational Behavior in Allais and Morlat-Type Problems," *Decision Sciences*, vol. 5, pp. 225–242.

Pratt, J. W. (1964): "Risk Aversion in the Small and in the Large," *Econometrica*, vol. 32, pp. 122–136.

Raiffa, H. (1968): *Decision Analysis*, Addison-Wesley, Reading, Mass.

Schlaifer, R. (1971): "Computer Programmes for Elementary Decision Analysis," Graduate School of Business, Harvard University, Boston.

Spetzler, C. S. (1968): "The Development of a Corporate Risk Policy for Capital Investment Decisions," *IEEE Transactions on System Science and Cybernetics*, vol. SSC-4, pp. 279–300.

Swalm, R. O. (1966): "Utility Theory—Insights into Risk Taking," *Harvard Business Review*, vol. 44, pp. 123–136.

√ Tversky, A. (1974): "Assessing Uncertainty," *Journal of the Royal Statistical Society*, vol. 36, pp. 148–159.

von Neumann, J., and O. Morgenstern (1947): *Theory of Games and Economic Behavior*, Princeton University Press, Princeton, N.J.

FOUR

SCREENING PROSPECTS BY DOMINANCE

4.1 DOMINANCE CRITERIA

We have met dominance criteria before. In Section 2.2 we discussed outcome dominance in the context of payoff matrix analysis. The example used was

	a_1	a_2	a_3
θ_1	6	3	8
θ_2	5	4	2
θ_3	7	6	3

Here we observed that action a_1 dominates a_2 in that whatever value of θ occurs, the payoff from a_2 is never greater than that from a_1. Outcome dominance is the weakest form of a decision criterion, assuming only a preference of more to less and some coherence reasoning. Evidently, it can be very useful in *screening* a set of decision options to eliminate the "nonstarters" for any subsequent decision analysis.

We also recall from Section 2.4 the brief discussion on mean-variance dominance. This is not undertaken in the framework of a payoff matrix, but on the basis of a set of payoff distributions $f_j(y)$ for each option j. The use of payoff distributions was developed to have wider applicability than the payoff matrix. We recall that it does not restrict all payoffs to be determined by one outcome probability distribution $P(\theta)$. Thus, a large manufacturing company might be comparing a_1, expand the existing facility in New Jersey, with a_2, develop a new plant in Algeria, the uncertainties of which are quite different. However, ultimately they can be reduced to two probability distributions on monetary payoff, $f_1(y)$ and $f_2(y)$. Mean-variance dominance works by eliminating either the option of higher variance for two options with equal means, or the option of lower mean for two options with equal variance. We also recall from that discussion how the object of a screening exercise is to obtain an "efficient" set of options that cannot be further reduced by dominance reasoning, and which will presumably then be subjected to analysis using a more explicit decision criterion.

In this section, we shall consider more thoroughly the dominance approach, both in terms of more types of dominance and in light of a closer look at the assumptions of each. At this stage, however, a general point on the validity of a dominance criterion needs to be clarified. Assuming the decision maker to be expected utility maximizing, if $f_j(y)$ dominates $f_i(y)$, then it is implicit that

$$\int_{-\infty}^{+\infty} U(y) f_j(y)\, dy \geq \int_{-\infty}^{+\infty} U(y) f_i(y)\, dy$$

that is,

$$U(a_j) \geq U(a_i)$$

Now what dominance tries to do is to make some general statement about the form of $U(y)$—which can be very weak, for example, $U(y)$ increases with y—such that certain conditions can be placed upon $f_j(y)$ and $f_i(y)$ for the above relation to hold. These are essentially the dominance conditions. Some of these will be considered below.

First-Degree Stochastic Dominance (FSD)

This is really just a generalization of the payoff dominance situation to deal with a set of payoff distributions. The basic assumption made is that $U(y)$ increases with y, that is, the decision maker prefers more of y to less. $U(y)$ is also assumed to be smooth and differentiable, a condition which is usually taken for granted. Thus, a_j dominates a_i in the sense of FSD if the condition

$$F_i(y) \geq F_j(y)$$

holds for all y.

In practice, all that needs to be done is to plot the cumulative distributions for each option in the usual way and eliminate those whose curves are completely to the left of another and do not intersect it. Frequently, however, curves will intersect, and the FSD screening method will be inconclusive. This is where second-degree stochastic dominance can further screen the set of options. Notice that if a_j does not dominate a_i, it does not imply the converse. All that can be said is that the weak assumptions of this type of dominance are not powerful enough to discriminate between these two options.

Second-Degree Stochastic Dominance (SSD)

In addition to FSD requirements, SSD requires the decision maker to be risk-averse over y. Under these assumptions, option j will dominate i if the condition

$$\int_{-\infty}^{z} [F_i(y) - F_j(y)]\, dy \geq 0$$

holds for all z over y.

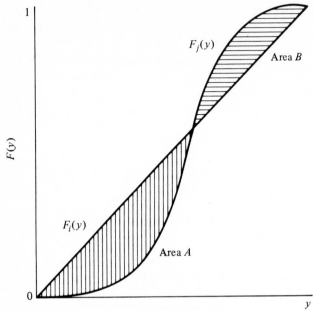

Figure 4.1 Second-degree stochastic dominance

In other words, the accumulated area under $F_i(y)$ should not be less than that of $F_j(y)$ for each point on y. In practice, this can be done quite simply by investigating the pattern of intersection of the two curves, and thus often avoiding the integration of the above expression. In Figure 4.1 it is clear that i is dominated. There is no way that j could be dominated since $F_i(y)$ is initially the steeper curve. All that has to be ascertained is that after the intersection, $F_j(y)$ does not overcompensate in accumulated area for what it "lost" before, that is, that area B is less than area A. Incidentially, if $A = B$, then i is still dominated. If B is greater than A, then the SSD test is inconclusive. This evaluation can often be done visually if the curves are plotted on squared graph paper.

One of the problems with SSD is the "left tail" sensitivity. We noted above that if one option has initially the steeper cumulative distribution (i.e., a longer left tail in its probability density function), there is no way, under SSD, that it can be the dominating option. To see how unreasonable this can be, consider the situation where you have the choice of $99 for certain or a risky outcome giving $98 with a 1 percent chance and $10,000 with a 99 percent chance. SSD would be inconclusive in this situation since the risky option has the longer left tail. Evidently, SSD admits any degree of risk aversion on the part of the decision maker. Thus, if SSD is going go be used in practice, greater care than usual must be taken in estimating the left tails of risky decision options.

Third-Degree Stochastic Dominance (TSD)

In addition to the risk aversion of SSD, TSD makes an assumption close to that of decreasing risk aversion. It will be recalled from Section 3.3 that for a decision maker with asset position Y_1 facing a small random prospect y_1 the risk premium is defined as

$$RP(y_1, Y_1) = EV(y_1) - CE(y_1, Y_1)$$

and that for decreasing risk aversion

$$RP(y_1, Y_1) > 0$$

and
$$RP(y_1, Y_1) > (y_1, Y_2)$$

if and only if $Y_1 < Y_2$.

It is quite easy to check for decreasing risk aversion. For example, if a decision maker's certainty equivalent for Z, where

$$Z \equiv \begin{cases} 0 \text{ with probability } \frac{1}{2} \\ 10 \text{ with probability } \frac{1}{2} \end{cases}$$

is 4 if total assets are 500, 4.5 when total assets are 1000, and 5 when total assets are 5000, he or she is exhibiting decreasing risk aversion.

Decreasing risk aversion is a *sufficient* condition for TSD but not a *necessary* one. In fact, TSD applies to a slightly larger class of utility functions. Mathematically, the assumptions for TSD are that the decision maker's utility function $U(y)$ should increase with y [i.e., the first derivative $U'(y)$ should be positive], be risk-averse [i.e., the second derivative $U''(y)$ should be negative], and have a non-negative third derivative $U'''(y)$. Fishburn and Vickson (1978) have shown that to test for $U'''(y) \geq 0$, in those circumstances where a differentiable mathematical equation for $U(y)$ was not assessed or fitted to the subjective responses of the decision maker, it is only necessary to show that

$$\tfrac{1}{4}U(Y) + \tfrac{3}{4}U(Y + 2\delta) \leq \tfrac{1}{4}U(Y + 3\delta) + \tfrac{3}{4}U(Y + \delta)$$

for $\delta > 0$ and all Y in the domain under consideration, where δ is a small positive increment to the decision maker's asset level Y.

Example Consider the two ventures V_1 and V_2 with this payoff matrix:

	Probabilities			
	$\frac{1}{4}$	$\frac{1}{4}$	$\frac{1}{4}$	$\frac{1}{4}$
V_1	100	120	120	120
V_2	130	110	110	110

If option V_2 is preferred to option V_1, then $U'''(100) \geq 0$. If this is repeated by the addition or subtraction of a constant amount to all payoff values, $U'''(Y) \geq 0$ can be verified for the applicable domain of Y. Thus, the exact conditions for TSD hold. The assumptions for TSD can therefore be evaluated exactly, or decreasing risk aversion can be used within the knowledge that even if decreasing risk aversion does not hold, it may still be the case that the exact conditions for TSD hold.

Given that the assumptions for TSD hold, option j will dominate option i if and only if the following conditions hold for all z' over y:

1.
$$E[f_j(y)] \geq E[f_i(y)]$$

2.
$$\int_{-\infty}^{z'} \int_{-\infty}^{z} [F_i(y) - F_j(y)] \, dy \, dz \geq 0$$

Condition 2, being a double integral, is not as easy to display as SSD and must be evaluated in full. Thus, TSD has not been so evident in practice, except in those cases where screening is a computer-based operation (which, incidentally, is becoming increasingly common).

Notice how, going from FSD to SSD and then on to TSD, we progressively "nest" the accumulated differences between $f_i(y)$ and $f_j(y)$. Thus, in FSD, for every point y we accumulated $f_i(y)$ and $f_j(y)$ to give $F_i(y)$ and $F_j(y)$ and then tested $F_i(y) \geq F_j(y)$. In other words, we accumulated the differences $[f_i(y) - f_j(y)]$ and checked that they never became negative. Similarly, in SSD we kept a running check on the accumulated differences $[F_i(y) - F_j(y)]$, let us call them $D(y)$, to see that they never became negative. Again, in TSD we keep a running check on the accumulated $D(y)$.

Example: TSD A simple example can be demonstrated from this payoff matrix:

θ	$P(\theta)$	a_1	a_2
θ_1	$\frac{1}{4}$	13	10
θ_2	$\frac{1}{4}$	11	12
θ_3	$\frac{1}{4}$	11	12
θ_4	$\frac{1}{4}$	11	12

The payoff values that can be taken by the variable y are thus (10, 11, 12, 13). Figure 4.2 shows $F_1(y)$ and $F_2(y)$. SSD is clearly inconclusive. Let

$$D(z) = \sum_{-\infty}^{z} [F_2(y) - F_1(y)]$$

where we have replaced the integral by the summation notation because of the discrete nature of the distribution. Examining the figure, we only need to evaluate the sum of differences at the points $z = 10, 11, 12,$ and 13, giving

$$D(10) = 0.25$$

$$D(11) = -0.25$$

$$D(12) = 0$$

$$D(13) = 0$$

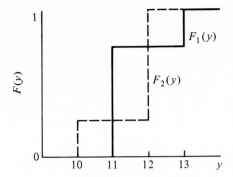

Figure 4.2 TSD screening example

where $D(11) = -0.25$ is the reason SSD failed.

It is now required to show that

$$\sum_{-\infty}^{z'} D(z) \geq 0$$

for $z' = 10, 11, 12$, and 13, if a_1 is to dominate a_2.

Clearly, for $z' = 10, 11, 12$, and 13 the summation is 0.25, 0, 0, and 0, respectively. Thus, TSD condition 2 is satisfied. To satisfy condition 1, we note that

$$E(a_1) = E(a_2) = 11.5$$

Thus, a_1 dominates a_2 in the sense of TSD.

Note that TSD is equally susceptible to the left tail sensitivity as SSD. The option whose cumulative distribution function ascends most quickly from the lowest value in the outcome space is never a candidate for the dominating option.

Nth-Degree Stochastic Dominance (NSD)

Theoretically, it is possible to consider a sequence of higher-order conditions of stochastic dominance making use of multiple integrals of the distribution functions. Tehranian (1980) considers these. It is, however, difficult to articulate the assumptions of such NSD procedures in terms of the risk attitudes they imply for $U(y)$. Needless to say, they all require computerized algorithms for screening.

Mean-Variance Dominance (MVD)

If a dominance criterion is to be based only upon consideration of the mean and the variance, then one of two conditions must be satisfied:

1. The decision maker's utility function is of a risk-averse quadratic form.
2. The probability density functions for the possible payoffs of all the decision options must be normal.

If one of these conditions holds, then for a given mean, the one with the higher variance will be dominated, whereas for a given variance, the one with the lower mean will be dominated.

The assumption of normality in the payoff distribution is common practice, and this ensures the popularity of the mean-variance method of dominance screening. In situations where normality does not hold, however, the assumption of a quadratic utility function must be carefully questioned. A quadratic utility function does not have decreasing risk aversion. Not only does a decision maker remain risk-averse, with a quadratic utility function he or she becomes in fact *more* risk-averse as his or her wealth increases (recall Section 3.3). As this seems counterintuitive to most conceptions of value and risk attitudes, an appeal to the assumption of a quadratic utility function to justify MVD is rarely very safe.

Furthermore, if all outcomes are described by the normal distribution, then MVD implies SSD. The reverse is not true, however. For example, we have two options X and Y, where X gives \$1 for certain and Y gives either \$1 or \$3 with equal probability. Evidently, MVD will fail to discriminate between these two options, even though Y dominates X under FSD (and hence, SSD). Thus, MVD is a weaker form of screening than SSD, but has nevertheless been very useful in practice.

4.2 APPLIED EXAMPLE IN SECURITIES ANALYSIS

In 1974, Porter and Carey published an account of a screening exercise on a sample of 16 randomly selected companies. These are listed below:

Company number	Company name
1	Federal Paper Board
2	American Machine and Foundry
3	Smith Kline/French Laboratories
4	Rayonier
5	American Tobacco
6	Crowell-Collier and Macmillan
7	American Seating
8	Emerson Electric
9	Riegel Textile
10	Cerro
11	American Distilling
12	American Investment
13	Johnson and Johnson
14	United Aircraft
15	Dresser Industries
16	Schering

Monthly rates of return ROR were calculated for the 54 periods from the last quarter of 1963 through the first quarter of 1968 according to the following formula:

$$\text{ROR}_t = \frac{(P_t - P_{t-1}) + D_t}{P_{t-1}}$$

where P_t = price per share in dollars at the end of period t

$\quad D_t$ = dividend in period t

and the probability distribution for each company's ROR was determined. These probability distributions were then analyzed for dominance. The results of FSD and SSD testing were as follows:

Company number		Company number
By first-degree stochastic dominance		
2	dominated	3
5	dominated	3
8	dominated	3, 5, 7
By second-degree stochastic dominance		
2	dominated	3
4	dominated	10
5	dominated	1, 2, 3, 7
7	dominated	1
8	dominated	1, 2, 3, 4, 5, 6, 7, 9, 10, 11, 13, 14, 15, 16
9	dominated	10
11	dominated	3
12	dominated	3, 11
13	dominated	1, 10
14	dominated	10
15	dominated	6, 9, 10, 14
16	dominated	1, 4, 6, 9, 10, 13, 14, 15
1, 3, 6, 10	dominated	none

Clearly, FSD only screened out three companies (3, 5, and 7). However, SSD reduced the efficient set to just two, namely, companies 8 and 12. These two are shown in Figure 4.3. Firm 8 has initially the steeper cumulative distribution function and therefore cannot dominate firm 12 under FSD, SSD, or TSD. However, most decision makers, on inspection of the curves, would not consider it to be significantly riskier than firm 12, whereas firm 12 clearly has a better chance of a larger rate of return. Thus, screening left the decision makers with two options, the choice between which is quite easy on inspection. It is interesting to observe that the mean-variance screening of these companies singled out firms 5, 8, and 12 as being efficient. We note however, that company 8 dominates company 5 in the sense of FSD.

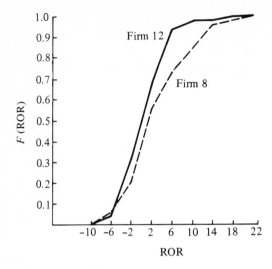

Figure 4.3 Cumulative probability functions of ROR for firms 3 and 12. (*Adapted from Porter and Carey, 1974.*)

4.3 COMMENT ON SCREENING AS DECISION AID

Screening out inferior options by a relatively crude mechanical but reliable procedure has evident value in reducing the dimension of a subsequently more thorough decision analysis. Indeed, in quite a few applications, the decision analysis purpose is to provide a short list of "good" candidate options for scrutiny at a higher level. This is particularly the case with many public policy analyses, such as siting decisions for a new airport or energy facility, where much of the analysis consists in providing a set of options for decision at a political level. One aspect of screening by dominance to be wary of is that of confusing the efficient set with a short list in the above sense. The connotation of a short list is that one expects it to contain approximately the top handful of options. If, for some unforeseen reason, the decision maker does not like the one that appears to come out best in an expected utility analysis, the "second best" (on expected utility grounds) will still be there for further examination. Unfortunately, the "efficient" set, while it will contain the most preferred option under an expected utility analysis, consistent with the assumptions of screening, will not necessarily contain the expected-utility-ranked second best. Clearly, screening by dominance can be misleading in situations where the efficient set becomes a focus of negotiation, with its analysis departing from the expected utility evaluation envisaged in the screening assumptions.

Screening by dominance works by attempting to eliminate options from the feasible set. In many cases the test will be inconclusive and will thus fail to show dominance. The screened subset will therefore consist of all those options where the test has failed. These will not necessarily all be preferable to those eliminated. In fact, we know from our own experiences that whenever we try to eliminate options, elimination tends to be of those which are similar in many respects but slightly worse in a few, thereby allowing an easy dominance discrimination to be made. Thus, it is easy to envisage a situation where screening by dominance leaves those options which under the full expected utility analysis would be ranked first and last. An illustrative example is given below to clarify this point.

Example Distribution functions of an outcome variable y are plotted in Figure 4.4 for four possible decision options.

Option 4 clearly dominates option 3 under FSD (the curves do not intersect), assuming that the decision maker's utility increases with y. Option 4 also clearly dominates option 2 under SSD (compare intersected areas as in Figure 4.1), assuming that the decision maker is risk-averse.

FSD and SSD fail to establish dominance between options 1 and 4, and thus the screened subset consists of these two options only.

With a particularly risk-averse utility function the ranking of option preference could quite conceivably be 4, 3, 2, 1. Thus, our screened set consists of the most desirable and the least desirable options.

It is possible that the option that would turn out on basic principles to be the most preferred may be disregarded for ulterior or incidental reasons, which makes it important in practice to be clear whether the screened subset has been derived via dominance criteria. If the options have been screened by dominance, then to find the second best, screening would have to start all over again.

Screening need not necessarily be done by dominance reasoning. Often a heuristic form of screening proceeds by utilizing a relatively crude form of decision criterion, such as the expected value, with a critical probability cutoff for risk elimination. The rationalization of using a surrogate decision criterion is that it should give a ranking sufficiently close to that of a thorough expected utility analysis such that its use will give a valid short list for further scrutiny. The advantage of using this screening by crude, or convenient, approximation is that the second best should still be in the short list. However, if the screening criterion is particularly crude, theoretically there is no guarantee that its short list will contain the proper expected-utility-preferred option. This is, of course, where dominance

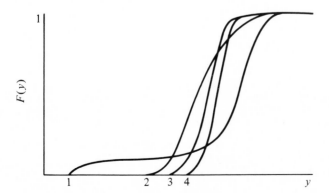

Figure 4.4 Screening by dominance

scores. However, as we have noted, the simplicity of its application must be weighted against the restrictions in interpreting the efficient set. The use of approximate decision criteria for screening is especially common in decisions with multiple objectives, which is our next topic.

EXERCISES

4.1 An investor has a choice of one of four ventures (V_1, V_2, V_3, or V_4), the outcomes of which depend upon the state of the economy E. Four scenarios for the future state of the economy are considered (E_1, E_2, E_3, and E_4) which, with their associated probabilities, give rise to the payoffs shown in the matrix:

E	E_1	E_2	E_3	E_4
$P(E)$	0.1	0.2	0.4	0.3
V_1	2	1	0	4
V_2	−1	2	1	0
V_3	−1	1	1	1
V_4	−1	2	0	0

Can any of the ventures be eliminated by dominance reasoning?

4.2 Consider the two ventures V_1 and V_2, of which each has six equally likely possible outcomes, with the following payoff matrix:

	P (outcome)					
	$\frac{1}{6}$	$\frac{1}{6}$	$\frac{1}{6}$	$\frac{1}{6}$	$\frac{1}{6}$	$\frac{1}{6}$
V_1	1	4	1	5	5	4
V_2	3	5	3	1	1	4

Which venture should be preferred?

4.3 Consider the two ventures V_1 and V_2 giving the following payoff matrix:

	Probability			
	$\frac{1}{4}$	$\frac{1}{4}$	$\frac{1}{4}$	$\frac{1}{4}$
V_1	1	1	4	4
V_2	0	2	3	3

If the decision maker is risk-averse, which venture should be chosen?

4.4 Consider the situation where decision A gives an outcome x equally likely between 0 and 1, and decision B gives an outcome x equally likely between -1 and a.

    (*a*) If $a = 2$, which decision dominates under (i) FSD, (ii) SSD?
    (*b*) If $a = \frac{4}{3}$, which decision dominates under (i) FSD, (ii) SSD?
    (*c*) If $a = \frac{3}{4}$, which decision dominates under (i) FSD, (ii) SSD?

4.5 Decision option A gives outcomes equally likely between -1 and $+1$, and decision option B gives outcomes equally likely between $-a$ and $+b$.

    (*a*) If $a = b = 2$, which option dominates under (i) FSD, (ii) SSD?

    (*b*) If $a = \frac{1}{2}$ and $b = \frac{3}{2}$, which option dominates under (i) FSD, (ii) SSD?

    (*c*) If $a = 2$ and $b = 3$, which option dominates under (i) FSD, (ii) SSD?

4.6 Two options V_1 and V_2 have this payoff matrix:

	Probability					
	$\frac{1}{6}$	$\frac{1}{6}$	$\frac{1}{6}$	$\frac{1}{6}$	$\frac{1}{6}$	$\frac{1}{6}$
V_1	0	1	2	3	3	3
V_2	1	2	2	2	2	2

The decision maker is decreasingly risk-averse. Which option should he or she prefer?

4.7 Show that if in a committee of two or more decision makers everyone screens the available options by dominance prior to a meeting, then the compromised option resulting from the committee discussion may be inferior to another option which never even got discussed. Hence suggest some guidelines for the group decision-making process where many options for decision occur regularly.

4.8 *Buckminster International Bank.* (This case has been adapted from one that originally appeared in P. G. Moore, H. Thomas, D. W. Bunn, and J. Hampton, *Case Studies in Decision Analysis*, Penguin, 1976, under the title "Property Redevelopment in Caracas: An Investment Decision.")

    Introduction. The board of Buckminster International Bank, at a meeting in 1970, was facing the problem of how best to reutilize the considerable property value of its main office building in Caracas. The building was an extremely fine 15-year-old block, architecturally splendid, and occupying a magnificent site in the city center. But, quite simply, the organization had grown too big for these offices and a much larger site was being developed a little way out from the center which would provide the necessary extra space and better facilities for the modern style of banking with its greater range of financial services, extensive computerization, and so on.

    As an alternative to selling the existing property outright in its present condition, the bank could keep the building as an investment and redevelop it as shops, apartments, offices, hotel, or some seemingly optimal mixture of these uses. Apart from these various configurations of space utilization, there were various structural changes which could be made to the building. Two extra floors could be added which, together with further modification, would increase the choice of possible space utilization configurations. A major reconstruction could also provide a more efficient utilization of the floor space, and a plan devised in 1967 had already been approved by the planning authorities. A more recent scheme submitted in 1969 had not yet been approved. However, with certain members of the board having considerable influence in the city, the possibility of the plans being turned down was described as "inconceivable."

    The options available. At this stage, the board decided to enlist the help of a consultant, Mr. R. B. Gale, to assist in analyzing and resolving the problem. His first act was to construct a list of the possible options open to the bank.

After considering systematically the possible space utilization configurations for each structural possibility, a set of apparent investment options was drawn as follows:

1. Sell the property in its present condition.
2. Retain and use as offices.
3. Retain and use as offices with slight modifications.
4. Add two floors and use as offices and retail shops.
5. As 4, with slight modifications.
6. As 5, but with apartments.
7. As 5, but incorporate a hotel.
8. Construct new building (1967 plan) for offices and retail shops.
9. As 8, but incorporate a hotel.
10. As 8, but with department store.
11. As 8, but with apartments.
12. As 8, but with just offices and department store.
13. Construct new building (1969 plan) for offices and retail shops.
14. As 13, but use for hotel.
15. As 13, but use for offices and department store.
16. As 13, but with apartments.
17. Construct new building (1970 plan), but with considerable expansion, and use it for department store.

A consideration persistently at the forefront of the board's thinking was that of maintaining the company's image and customer goodwill. For this reason they would only be prepared to let the property out to prestige hoteliers and retailers. Hence in estimating the value of outright sale (option 1), the need to find the right sort of buyer who would not pull it down immediately, but maintain it in first class condition and use it for highly respectable purposes, had to be taken into account. As a consequence, the subjective probability distribution of the sale value was found to have the rather high variance of 1 against the mean of 6. Furthermore, many members of the board had expressed strong opposition to those options which involved demolishing and redeveloping the existing building. Their argument, perhaps owing more to sentiment than to economic reality, was that the building symbolized the immortal and impregnable security of the bank, and they should avoid even the slightest tones of transience.

As a starting point, however, the net present value was considered to be an appropriate criterion with which to evaluate these investment options. A 20-year planning horizon was taken. The costs and rent revenues associated with each option were assessed and discounted at 10 percent to give present values. The probability distributions were assessed in each case as being normal. The terminal ("resale") value of each investment option proved the most difficult to estimate. Clearly, 20 years hence the value of the property would depend not only upon the general trend in land prices, but also on how a potential buyer in 20 years' time would assess the revenue possibilities of the property. A city like Caracas changes its character rapidly, and with many of the other large financial and commercial organizations also planning new headquarters outside the center, there were already signs of the city shifting its center of gravity. Even if a new building on the 1969 code were constructed, the market value of the property in 20 years would clearly have to be based solely upon its redevelopment potential. The board finally agreed upon a terminal value of 6.5 million bolivars in present-day terms, again normally distributed, with a variance of 4.

Thus, the total net present value (NPV) of each option was finally evaluated as being normally distributed with means and variances as follows:

Option	Rent (mean) (a)	Cost (mean) (b)	Resale (mean) (c)	Equity (mean) (d)	Total NPV* Mean[†]	Total NPV* Variance[‡]
1		−6.00			6.00	1
2	9.43	1.55	6.5		14.38	5
3	10.96	4.53	6.5		12.93	6
4	15.82	6.9	6.5		15.42	7.5
5	17.74	13.35	6.5		10.89	13
6	15.37	12.70	6.5		9.17	11.5
7	15.82	12.85	6.5		9.47	11.5
8	28.92	19.30	6.5		16.12	24
9	21.40	18.20	6.5		9.70	21
10	32.20	20.95	6.5		17.75	32
11	23.70	18.22	6.5		11.98	21
12	31.20	20.50	6.5		17.20	31
13	22.60	18.37	6.5		10.73	21
14	20.80	18.29	6.5		11.01	21
15	28.20	19.20	6.5		15.50	24
16	22.80	18.20	6.5		11.10	21
17	55.90	40.60	6.5	3	24.80	71

All units are million bolivars.

*Net present value at the discount rate of 10 percent.

[†] Mean NPV is equal to $(a) − (b) + (c) + (d)$.

[‡] Variance NPV is sum of variances for rent, cost, resale, and equity.

(a) Screen the options. You can assume the board to be risk-averse.

(b) If the board wished to minimize the chance of a negative net present value, which option(s) should they consider?

(c) If you are in Mr. Gale's position, how would you summarize your advice to the board?

(d) How should the discount rate have been interpreted for this analysis?

(e) How could objectives other than net present value be taken into consideration more explicitly?

REFERENCES

Fishburn, P. C., and R. G. Vickson (1978): "Theoretical Foundations of Stochastic Dominance," in G. A. Whitmore and M. C. Findlay (eds.), *Stochastic Dominance*, D. C. Heath, Lexington, Mass.

Porter, R. B., and K. Carey (1974): "Stochastic Dominance as a Risk Analysis Criterion," *Decision Sciences*, vol. 5, pp. 10–21.

Tehranian, H. (1980): "Empirical Studies in Portfolio Performance Using Higher Degrees of Stochastic Dominance," *The Journal of Finance*, vol. 35, no. 1, pp. 159–171.

Whitmore, G. A., and M. C. Findlay (1978): *Stochastic Dominance*, D. C. Heath, Lexington, Mass.

FIVE

MULTIPLE-ATTRIBUTE UTILITY DECOMPOSITION

5.1 INTRODUCTION

Milan Zeleny (1982) opens his book *Multiple Criteria Decision Making* with the sentence: "It has become more and more difficult to see the world around us in a unidimensional way and to use only a single criterion when judging what we see."

We noted earlier that many decisions in the public sector appear to involve payoff assessments in more than just monetary values. Siting a nuclear power plant, for example, involves issues of safety, health, environment, and reliability as well as cost. We must therefore look at decision criteria that are multidimensional, that can cope with the many often conflicting objectives with which decision makers are sometimes faced. This seems to apply to the private sector as well. Thus, Peter Drucker (1974) states: "To manage a business is to balance a variety of needs and goals. And this requires multiple objectives."

For example, in a case study on the management of research and development (Moore et al., 1976), the following list of company objectives was obtained for the R & D activity:

1. Profitability
2. Growth and diversity of the product line
3. Offensive research mounted to anticipate competition
4. Increased market share
5. Maintained technical capability
6. Increase in firm's reputation and image
7. Provision of interesting research work to maintain engineer creativity

Not everyone sees it this way, however. Milton Friedman (1970), writing on the responsibility of business managers, has stated: "that responsibility ... will be to make as much money as possible while conforming to the basic rules of the society." Friedman does not argue that objectives such as those listed in the above R & D example should not exist, but rather that they all represent an ulterior desire for money. A company should develop social objectives, but only to the extent that they make an economic return, since improved company morale promotes greater productivity. Likewise, many politicians believe that all public spending should be directed to increasing the GNP, subject to minimal constraints of safety, poverty, security, and so forth.

We do not wish to enter into the realm of political economy here, since it suffices to observe, for our purposes, that even those who recognize the implicit monetary goal of all the objectives may still prefer to deal explicitly with these multiple objectives because of the difficulties involved in converting them into pure monetary values. To appreciate this, it is worth spending a moment or two looking at the technique of *cost-benefit analysis*, which has been popular in public policy analyses since the 1930s. It has been subject to much criticism, but not entirely discredited. Essentially, it attempts to measure all the costs and benefits, widely interpreted, associated with a proposal in monetary amounts (e.g., Layard, 1972).

Given the monetary total of all the costs C and benefits B, then public projects will be ranked either according to the ratio B/C or to the difference $B - C$. Thus, large public schemes, such as new airports, will have monetary values placed not only upon construction costs but also upon noise, time saved by commuters, expected accidents and deaths, and displaced industries and households, as well as on the economic effects of the associated increased traffic growth.

In Britain in the late 1960s, a major study (the Roskill Commission) was undertaken to find a site for a third London airport. The study used the cost-benefit analysis (CBA) approach. After considerable discussion, the Roskill report was finally disregarded and much of its methodology considerably discredited. Speaking at the Royal Statistical Society some years later (1980), George Stern made several incisive remarks on details of the CBA approach, including the following:

Noise is peace. The Roskill Commission, in examining the third London airport, assessed the cost of noise by comparing market prices of houses near airports with those of similar houses elsewhere. On this basis, when the entire country is covered with a uniformly high level of noise, the cost of this noise will be found to be zero.

Death is dollars. The Roskill Commission assessed the value of a death as £9300. This figure consisted of lost net output added to the funeral and other expenses associated with killing the person, with an additional £5000 added to the sum so calculated. The £5000 was needed as otherwise it would actually "pay" to kill those people, such as the old, whose expected future net output is so negative as to outweigh the costs associated with killing them. The pre-£5000 planner aimed to kill as many oldsters as possible; the more humane post-£5000 planner will merely prefer killing oldsters.

The reverse Robin Hoods. Roskill decided that in assessing the value of time saved, the time of richer people was worth more. In assessing costs of noise, Roskill observed that more expensive houses depreciate more than cheaper ones. Hence cost-benefit-driven planners must choose the scheme which speeds the rich more than the poor, while affecting the poorer area more and, as we have seen, killing more of the older.

Thus, in many multiple-objective situations, decision makers may wish to avoid using an explicit procedure of converting all attributes to a common montary base. Forms of preference scaling have been quite widely used to this end.

A fairly common type of multiple-attribute decision model is the achievement matrix, which is quite thoroughly reviewed in Baecher et al. (1978). This consists of subjectively assessed scores for each option (defining the rows) against each relevant attribute (objective) in the decision problem (defining the columns). In assigning relative weights to each attribute, a weighted score can be computed for each option and thereby provide a ranking. In formal terms, if s_{ij} denotes the score of option i on the jth attribute and w_j the relative weight given to attribute j, then the score s_i for option i,

$$s_i = \sum_j w_j s_{ij}$$

gives a complete ranking of the options according to this criterion. This procedure was, in fact, used in the R&D example mentioned earlier (Moore et al., 1976). Clearly, this is a generalization of cost-benefit analysis, for if the w_j were assessed as monetary conversion factors and the s_{ij} as quantified impacts of the ith option on the jth attribute, then the s_i would provide an equivalent monetary ranking of the options.

The main value of this achievement matrix procedure lies in its intuitive appeal as a simple formalization of the decision situation and the decision maker's preference model, and it is therefore quite popular in practice. As a decision model, however, it does assume that the attributes are considered independent and that the decision maker's preferences are adequately represented by the implicitly linear scoring measure. The decision maker may argue that although these assumptions are not strictly true, the model is a sufficiently good approximation to bring the truly best option close to the top of the ranking. Thus, this procedure is quite useful for screening purposes.

A serious deficiency in this methodology, however, is its lack of attention to uncertainty and risk. Basically it assumes that the decision maker has a linear utility function and is therefore risk-neutral. Evidently risk could be treated as one of the attributes, but that would beg the question of its definition. Even if its measurement could be reduced to a single value, each uncertain attribute would need a risk index associated with it, and this could double the number of columns in the matrix.

Ideally, what we should like to do is to generalize the expected utility theory to the multiple-attribute problem. Thus if x_i is the measure of effectiveness on attribute i and there are n attributes, then a utility function of the form $U(x_1, \ldots, x_n)$ is required. There are no easy guidelines currently available for assessing such a general multiple-attribute utility function. In many circumstances, however, certain conditions can be satisfied in order to decompose the joint utility function into a function of individual single-attribute utility functions, namely,

$$U(x_1, \ldots, x_n) = f(U_1(x_1), U_2(x_2), \ldots, U_n(x_n))$$

such as the linear case

$$U(x_1, \ldots, x_n) = \sum_{i=1}^{n} k_i U(x_i)$$

where

$$1 = \sum_{i=1}^{n} k_i$$

or the multiplicative form

$$U(x_1, \ldots, x_n) = \frac{\prod_{i=1}^{n} [1 + Kk_i U_i(x_i)] - 1}{K}$$

For example, our first objective may be job satisfaction, and we may choose to measure it by x_1, the annual rate of employee turnover. Our second may be market share x_2, and so on. If the above simplification of the joint utility function can be made, it will have considerable computational value.

5.2 SEPARABILITY CONDITIONS

A necessary condition for the type of separability indicated above is that of *mutual preferential independence*. An attribute x_1 is said to be preferentially independent of x_2 if preferences for specific outcome values of x_1 do not depend upon x_2. For example, let x_1 be the time to completion of a project and x_2 its cost. Now if we prefer a project time of 5 days to one of 10 days, assuming that the cost is 100 in both cases, and if we also prefer a project time of 5 days to one of 10 days if in both cases the cost is 200 or any other value of x_2, then x_1 is preferentially independent of x_2. If x_2 is also preferentially independent of x_1, then we refer to x_1 and x_2 as being mutually preferentially independent.

Further insight into preferential independence may be gained from considering a situation where it may not hold. A rather contrived example could be a personal decision with outcomes which affect both the place where you live and the automobile that you drive. Let x_1 be an outcome variable which could denote either Los Angeles or an African farm and x_2 an outcome variable denoting either a Cadillac or a Land Rover. The value of x_1, namely, whether you live in Los

Angeles or on an African farm, may well affect your preference for a Cadillac or a Land Rover. Therefore x_2 would not be preferentially independent of x_1. The reverse case may still be preferentially independent, however. You may well prefer Los Angeles to an African farm, regardless of which car you currently own. Mutual preferential independence has been found to hold in many decision-making situations, but one must never assume its applicability to be a matter of course.

It is particularly useful to consider preferential independence with respect to sets of attributes. We can talk of the set (x_1, x_2) being preferentially independent of x_3 if the decision maker's preferences for outcomes in (x_1, x_2) are independent of a fixed x_3. Thus, for a given x_3, the rate of tradeoff between x_1 and x_2 should not depend upon the level at which x_3 is fixed. Using the project evaluation example with x_3 now the reliability of the project, if the most that the decision maker will pay for a day's reduction in project time is 20, this should still be 20, whatever the reliability is assessed to be. If x_3 is preferentially independent of (x_1, x_2), then we can refer to (x_1, x_2) and x_3 as being mutually preferentially independent. A special case of this, to be considered later, is the preferential independence of a subset Y of $(x_1, \ldots, x_n)$ to its complement $\overline{Y}$. This will be denoted for brevity as Y is PI. A set of attributes X will be considered mutually preferentially independent if Y is PI for all possible subsets Y of X.

The mutual preferential independence of a set of attributes is a necessary condition for the type of separability indicated in Section 5.1, but is far from sufficient. A sufficient condition for the joint utility function to decompose into either the multiplicative or the additive form is the stronger one of *mutual utility independence*. This condition implies the mutual preferential independence of the set of attributes X. Incidentally, mutual preferential independence is a sufficient condition for the additive decomposition of a joint *value* function as opposed to a joint *utility* function, that is,

$$V(x_1, \ldots, x_n) = \sum_{i=1}^{n} v_i(x_i)$$

where the joint value function $V(x_1, \ldots, x_n)$ is assessed under circumstances where uncertainty in the outcome variables x_i is not considered or is irrelevant. When there is no uncertainty in the outcomes and the problem is only one of reconciling conflicting objectives, the use of value functions is appropriate. In general decision problems, however, where there is considerable uncertainty, the use of such value functions would be incoherent with expected utility principles for the same reason that the simple expected payoff criterion can be incoherent, as shown in Section 2.3.

An attribute x_1 is considered *utility independent* of x_2 if preferences for uncertain scenarios involving different levels of x_1 are independent of the value of x_2. In other words, if the certainty equivalent for an outcome involving equal chances of the worst and best values of x_1, that is, x_{1*} and x_1^*, respectively, is assessed for any fixed level of x_2 and found to be the same, regardless of how x_2 is varied throughout the domain of x_2, then x_1 is utility independent of x_2. If x_2 is also utility independent of x_1, then the pair are said to be mutually utility independent.

This is clearly analogous to preferential independence, except that the trade-offs and preferences are considered under conditions of uncertainty. For the project evaluation example, if we require the completion time x_1 to be utility independent of the cost x_2, then we need to ascertain that the certainty equivalent for an option giving a 50 percent chance of $x_1 = 5$ and a 50 percent chance of $x_1 = 10$ should not depend upon the level at which x_2 is fixed.

For a counterexample suppose x_1 and x_2 are the rates of serious crime in two precincts of a metropolitan police division. In determining the joint utility function for this region's police chief, the issue of utility independence for x_1 and x_2 would be faced. With x_2 fixed at 5, a relatively low rate of crime, he may be quite risk-averse to rates of crime in x_1 for political reasons associated with any apparent neglect of a particular precinct. Thus, his certainty equivalent for an option giving a 50 percent chance of $x_1 = 0$ and a 50 percent chance of $x_1 = 30$ may be 22 when x_2 is fixed at 5. If x_2 were fixed at the higher rate of 15, however, his certainty equivalent may be less risk-aversely assessed at 17. Thus, one must not assume that utility independence will hold in all cases despite the large number of reported practical studies describing its application.

This term can apply to subsets of X in a way analogous to the case of preferential independence. Thus if Y is utility independent of its complement $\bar{Y}$ in X, then this is often denoted as Y is UI. Furthermore, we can refer to a set of attributes being mutually utility independent if Y is utility independent for all possible Y in X.

Mutual utility independence of a set of attributes is a necessary and also sufficient condition for multiplicative decomposition, that is,

$$U(x_1, \ldots, x_n) = \frac{\prod_{i=1}^{n} [1 + Kk_i U_i(x_i)] - 1}{K}$$

which reduces to the additive form

$$U(x_1, \ldots, x_n) = \sum_{i=1}^{n} k_i U_i(x_i)$$

when

$$1 = \sum_{i=1}^{n} k_i$$

In practice, therefore, it is first of all necessary to test for the mutual utility independence of X. If we were to test this by considering whether every Y is utility independent, we would have $2^n - 2$ tests to undertake, where each test demonstrates the independence of a certainty equivalent for uncertain prospects involving Y over the level of $\bar{Y}$. In the two-attribute case, only two such tests are required, but for $n \geq 3$, the number of such tests can become tedious if not prohibitive. Fortunately, in this latter case we can make use of a theorem described in Keeney and Raiffa (1976).

Essentially, it can be shown that if the set X consists of $(x_1, \ldots, x_n)$, then the following statements are equivalent:

1. Attributes X are mutually utility independent.
2. x_1 is utility independent and (x_1, x_i) is preferentially independent for $i = 2, 3, \ldots, n; n \geq 3$.

This condition is a great simplification when n is greater than 2. All that is required is to focus attention on one attribute, arbitrarily listed as x_1, show that it is utility independent of its complement $\overline{X}_1$, and then show that all $n - 1 \, (x_1, x_i)$ pairs are preferentially independent of their complements. Thus, we have just n tests, all but one of which are the simpler preferential independence tests, instead of the $2^n - 2$ utility independence tests which would follow from basic principles.

Having established mutual utility independence in the above way, plus several further checks for consistency, we know that the decomposition is of the multiplicative form, and all that is required is to assess the scaling constants k_i. If the k_i sum to 1, then the decomposition falls out as the additive form.

It is often useful to test for additivity beforehand as the knowledge of an additive form can aid the assessment task insofar as only $n - 1$ scaling constants need be assessed. For the additive decomposition to be appropriate,

$$U(x_1, \ldots, x_n) = \sum k_i u_i(x_i)$$

the separability condition of *additivity independence* must hold. Following Fishburn (1970), additive independence occurs if preferences over lotteries on $\{X\}$ depend only upon the marginal probability distributions of the x_i, not on the overall joint probability distribution $\{X\}$. This marginalization is often difficult to see in practice. An easier set of necessary and sufficient conditions for additivity can be set up as follows:

1. $\{X\}$ is mutually preferentially independent.
2. Select any two attributes x_1 and x_2, with the best and worst outcomes x_1^*, x_{1*}, x_2^*, x_{2*}, denoted as before. Test for indifference of preferences between options A and B:

$$A \begin{cases} (x_1^*, x_2^*) \text{ with probability } \tfrac{1}{2} \\ \text{or} \\ (x_{1*}, x_{2*}) \text{ with probability } \tfrac{1}{2} \end{cases}$$

$$B \begin{cases} (x_1^*, x_{2*}) \text{ with probability } \tfrac{1}{2} \\ \text{or} \\ (x_{1*}, x_2^*) \text{ with probability } \tfrac{1}{2} \end{cases}$$

with all other $n - 2$ attributes being held constant throughout. If options A and B are equally preferable, then additivity independence holds.

With the usual scaling of

$$U(x_{1*}, \ldots, x_{n*}) = 0 \qquad \text{that is, all attributes at worst levels}$$

$$U(x_1^*, \ldots, x_n^*) = 1 \qquad \text{that is, all attributes at best levels}$$

$$U_1(x_1^*) = 1$$

$$U_1(x_{1*}) = 0$$

then it is clear that both A and B have an equal expected utility.

$$
\begin{aligned}
U(A) &= \frac{1}{2}\left[k_1 U_1(x_1^*) + k_2 U_2(x_2^*) + \sum_{i=3}^{n} k_i U_i(\bar{x}_i) \right] \\
&\quad + \frac{1}{2}\left[k_1 U_1(x_{1*}) + k_2 U_2(x_{2*}) + \sum_{i=3}^{n} k_i U_i(\bar{x}_i) \right] \\
&= \frac{1}{2}\left[k_1 U_1(x_1^*) + k_2 U_2(x_{2*}) + \sum_{i=3}^{n} k_i U_i(\bar{x}_i) \right] \\
&\quad + \frac{1}{2}\left[k_1 U_1(x_{1*}) + k_2 U_2(x_2^*) + \sum_{i=3}^{n} k_i U_i(\bar{x}) \right] \\
&= U(B)
\end{aligned}
$$

where $\bar{x}_i$ is the arbitrary level selected for x_i.

Notice also that the additive form can be written as

$$
\begin{aligned}
U(x_1, x_2) &= k_1 U_1(x_1) + (1 - k_1) U_2(x_2) \\
&= U(x_1, x_{2*}) + U(x_{1*}, x_2)
\end{aligned}
$$

and that the scaling constant is

$$k_1 = U(x_1^*, x_{2*})$$

This interpretation of the scaling constant also holds in the multiplicative form, which in the two-attribute case can be written as

$$
\begin{aligned}
U(x_1, x_2) &= k_1 U_1(x_1) + k_2 U_2(x_2) + (1 - k_1 - k_2) U_1(x_1) U_2(x_2) \\
&= U(x_1, x_{2*}) + U(x_{1*}, x_2) \\
&\quad + \frac{U(x_1, x_{2*}) U(x_{1*}, x_2)[1 - U(x_1^*, x_{2*}) - U(x_{1*}, x_2^*)]}{U(x_1^*, x_{2*}) U(x_{1*}, x_2^*)}
\end{aligned}
$$

and again the scaling constant is

$$k_1 = U(x_1^*, x_{2*})$$

The assessment of the scaling constants is thus relatively easy in principle. Consider option Z as

$$Z \begin{cases} (x_1^*, x_2^*, \ldots, x_n^*) \text{ with probability } p \\ \text{or} \\ (x_{1*}, x_{2*}, \ldots, x_{n*}) \text{ with probability } 1 - p \end{cases}$$

and find that value of p for which the certainty equivalent of Z is equivalent to the outcome $(x_1^*, x_{2*}, x_{3*}, \ldots, x_{n*})$ for certain. When such a p is identified, then

$$U(Z) = pU(x_1^*, \ldots, x_n^*) + (1 - p)U(x_{1*}, \ldots, x_{n*})$$

$$= p$$

which is equivalent, by the assessment of p, to $U(x_1^*, x_{2*}, \ldots, x_{n*})$ and therefore equal to k_1. Such assessments can easily be repeated for the other k_i as needed.

Worked examples are given in the following sections for the two-attribute and four-attribute cases, both multiplicative and additive, which may make the above theory easier to grasp. For further reading and proofs the reader is referred to Keeney and Raiffa (1976), Fishburn (1970), and Farquhar (1977).

The basic key to the development of this theory is the fact that the von Neumann and Morgenstern expected utility is arbitrary up to a linear transformation. Thus, if a utility function is assessed as $U^a(x)$, it can be rescaled as $U^b(x)$ without affecting the expected utility theory, since

$$U^b(x) = a + bU^a(x)$$

If we have two attributes x and y which are mutually utility independent, then it follows that

$$U(x, y) = c_1(y) + c_2(y)U(x, y_*)$$
$$U(x, y) = d_1(x) + d_2(x)U(x_*, y)$$

and by definition,

$$U(x_*, y_*) = 0$$
$$U(x^*, y^*) = 1$$

The multiplicative form can then be derived by appropriate substitutions in the above formulas.

5.3 ASSESSMENT OF A TWO-ATTRIBUTE UTILITY FUNCTION

One of the earliest published case studies of a two-attribute utility function assessment procedure was by Keeney (reprinted in 1976) in the context of a management decision involving a hospital blood bank. In deciding how large an inventory of blood to stock, the decision maker must consider the possibility of shortage

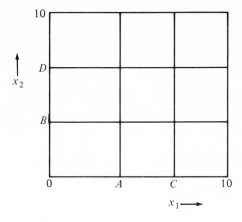

Figure 5.1 Display scheme for utility independence

x_1, which involves a special order to a central blood bank, or outdating x_2, which is the loss of all blood kept over the legal lifetime of three weeks. The problem is thus an example of the perishable inventory problem, rather like Ferret's Newstand (Exercise 2.1), although in this case under- and overstocking cannot be expressed easily in monetary terms.

In order to see whether $U(x_1, x_2)$ can be expressed in a tractable form, the decision maker's preference structure over all the outcomes (x_1, x_2) can be tested for mutual utility independence. A convenient visual way to do this is shown in Figure 5.1. The shortage and outdating scales both go from 0 to 10, and thus the outcomes can be represented by any point defined by the x_1, x_2 axes.

Let us suppose that the decision maker was asked what the certainty equivalent would be for option Z if x_2 is fixed at 5, where

$$Z \begin{cases} x_1 = 0 \text{ with probability } \frac{1}{2} \\ x_1 = 10 \text{ with probability } \frac{1}{2} \end{cases}$$

If he or she answers that $x_1 = A$ would be the certainty equivalent, then it is necessary to show that this would stay the same if x_2 takes any other value from 0 to 10. Thus, if the certainty equivalent for option Z is given by the straight line $x_1 = A$ for all conceivable values of x_2, then x_1 is utility independent of x_2.

Likewise, if the certainty equivalent for option Y with $x_1 = 5$,

$$Y \begin{cases} x_2 = 0 \text{ with probability } \frac{1}{2} \\ x_2 = 10 \text{ with probability } \frac{1}{2} \end{cases}$$

is assessed as $x_2 = B$, and this also holds over all conceivable values of x_1, then x_2 is utility independent of x_1. Assessments such as $x_1 = C$ and $x_2 = D$ should also be undertaken as consistency checks.

Once it has been ascertained that (x_1, x_2) are mutually utility independent, then it will be possible to separate $U(x_1, x_2)$ into the multiplicative form,

$$U(x_1, x_2) = k_1 U_1(x_1) + k_2 U_2(x_2) + (1 - k_1 - k_2) U_1(x_3) U_2(x_2)$$

with the additive decomposition as the special case, if

$$1 = k_1 + k_2$$

In order to test for additivity independence, it is necessary to show that the options U and V involving (x_1, x_2),

$$U \begin{cases} (0, 0) \text{ with probability } \frac{1}{2} \\ (10, 10) \text{ with probability } \frac{1}{2} \end{cases}$$

$$V \begin{cases} (0, 10) \text{ with probability } \frac{1}{2} \\ (10, 0) \text{ with probability } \frac{1}{2} \end{cases}$$

are equally preferred by the decision maker.

Let us suppose that additivity holds in this case. Thus, only k_1 needs to be ascertained. The following question can be posed. Ask the decision maker to state the value of p which makes a certainty of $(0, 10)$ equally preferred to option W,

$$W \begin{cases} (0, 0) \text{ with probability } p_1 \\ (10, 10) \text{ with probability } 1 - p_1 \end{cases}$$

In Section 5.2 it was shown that this value of p_1 will equal k_1, with the usual scaling:

$$U(0, 0) = 1 \qquad U_1(0) = 1 \qquad U_2(0) = 1$$

$$U(10, 10) = 0 \qquad U_1(10) = 0 \qquad U_2(10) = 0$$

If the utility function $U(x_1)$ was determined as in Section 2.3, regardless of the value of x_2 fixed during the assessment, and likewise $U_2(x_2)$, as shown in Figure 5.2, then the joint utility function can be determined as

$$U(x_1, x_2) = k_1 U_1(x_1) + (1 - k_1) U_2(x_2)$$

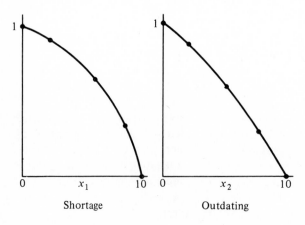

Figure 5.2 Utility functions for the blood bank problem

Incidentally, had additivity independence not held, the value of k_2 would have to be determined to describe the multiplicative decomposition. This would be done in the same way as for k_1. The value of p_2, which makes a certainty of $(10, 0)$ equally preferred to option x,

$$x \begin{cases} (0, 0) \text{ with probability } p_2 \\ (10, 10) \text{ with probability } 1 - p_2 \end{cases}$$

is identified and will equal k_2. Thus, the multiplicative form would have been determined as

$$U(x_1, x_2) = k_1 U_1(x_1) + k_2 U_2(x_2) + (1 - k_1 - k_2)U_1(x_1)U_2(x_2)$$

5.4 ASSESSMENT OF AN n-ATTRIBUTE UTILITY FUNCTION

To see how the above two-attribute decomposition can easily be extended to the n-attribute case ($n \geq 3$), it may help first of all to work through a simplified example. Suppose that potential sites for a new city airport are under consideration and four attributes are identified as important:

x_1 Cost
x_2 Noise impact on local residents
x_3 Accessibility from city center
x_4 Airport capacity

Thus, preferences over the outcomes will be a function of $U(x_1, x_2, x_3, x_4)$. In order to test the separability of this joint utility function, use can be made of the simplification theorem given in Section 5.2 for the mutual utility independence condition.

First of all we must focus on the utility independence of just one attribute selected arbitrarily, let us say x_1. If the certainty equivalent of the option

$$\begin{cases} x_{1*} \text{ with probability } \frac{1}{2} \\ x_1^* \text{ with probability } \frac{1}{2} \end{cases}$$

is independent of any fixed (x_2, x_3, x_4), then we can say x_1 is utility independent.

We must then test the preferential independence of all pairs (x_1, x_i). Thus, for (x_1, x_2) if the maximum that we would pay in money (i.e., increase in x_1) for a unit reduction in noise (i.e., reduction of x_2) is independent of any fixed level of (x_3, x_4), then (x_1, x_2) is preferentially independent. In other words, the rate of tradeoff of x_1 for x_2 is independent of the other attributes. Likewise, if (x_1, x_3) is preferentially independent and (x_1, x_4) is preferentially independent, then the minimum conditions for mutual utility independence of (x_1, x_2, x_3, x_4) have been satisfied. A few other assessments should, of course, be undertaken as consistency checks.

We now know that $U(x_1, x_2, x_3, x_4)$ can be separated into multiplicative or additive decompositions. In order to test for additivity independence, any pair of attributes, say, x_1 and x_2 can be taken. Then, holding x_3 and x_4 fixed at some level, test for the preference between options U and V,

$$U\begin{cases} x_{1*}, x_{2*} \text{ with probability } \frac{1}{2} \\ x_1^*, x_2^* \text{ with probability } \frac{1}{2} \end{cases}$$

$$V\begin{cases} x_1^*, x_{2*} \text{ with probability } \frac{1}{2} \\ x_{1*}, x_2^* \text{ with probability } \frac{1}{2} \end{cases}$$

If they are equally preferred, then the set of attributes can be decomposed as

$$U(x_1, x_2, x_3, x_4) = \sum_{i=1}^{4} k_i U_i(x_i)$$

and since

$$1 = \sum_{i=1}^{4} k_i$$

this means that only k_1, k_2, and k_3 need to be assessed. If additivity independence does not hold, then the multiplicative form

$$U(x_1, x_2, x_3, x_4) = \frac{\prod_{i=1}^{4} [1 + Kk_i U_i(x_i)] - 1}{K}$$

requires all k_i to be assessed.

Let us assume that additivity independence did not hold and that each k_i needs to be assessed. These values can be assessed exactly, as before, by finding that value of p_i which gives the certainty equivalent for

$$\begin{cases} (x_1^*, x_2^*, x_3^*, x_4^*) \text{ with probability } p_i \\ (x_{1*}, x_{2*}, x_{3*}, x_{4*}) \text{ with probability } 1 - p_i \end{cases}$$

equal to the certainty of x_i at its best level and all others at the worst. With the usual scaling

$$U(x_{1*}, x_{2*}, x_{3*}, x_{4*}) = 0 \qquad U_i(x_{i*}) = 0$$
$$U(x_1^*, x_2^*, x_3^*, x_4^*) = 1 \qquad U_i(x_i^*) = 1$$

p_i then equals k_i.

Let us suppose that the $u_i(x_i)$ have been assessed as in Figure 5.3 and that

$$k_1 = 0.3$$
$$k_2 = 0.2$$
$$k_3 = 0.1$$
$$k_4 = 0.1$$

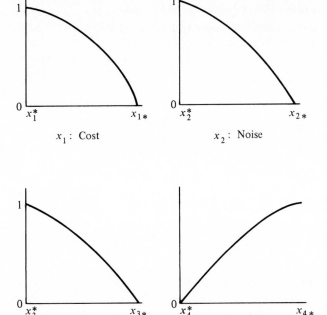

x_1: Cost

x_2: Noise

x_3: Access

x_4: Capacity

Figure 5.3 Utility functions for the airport siting attribute

Thus, from our scaling,

$$U(x_1^*, x_2^*, x_3^*, x_4^*) = \frac{\prod_{i=1}^{4} [1 + Kk_i U_i(x_i^*)] - 1}{K} = 1$$

that is,

$$K = (1 + 0.3K)(1 + 0.2K)(1 + 0.1K)(1 + 0.1K) - 1$$

In general, solving this equation for K is the most difficult mathematical aspect of assessing the multiplicative form, and use is usually made of an iterative computational procedure. Such procedures are now readily available on small computers and even on some pocket calculators.

It is easy to show that if

$$\sum k_i > 1$$

then the solution exists within

$$-1 < K < 0$$

and if

$$\sum k_i < 1$$

then the solution for K must be > 0. Furthermore, there will be a unique solution for K in each case, and so an iterative procedure is appropriate.

In the above example the equation can be set up iteratively by initially substituting any reasonable positive value in the right-hand side of the equation, computing the left-hand side, substituting this in the right-hand side to give a new left-hand side, and repeating this until the computed left-hand side differs little from the right-hand side.

One point to remember in practice is that $K = 0$ will always be a solution, and so if it is clear that the iterative procedure is converging to $K = 0$, it means that the initially selected value was not far enough away from zero.

In our example, let us try $K = 1$. Thus recomputing K gives

$$K = (1.3)(1.2)(1.1)(1.1) - 1 = 0.88$$

Clearly, substituting this will give an even smaller recomputed K, and the process will converge to $K = 0$.

Let us now try $K = 1.2$, giving

$$K = (1.36)(1.24)(1.12)(1.12) - 1 = 1.11$$

which is still less than 1.2 and may also converge to $K = 0$. Try $K = 1.5$,

$$K = (1.45)(1.30)(1.15)(1.15) - 1 = 1.49$$

which is close enough for our purposes. Thus K is estimated as 1.5, and the joint utility function is decomposed as

$$U(x_1, x_2, x_3, x_4)$$
$$= \frac{[1 + 0.45U_1(x_1)][1 + 0.3U_2(x_2)][1 + 0.15U_3(x_3)][1 + 0.15U_4(x_4)] - 1}{1.5}$$

Further consistency checks would, of course, be made on the validity of the decomposition. The multiple-attribute utility assessment procedure also helps to clarify the decision maker's ideas on the subject in addition to encoding them in a mathematical equation, and thus the decision maker may wish to change some of the earlier assessments in light of the greater insights obtained in going through the procedure.

5.5 EXTENSIONS

The preceding sections have concentrated upon practical methods of separability in multiple-attribute utility problems. In those cases where the above conditions of separability cannot be satisfied, the decision maker must still, in practice, do the best that he or she can to model the utility tradeoffs. One possibility, which always remains open, is to use an approximation in the direct assessment of the multiple-attribute utility function. Essentially, this just means assessing the utilities for a set of particular outcomes and then interpolating whatever may subsequently be required for analysis. An example of this procedure in a two-attribute problem may make it clear.

Given two attributes x_1 and x_2, both of which measure outcomes on a scale of 0 to 10, and assuming that utility increases with both variates. Then

$$U(0, 0) = 0$$

$$U(10, 10) = 1$$

as usual. Now, the utility of any particular outcome can be found from the value of p which equates this outcome to the certainty equivalent of Z,

$$Z \begin{cases} x_1 = 0, x_2 = 0, \text{ each with probability } 1 - p \\ x_1 = 10, x_2 = 10, \text{ each with probability } p \end{cases}$$

Thus suppose that for $x_1 = x_2 = 5$ a value of $p = 0.4$ equates this to Z. Then $U(5, 5)$ is directly assessed to be 0.4. For a set of (x_1, x_2) pairs a matrix of such directly assessed utilities could be set up as follows:

		0	3	x_1 5	7	10
	0	0	0.1	0.2	0.3	0.35
	3	0.1	0.2	0.25	0.35	0.4
x_2	5	0.2	0.25	0.4	0.45	0.5
	7	0.3	0.35	0.45	0.5	0.6
	10	0.35	0.4	0.5	0.6	1

If in the decision analysis the value of $U(0, 4)$ is required, this could be interpolated as 0.15. It is clear, however, that for many attributes such a procedure will require numerous direct estimates, even for quite crude approximations. It is thus a method of last resort only.

There are other possible approaches to the nonseparability problem, most of which are discussed in Keeney and Raiffa (1976). These usually involve transformations or reaggregations of the attributes. For example let us refer back to the illustration of utility nonindependence for precinct crime rates given in Section 5.2, where x_1 and x_2 are the rates of serious crime in two precincts of a metropolitan police region. If we transform these attributes to v, the average rate of crime,

$$v = \frac{x_1 + x_2}{2}$$

and w, the balance of criminal activity,

$$w = |x_1 - x_2|$$

then these two transformed attributes may well satisfy the utility independence requirements for separability. As in all aspects of decision analysis modeling, some inspiration in the derivation of alternative formulations can often reap significant rewards in terms of simplicity of computation.

The purpose of this chapter has been to indicate how multiple attributes or objectives can be brought into the expected utility ideal in decision analysis. We recall from our development of utility theory that circumstances in practice sometimes appear to violate its assumptions, but that in many of those cases it was the introduction of extra considerations, that is, attributes, which caused the difficulties. We now see how utility theory can survive with these difficulties.

The practice of multiple-attribute utility analysis is characterized by considerable skill in formulating a set of attributes which is complete, minimal, and tractable. We require completeness in a decision model for it to be relevant. All objectives and attributes that the decision maker believes to be important should be included. Often this may be the heart of the problem: discovering what are the real objectives. Sometimes it is helpful to pose such questions as "If all the uncertainties that we have modeled could be magically resolved, would you then be able to make a clear choice?" or, "Are there any factors that you feel you would like to insure against that we have not yet modeled?", in order to elucidate further considerations that have not been modeled. However, we do not want too many attributes as this compounds disproportionately the assessment tasks. Often similar attributes can be grouped together successfully. Such judicious grouping can also help achieve tractability through convenient separability, as we have seen above. The increasing use of user-friendly interactive computer assessment procedures in multiple-attribute utility applications is rendering this methodology one of the most useful in decision analysis. As in all decision analysis, it is not so much the power of the technique itself in "solving the problem," but the structured way in which the problem is approached and the decision maker interrogated that gives it value. In many of these multiple-objective applications, once the decision maker has studied his or her objectives, their tradeoffs, and his or her attitude to risk, the right course of action becomes quite apparent. It does not always succeed, needless to say, but in such cases the failure to develop useful insights is often due to attempts at modeling too many attributes. Simple models, concentrating upon essential features, are easier to understand. Recalling the discussion in Chapter 1, modeling needs only to be "requisite" to be effective. This point will be reexamined in later chapters in the context of modeling evaluation.

EXERCISES

5.1 Describe in terms understandable by executives the meaning of preferential, utility, and additivity independence of attributes.

5.2 Construct a hypothetical dialogue between a decision maker and a decision analyst attempting to derive a three-attribute utility function.

5.3 The linear additive function has the form

$$f(x_1, x_2, \ldots, x_n) = \sum_{i=1}^{n} a_i x_i$$

Under what conditions would this be a valid (a) utility function, (b) value function? How does this relate to the achievement matrix methods?

5.4 Some writers on this subject distinguish between an individual's personal utility function which underlies his or her action and a "social welfare function" which is assumed to underly his or her more altruistic beliefs. Can you find any evidence to support this theory? How would you reconcile it with coherence?

5.5 The achievement matrix approach to multiple attributes in a decision analysis involves developing a weighted score for each option j as

$$s_j = \sum_{i=1}^{n} w_i s_{ij}$$

where s_{ij} is the subjective score given to option j on attribute i, and w_i is an importance weight given to the ith attribute. Thus, if an R&D manager is evaluating the worth of four projects ($j = 1, 2, 3, 4$) on four attributes, namely, (1) profitability, (2) growth and diversity company, (3) competitiveness, and (4) technical interest, the following matrix of scores may have been assessed:

	Attributes			
	1	2	3	4
Projects				
1	5	4	7	9
2	3	8	2	1
3	7	9	4	1
4	8	7	7	5

The attribute importance weights are 12, 10, 7, and 7 for $i = 1, 2, 3$, and 4, respectively. What would be the most preferred option under this criterion? Under what conditions is the decision criterion a rational (*a*) utility and (*b*) value decomposition of the problem?

5.6 The administrator of a postal service is investigating planning options. Two attributes are of interest:

x_1 revenue (0–100 units)

x_2 proportion of next-day deliveries (0–100 percent)

Preliminary testing has shown these to be mutually utility independent. Conditional utility functions $u_1(x_1)$ and $u_2(x_2)$ were derived in the usual way, in each case holding the other attribute constant. The administrator was then found to be indifferent between the certainty of $x_1 = 100, x_2 = 0$ and

$$\begin{cases} x_1 = 100, x_2 = 100 \text{ with probability } 0.4 \\ x_1 = 0, x_2 = 0 \text{ with probability } 0.6 \end{cases}$$

The administrator was also indifferent between the certainty of $x_1 = 0, x_2 = 100$ and

$$\begin{cases} x_1 = 100, x_2 = 100 \text{ with probability } 0.3 \\ x_1 = 0, x_2 = 0 \text{ with probability } 0.7 \end{cases}$$

What is the decomposed form of this two-attribute utility function?

5.7 A large city is considering possible sites for a new airport. The decision-making body requires a multiple-attribute utility function on accessibility x_1 (rated on a scale from 0 to 100) and urban quietness x_2 (also rated on a scale from 0 to 100). Conditional utility functions $U_1(x_1)$ and $U_2(x_2)$ were derived separately in the usual way, just holding the other attribute constant in each case. Additivity independence was found to hold, and $U(60, 0)$ was indifferent to $U(0, 100)$. What is the utility function $U(x_1, x_2)$ in terms of $U_1(x_1)$ and $U_2(x_2)$? [$U_1(60) = 0.9$.]

5.8 In evaluating possible sites for a new electricity generating facility, the attributes x_1 (air pollution), x_2 (land use), x_3 (water evaporation), and x_4 (safety) were found to be mutually utility independent. The constants were assessed as $k_1 = 0.35$, $k_2 = 0.3$, $k_3 = 0.15$, and $k_4 = 0.4$. What is the form of the joint utility function $U(x_1, x_2, x_3, x_4)$ in terms of the individual functions $U_i(x_i)$?

5.9 A very common procedure for evaluation decisions which involve cash flows at different points in time is that of discounting future returns to give a net present value. If x_i is the cash flow at year i and r the discount rate, supposedly the decision maker's time preference for money, then the net present value NPV is given by

$$\text{NPV} = \sum \frac{x_i}{(1 + r)^i}$$

where the summation is over all future cash flows including x_0, the current one. Discuss the rationality of the net present value criterion from a decision analysis perspective.

5.10 Using the basic notion of utility independence and the properties of von Neumann and Morgenstern utility functions, derive the multiplicative decomposition for two attributes,

$$U(x, y) = aU(x) + bU(y) + (1 - a - b)U(x)U(y)$$

5.11 Suppose there are two individuals with utilities $U_1(x)$ and $U_2(x)$ for outcome x and the decision maker has the additive utility function

$$U_d(x) = 0.5U_1(x) + 0.5U_2(x)$$

If (v, w) denotes the outcome x, giving $U_1(x) = v$, and $U_2(x) = w$, then consider the two options:
(a) $(1, 0)$ with probability $\frac{1}{2}$, $(0, 1)$ with probability $\frac{1}{2}$
(b) $(1, 1)$ with probability $\frac{1}{2}$, $(0, 0)$ with probability $\frac{1}{2}$
The decision maker is indifferent between these two options. Note, however, that option (b) is equitable in terms of its impact on the two groups. Thus, show that the additive reconciliation of multiple interest groups is not compatible with any preference for equity on the part of the decision maker.

5.12 A decision maker who is very sensitive to equity among differently impacted groups of people, assigned the following utility function:

$$U_d(x) = 0.3U_1(x) + 0.3U_2(x) + 0.4U_1(x)U_2(x)$$

where $U_1(x)$ is the utility of group 1 and $U_2(x)$ that of group 2.
With (v, w) denoting the outcome $U_1(x) = v$, $U_2(x) = w$, the decision maker had these two options: (a) $(0.4, 0.4)$; and (b) $(1, 0)$ with probability $\frac{1}{2}$, $(0, 1)$ with probability $\frac{1}{2}$. Which of these options does each group prefer? Which option does the decision maker prefer? Can you isolate the cause of this dilemma and suggest how it may be avoided in practice?

REFERENCES

Baecher, G. B., J. G. Gros, and K. McCusker (1978): "Methodologies for Facility Siting Decision," in D. W. Bunn and H. Thomas, Eds., *Formal Methods in Policy Formulation*, Birkhauser, Basel.

Drucker, Peter G. (1974): *Management: Tasks, Responsibilities, Practices,* Harper and Row, New York.

Farquhar, P. (1977): "A Survey of Multiattribute Utility Theory and Applications," *TIMS Studies in the Management Sciences,* vol. 6, pp. 57–89.

Fishburn, P. (1970): *Utility Theory for Decision Making,* Wiley, New York.

Friedman, Milton (1970): "The Social Responsibility of Business Is to Increase Its Profits," *The New York Times Magazine,* Sept. 13, pp. 32–30, 123, 124, 126.

Keeney, R., and H. Raiffa (1976): *Decisions with Multiple Objectives,* Wiley, New York.

Layard, R. (1972): *Cost-Benefit Analysis,* Penguin, Harmondsworth, U.K.

Moore, P. G., H. Thomas, D. W. Bunn, and J. Hampton (1976): *Case Studies in Decision Analysis,* Penguin, Harmondsworth, U.K.

Zeleny, Milan (1982): *Multiple Criteria Decision Making.* McGraw-Hill, New York.

SIX

DECISIONS INVOLVING HUMAN LIFE

6.1 CASE STUDY: THE REACTOR SAFETY STUDY

Reprinted below is part of the "Executive Summary" of the 1975 report published by the U.S. Nuclear Regulatory Commission (WASH-1400 NUREG 75/014) subtitled "An Assessment of Accident Risks in U.S. Commercial Power Plants."

The Reactor Safety Study was sponsored by the U.S. Atomic Energy Commission[1] to estimate the public risks that could be involved in potential accidents in commercial nuclear power plants of the type now in use. It was performed under the independent direction of Professor Norman C. Rasmussen of the Massachusetts Institute of Technology. The risks had to be estimated, rather than measured, because although there are about 50 such plants now operating, there have been no nuclear accidents to date resulting in significant releases of radioactivity in U.S. commercial nuclear power plants. Many of the methods used to develop these estimates are based on those that were developed by the Department of Defense and the National Aeronautics and Space Administration in the last 10 years and are coming into increasing use in recent years.

The objective of the study was to make a realistic estimate of these risks and, to provide perspective, to compare them with non-nuclear risks to which our society and its individuals are already exposed. This information may be of help in determining the future reliance by society on nuclear power as a source of electricity.

The results from this study suggest that the risks to the public from potential accidents in nuclear power plants are comparatively small. This is based on the following considerations:

a. The possible consequences of potential reactor accidents are predicted to be no larger, and in many cases much smaller, than those of non-nuclear accidents. The consequences are predicted to be smaller than people have been led to believe by previous studies which deliberately maximized estimates of these consequences.

[1] The work, originally sponsored by the U.S. Atomic Energy Commission, was completed under the sponsorship of the U.S. Nuclear Regulatory Commission, which came into being on January 19, 1975.

b. The likelihood of reactor accidents is much smaller than that of many non-nuclear accidents having similar consequences. All non-nuclear accidents examined in this study, including fires, explosions, toxic chemical releases, dam failures, airplane crashes, earthquakes, hurricanes and tornadoes, are much more likely to occur and can have consequences comparable to, or larger than, those of nuclear accidents.

Figures 1-1, 1-2, and 1-3 compare the nuclear reactor accident risks predicted for the 100 plants expected to be operating by about 1980 with risks from other man-caused and natural events to which society is generally already exposed. The following information is contained in the figures:

a. Figures 1-1 and 1-2 show the likelihood and number of fatalities from both nuclear and a variety of non-nuclear accidents. These figures indicate that non-nuclear events are about 10,000 times more likely to produce large numbers of fatalities than nuclear plants.[2]
b. Figure 1-3 shows the likelihood and dollar value of property damage associated with nuclear and non-nuclear accidents. Nuclear plants are about 1000 times less likely to cause comparable large dollar value accidents than other sources. Property damage is associated with three effects:

1. The cost of relocating people away from contaminated areas
2. The decontamination of land to avoid overexposing people to radioactivity
3. The cost of ensuring that people are not exposed to potential sources of radioactivity in food and water supplies

In addition to the overall risk information in Figs. 1-1 through 1-3, it is useful to consider the risk to individuals of being fatally injured by various types of accidents. The bulk of the information shown in Table 1-1 is taken from the 1973 *Statistical Abstracts of the U.S.* and applies to the year 1969, the latest year for which these data were tabulated when this study was performed. The predicted nuclear accident risks are very small compared to other possible causes of fatal injuries.

In addition to fatalities and property damage, a number of other health effects could be caused by nuclear accidents. These include injuries and long-term health effects such as cancers, genetic effects, and thyroid gland illness. The early illness expected in potential accidents would be about 10 times as large as the fatalities shown in Figs. 1-1 and 1-2; for comparison there are 8 million injuries caused annually by other accidents. The number of cases of genetic effects and long-term cancer fatalities is predicted to be smaller than the normal incidence rate of these diseases. Even for a large accident, the small increases in these diseases would be difficult to detect from the normal incidence rate.

Thyroid illnesses that might result from a large accident are mainly the formation of nodules on the thyroid gland; these can be treated by medical procedures and rarely

---

[2] The fatalities shown in Figs. 1-1 and 1-2 for the 100 nuclear plants are those that would be predicted to occur within a short period of time after the potential reactor accident. This was done to provide a consistent comparison to the non-nuclear events which also cause fatalities in the same time frame. As in potential nuclear accidents, there also exist possibilities for injuries and longer term health effects from non-nuclear accidents. Data or predictions of this type are not available for non-nuclear events and so comparisons cannot easily be made.

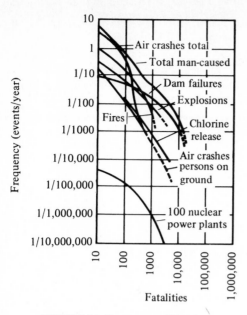

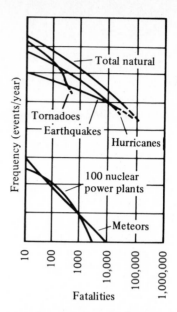

FIGURE 1-1 Frequency of Fatalities
due to Man-Caused Events

Notes:

1. Fatalities due to auto accidents are not
   shown because data are not available.
   Auto accidents cause about 50,000
   fatalities per year.

2. Approximate uncertainties for nuclear events
   are estimated to be represented by factors of
   1/4 and 4 on consequence magnitudes and
   by factors of 1/5 and 5 on probabilities.

3. For natural and man-caused occurrences the
   uncertainty in probability of largest recorded
   consequence magnitude is estimated to be
   represented by factors of 1/20 and 5.
   Smaller magnitudes have less uncertainty.

FIGURE 1-2 Frequency of Fatalaties
due to Natural Events

Notes:

1. For natural and man-caused occurrences the
   uncertainty in probability of largest recorded
   consequence magnitude is estimated to be
   represented by factors of 1/20 and 5.
   Smaller magnitudes have less uncertainty.

2. Approximate uncertainties for nuclear events
   are estimated to be represented by factors of
   1/4 and 4 on consequence magnitudes and by
   factors of 1/5 and 5 on probabilities.

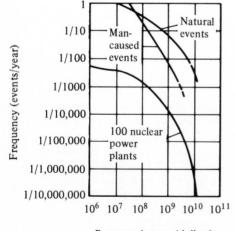

FIGURE 1-3

Frequency of Property Damage due to
Natural and Man-Caused Events

Notes:

1. Property damage due to auto accidents is not
   included because data are not available for low-
   probability events. Auto accidents cause about
   $15 billion damage each year.

2. Approximate uncertainties for nuclear events are
   estimated to be represented by factors of 1/5 and
   2 on consequence magnitudes and by factors of
   1/5 and 5 on probabilities.

3. For natural and man-caused occurrences the
   uncertainty in probability of largest recorded
   consequence magnitude is estimated to be
   represented by factors of 1/20 and 5. Smaller
   magnitudes have less uncertainty.

Table 1-1 Average risk of fatality by various causes

Accident type	Total number	Individual chance per year
Motor vehicle	55,791	1 in 4,000
Falls	17,827	1 in 10,000
Fires and hot substances	7,451	1 in 25,000
Drowning	6,181	1 in 30,000
Firearms	2,309	1 in 100,000
Air travel	1,778	1 in 100,000
Falling objects	1,271	1 in 160,000
Electrocution	1,148	1 in 160,000
Lightning	160	1 in 2,000,000
Tornadoes	91	1 in 2,500,000
Hurricanes	93	1 in 2,500,000
All accidents	111,992	1 in 1,600
Nuclear reactor accidents (100 plants)	—	1 in 5,000,000,000

lead to serious consequences. For most accidents, the number of nodules caused would be small compared to their normal incidence rate. The number that might be produced in very unlikely accidents would be about equal to their normal occurrence in the exposed population. These would be observed during a period of 10 to 40 years following the accident.

While the study has presented the estimated risks from nuclear power plant accidents and compared them with other risks that exist in our society, it has made no judgment on the acceptability of nuclear risks. The judgment as to what level of risk is acceptable should be made by a broader segment of society than that involved in this study.

6.2 ISSUES FOR DISCUSSION AND EXERCISES

6.1 The final sentence in the above extract reiterates the position of the report in that it seeks to estimate only the risks and not to assess their public acceptability. However, we observe that in the framing of this question, certain underlying assumptions on how this assessment should be formulated were introduced. Two of these are:

(a) *The standard decision analysis perspective of separating the chance of an event occurring and the evaluation of its impact.* Thus, a fatality is the same, no matter how it is caused. This allows making comparisons between fatality risks due to nuclear reactor failures and those due to other hazards such as airplanes, earthquakes, etc. But does this really reflect public attitude to risk? Individuals seem happier to tolerate risks which they choose to take, for example, an automobile journey, than those which are placed by official decision. Because a mountaineer faces a particular probability of death as part of his or her hobby, does this mean that he or she will accept the same probability of mortality from the local siting of a nuclear reactor?

(b) *Risk as a constraint not an objective.* In posing the very question of whether the hazards associated with nuclear reactors are *acceptable*, it is clear that such risks are being considered as a constraint in any policy evaluation. Implicit is the reasoning that, provided that the risks to life, property, etc., are below a critical level, evaluation can proceed on primarily cost-effective grounds. Thus, mortality, property damage, and so on, are not to be considered as part of the objective function in policy evaluations. This avoids implicit, or explicit, numerical comparisons between money and human life, but does involve the setting of standards (i.e., constraints) for nuclear risks. The implications of transforming an outcome attribute into a constraint should be considered carefully in both this and the wider context.

More recently the Nuclear Regulatory Commission has taken a step further (NUREG-0880) by stipulating "acceptability" in terms of "safety goals," namely:

1. Individual members of the public should be provided a level of protection from the consequences of nuclear power plant accidents such that no individual bears a significant additional risk to life and health.
2. Societal risks to life and health from nuclear power plant accidents should be as low as reasonably achievable and should be comparable to or less than the risks of generating electricity by viable competing technologies.

The primary numerical guidelines relate to prompt and delayed mortality risks, the latter being attributed to induced cancer. Prompt fatalities "should not exceed 0.1 % of the sum of early fatality risks resulting from other accidents to which members of the U.S. population are generally exposed." Similarly, cancer fatalities "should not exceed 0.1 % of the sum of cancer fatality risks resulting from all other causes."

Two secondary guidelines are also proposed. One states that the "benefit of an incremental reduction of risk below the numerical guidelines for societal mortality risks should be compared with the associated costs on the basis of $1,000 per man-rem averted." The other states that the "likelihood of a nuclear reactor accident that results in a large-scale core melt should normally be less than one in 10,000 per year of reactor operation." [*RISK* newsletter, April 1982, p. 3]

By considering these and other issues of problem formulation, discuss the appropriateness of this approach to risk assessment in the context of public decision making. How should we make such decisions?

6.2 Is there any rational way to avoid the assessment of the economic value of life, either explicitly or implicitly, in hazardous project evaluations? Why? How?

6.3 In seeking to compare alternative methods of computing the value of human life, list several criteria that such a measure should satisfy. For example, such a measure should be, in a sense, *efficient* in that it measures that which should be measured. Thus, should we be measuring:

(a) The value of life or the value of a life-year?
(b) The value of life to an individual, to his or her dependents, or to society as a whole?
(c) The value of an identifiable individual's life or that of an unidentified statistical life?

Similarly, a measure should be *feasible*. There is no operational value to a highly developed concept of the value of life if it cannot be measured in practice. What conditions should a value of life measure fulfill?

6.4 Using the above criteria, evaluate the following candidate procedures for measuring the value of human life:

(a) Court decisions on damages for loss of life.
(b) Life insurance premiums.

(c) The imputed cost per life saved of public programs exclusively designed to increase life expectancies, such as emergency medical facilities or improved regulations for occupational risks.

(d) The *human capital* approach. Under the assumption that an individual's value to society is reflected in the discounted net sum of future earnings, the value of life $h(j)$ for an individual of age j becomes

$$h(j) = \sum_{i=j+1}^{n} \frac{P(i|j)Y(i)}{(1 + r)^{i-j}}$$

where $P(i|j)$ = probability that an individual of age j will live to be age i

$Y(i)$ = annual earnings at age i

r = discount rate

n = age of retirement

(e) The *willingness-to-pay* criterion. The idea behind this rests upon the observation that individuals regularly make choices between higher or lower consumption and the probability of mortality. Thus, the idea is to obtain, explicitly or implicitly, from individuals tradeoffs such as "in return for an increase of $500 in income now, an individual is willing to incur an increase of 0.001 in the probability of death." This is a marginal rate of substitution in that it does not imply that the value of life in a society of 1000 similar people is equal to $500,000 since, statistically, one extra person's life would be lost.

6.5 Can the reasoning for deriving an economic value of life be extended to (a) computing salary adjustments for individuals facing occupational risks? (b) risks of injury rather than of mortality?

6.6 Are there any injuries that you consider worse than death? What implications does this have for human risk evaluations?

6.7 On a technical issue, how can Figures 1-1 and 1-2 in the above extract be interpreted as "risk profiles" and how can the "chances" in Table 1-1 be computed from them?

6.8 The benefits of major public facilities such as nuclear reactors accrue, because of geographical reasons, mostly to those who do not have to bear the major risks. How should this distributional aspect be taken into account in evaluating the acceptability of risk?

6.9 The publication of the "Reactor Safety Study" preceded the Three Mile Island incident in 1979. Such an incident had been predicted by the study to occur once in 33,000 reactor-years. In fact, it occurred after only 500 reactor-years. What implications does this have for any revision of the assessed probabilities in the 1975 study?

SEVEN

SUBJECTIVE PROBABILITY
AND BAYESIAN INFERENCE

7.1 SUBJECTIVE PROBABILITY

In making the alarming statement that "probability does not exist," De Finetti (1976) emphasized the pragmatic decision-making perspective. In decision analysis, the probabilities are statements of personal belief, reflecting the decision maker's uncertainties on some of the variables. They are not estimates of some absolute, physical constant. Whenever a brand manager assesses a probability for the success of a new product, this is a measure of opinion, one upon which his or her managerial performance will be established; it is not a numerical constant upon which the whole community of brand managers should necessarily agree. Thus, in that sense it (the probability) is not an issue of scientific inquiry. The speed of light is considered to be an absolute constant, and the scientific idealism of physicists requires that they should all come to some objective agreement on its value. The speed of light is an entity which exists in a real sense, and so scientists endeavor to estimate its value with increasing accuracy. De Finetti is debunking this line of reasoning for the decision-making context.

There has been a long, and quite partisan, debate in the philosophy of inference upon whether probability is a "relative frequency," a "logical implication," "a degree of confirmation," or an "intrinsic property" of a particular random variable. As far as we are concerned in decision making, however, the issue is not an existential one of the nature of probability. *Uncertainty* exists for the decision maker, and *probability* is just a way of measuring it.

Decision making apart, other notions of probability may be suitable. In particle physics, for example, the view is often taken that there are intrinsic probabilities (relating to movements and location) that are physical properties just like mass and velocity. Similarly, in societal models it is often useful to consider probability as a definite entity for scientific investigation, for example, the probability that an individual watches a commercial break during a television program.

We recall, however, from Chapter 1 the distinction between descriptive and normative models and the manner in which the pragmatic orientation of decision making requires a special line of reasoning. A decision maker, acting responsibly, is effectively taking the approach of subjective probability whenever uncertainties are quantified in his or her analysis. A decision analysis is, in essence, just a procedure for subjecting a decision maker's personal preferences and beliefs to explicit tests of coherence.

7.2 ASSESSMENT OF SUBJECTIVE PROBABILITIES

In considering the assessment of subjective probability distributions, it is easier to look at the discrete version before considering the continuous one. It may be thought that the simplest assessment procedure would be one in which the decision maker responds by directly articulating a set of numerical probabilities. Unfortunately psychologists have suggested that this is not necessarily the simplest conceptual task, particularly for a decision maker with little experience in probability. For example, different measures are obtained if the individual responds in terms of odds ratios or direct probabilities. For this reason, the use of standard devices is generally advocated as a medium of expression. A *standard device* is some physical instrument or conceptual situation where the probabilities of outcomes are easily understood and computed. It provides a comparative situation to the decision maker's problem and, in a sense, serves as a measuring instrument for subjective uncertainty in terms of probabilities.

A useful conceptual standard device is an urn filled with 1000 identically shaped balls. Each ball is identified with a number, from 1 to 1000. The simple experiment of drawing blind one ball from the urn is to be performed. Phillips and Thomas (1973) describe this method as it is often presented by a decision analyst in practice:

To see how the standard device can be used to measure degrees of belief, we must consider two bets, one involving the event whose probability you wish to assess, and one involving the standard device.

Suppose, for example, you want to determine the probability that it will rain tomorrow. Imagine that the following bet has been offered to you:

$$\text{Bet } A \begin{cases} \text{If it rains tomorrow, you win 1000} \\ \text{If no rain tomorrow, you win nothing} \end{cases}$$

Now imagine that balls 1 through 500 in the standard urn have been painted red while the remaining 500 balls have been colored blue. The balls are thoroughly mixed, and one is to be drawn by a blindfolded observer as tomorrow draws to a close. Now consider this bet:

$$\text{Bet } B \begin{cases} \text{If the ball drawn is red, you win 1000} \\ \text{If the ball is blue, you win nothing} \end{cases}$$

Consider both bets. Which do you prefer, *A* or *B*? Suppose you prefer *B*. Then there must be a better chance for you to win 1000 with Bet *B* than Bet *A*. Thus, the probability of rain tomorrow in your judgment is clearly less than 0.5.

By changing the proportion of red balls in the urn, it is eventually possible to find a mix of red and blue balls that make you indifferent between the two bets. When this point is reached, then we are justified in assigning the same probability to the event "red ball is drawn" as we are to the event "rain tomorrow." At no time is it necessary to ask a question more complex than "do you prefer this bet or that one, or are you indifferent between them?" Numerical measurement of an individual's subjective probability can be obtained simply by asking questions of preference.

Other standard devices have been popular. A pie diagram or spinner has been a favorite with the Stanford Research Institute. A circle is divided into two sectors and the relative sectors can be adjusted. A spinner randomly selects one of the two sectors, and hence the larger a sector, the greater its chance of being chosen. The same bets as those in the above example can be offered, but the outcomes for bet *B* are determined not by drawing a ball from an urn, but by noting which sector is chosen. The relative sizes of the sectors are adjusted until the indifference point is reached: The sector sizes then represent the probabilities of the event being assessed and its complement.

The prerequisite of a standard device is that it should have easily perceived probabilistic implications, otherwise it will introduce bias. Thus, Phillips and Thomas (1973) report some preliminary investigations which suggest that assessments using the urn device are 0.02 to 0.07 larger than the probabilities from the SRI spinner.

It is possible to distinguish between task bias, which is characteristic of the assessment method itself, and conceptual bias, which is idiosyncratic to the individual. Task bias could be caused by the standard device having misunderstood probabilistic implications or because it also structures thinking and maybe changes the fundamental beliefs of the individual in some systematic way. Conceptual bias is caused by the various heuristics that an individual might use to process information and make judgments upon various prospects. Much recent work has been done on this subject by Tversky and Kahnemann (1973) who have postulated three types of heuristics in this context:

1. *Representativeness.* Individuals apparently formulate probabilistic judgments to a greater or lesser extent by means of a representativeness heuristic. If *x* is considered highly representative of a set *A*, then it is given a high probability of belonging to *A*. However, this approach to the uncertainty judgment leads to serious bias because many of the factors important in the assessment of probability play no role in such judgments of similarity. One factor is the base rate frequency. For example, given a neutral description of a person and being asked to estimate the probability of his or her being a lawyer or engineer, subjects were found to answer 0.5 regardless of prior information on the relative number of lawyers and engineers in the population. Similarly, the representativeness heuristic does not take any account of sample size. Thus the manifestation of

the gambler's fallacy can be ascribed to the belief that randomness is expected to be represented in even very small samples. Tversky and Kahnemann describe many fascinating cases of such bias.

2. *Availability.* Reliance on the availability heuristic introduces bias through the inadequacy of the cognitive process in conceptualizing all of the relevant information. There is a memory retrievability problem which can introduce a bias. The assessed probability of a road accident increases dramatically after the subject has witnessed such an event, and by much more than if the individual were just to read about it. The limitations of the memory search process cause people to judge that there are more words beginning with "r" than there are with "r" in the third place, when in fact the converse is true. Conceptual limitations of imaginability and scenario formulation encourage subjects to believe, for example, that many more committees can be constructed of size 2 from 10 than of size 8. Again Tversky and Kahnemann relate many interesting examples.

3. *Adjustment and anchoring.* In most situations it is found that individuals formulate their general belief structure by starting from some obvious reference point and adjusting for special features. Typically, however, the adjustment is not sufficient, and a bias toward these initial values is described as anchoring. Thus, when subjects were asked to estimate within 5 seconds the product $8 \times 7 \times 6 \times \cdots \times 1$, they gave a much higher answer than those asked the product $1 \times 2 \times 3 \times \cdots \times 8$. Anchoring is, in fact, a form of bias which is most often introduced by the sequential way that the assessment proceeds. Thus, it is often as much, if not more, a form of task as a form of conceptual bias.

The cognitive process of formulating judgments of uncertainty is poorly understood by psychologists. Thus, the current state of fundamental understanding in subjective probability assessment is sketchy and mostly inconclusive. However, certain general features are beginning to emerge (see Morgan et al., 1979). One of them is a widespread tendency for individuals to be "overconfident." In situations where a large "track record" of assessments and actual outcomes is available for comparison, individuals seem generally prone to too many surprises. In other words, the assessed probability distributions are too tight (too small a variance) such that events of low assessed probability (those in the tails of the distribution) actually turn out to occur with higher frequencies than the distributions predict. The reasons for this are not completely understood. There may well be an anchoring effect through assessors focusing initially upon the mode or median. Representativeness and availability heuristics may limit the broad-minded view necessary to accommodate a wider range of probabilities. Individual characteristics involving an intolerance of ambiguity, dogmatism, a desire not to appear unsure of oneself, and cultural factors may also play a part in this.

A common way of assessing a continuous probability distribution is to break it up into a series of discrete assessments. This evidently makes the task particularly susceptible to adjustment bias, and indeed, overconfidence has been a pervasive problem. The procedure described below is especially common in that it requires only an analogy to equiprobable prospects (compare the assessment of utility functions in Section 3.3). Thus, if x is the variable under consideration, for example, tomorrow's temperature or the price of gold next month, and $F(x)$ is its cumulative distribution function, then we can proceed in the following fashion to assess $F(x)$:

1. Determine the value x_1 for which the decision maker believes there is 50 percent chance of x exceeding x_1. This gives $F(x_1) = 0.5$.
2. Determine the value x_2 for which the decision maker believes there is an equal chance of x being less than x_2 and x being between x_2 and x_1. This gives $F(x_2) = 0.25$.
3. Determine the value x_3 for which the decision maker believes there is an equal chance of x falling below x_3 as falling between x_3 and x_2. This gives $F(x_3) = 0.125$.

Evidently this procedure can continue up from the median to give similarly the points $F(x) = 0.75$ and $F(x) = 0.875$. Depending upon the number of points required, such a procedure of successively bisecting intervals into equiprobable halves will yield quartiles (four intervals), octiles (eight intervals) and so on. These are all special cases of *fractile assessments*. Recall that the point $F(x) = 0.75$ is known as the 0.75 fractile of the distribution. Another type of fractile assessment procedure which has been found by some workers to produce less anchoring bias is the *tertile* method. In this method, the decision maker is asked to give two points that split the range of x into three equally likely segments. The motivation behind this is to avoid anchoring at the median.

An alternative to the fractile method of splitting up the range of x according to fixed probabilities is to fix the points $x_1, x_2, \ldots, x_m$ (depending on the number of intervals required) and ask the decision maker to assess the probabilities of x being between x_1 and x_2, x_2 and x_3, and so on. This is known as the *histogram* method, in recognition of the way that discrete probability distributions are usually displayed. Note that with this method we are in fact assessing a probability distribution, as opposed to the cumulative distribution function in the fractile method. Some decision analysts with access to interactive visual display units can ask the decision makers to sketch out the probability function directly, switch quickly to and from the cumulative function, and perform various consistency checks.

No single "best" assessment procedure has yet emerged. Experimental evidence seems well divided over the relative merits of the fractile or histogram methods (Morgan et al., 1979). Unfortunately, much of this evidence is from artificial experiments, particularly on college students, where the subjects do not have the same degree of motivation and personal involvement in the consequences of their probability estimates as they would in a real decision-making situation. There is an obvious need in this area for more research to be undertaken in the real decision-making process. A couple of applied studies that have been undertaken are those of von Holstein (1970) and Winkler and Murphy (1973).

Von Holstein was able to use professional investment analysts in his ongoing stock market forecasting and portfolio selection activity. The histogram method was used, and significant anchoring bias was reported. Winkler and Murphy were able to compare the quartile and histogram methods in the real-world situation of weather forecasting. They reported that the histogram method exhibited greater anchoring bias than the quartile method for which, in fact, the 50 percent interval captured the true value 45 percent of the time. They were fortunate, however, in having subjects with considerable experience in-probabilistic forecasting; training and practice appear to have a significant effect in reducing anchoring bias.

One factor which may reinforce anchoring bias is the importance generally placed upon self-consistency within the assessments. In a straightforward assessment method, it is easy for the subject to be pseudo-consistent precisely because he or she can perceive what they should believe in order to be consistent with their previous responses. In this way, their responses become firmly anchored from the starting point.

Ways by which decision analysts can go about reducing bias in assessments are described in Bunn (1975) and Morgan et al. (1979). These include various forms of preassessment "conditioning" including tutorials on assessment bias, dialectical processes whereby the assessor lists arguments for and against the propositions and discusses the extreme values in detail. These procedures attempt to put the assessor in a frame of mind which should be less prone to anchoring. The assessment task itself is sometimes structured to work from the tails rather than the center of the distribution and sometimes to include hybrid types of consistency checks (mixing fractile and histogram type questions). As in the assessment of utility, the process of subjective probability elicitation is an iterative procedure—the very act of assessment concentrates the decision maker's mind on a variable, often causing a reevaluation of its uncertainty.

7.3 THE IMPACT OF NEW INFORMATION (BAYES' THEOREM)

The subjective probability distribution that a decision maker assesses upon a variable should embody a synthesis of all his or her information relevant to its outcome. This follows from the coherence ideal. An issue which we now want to consider is how new information should revise an individual's probability assessments. This clearly gets to the heart of the rational formulation of belief.

Suppose you were thinking of going to the beach tomorrow and would therefore be interested in the chances of it being sunny. You assess the probability of it being sunny as $P(S) = 0.6$. You then turn on the television forecast, which is not infallible, and find that a cloudy day is predicted. How should you change your probability $P(S)$?

For simplicity, let us assume that you are only interested in two mutually exclusive and collectively exhaustive events, namely, that it is sunny S or not $\bar{S}$. Recall that mutual exclusivity means that if S occurs, $\bar{S}$ cannot, and vice versa.

Collectively exhaustive renders it certain that one of the events must occur. These two conditions, sometimes referred to as a partition of the outcomes, allow us to assign a probability distribution over the set of events. Thus, since probabilities must add up to 1 over a valid partition of the outcome, we know that $P(\bar{S}) = 0.4$. Likewise, let us assume that the weather forecaster either predicts a bright B or a cloudy C day. Thus, the events (B, C) also form a partition of the outcome (tomorrow's weather). We further recall from elementary probability that when an outcome can be partitioned in two different ways, we can analyze the situation by means of a *joint probability table*, as shown below:

	S	$\bar{S}$	
C	$P(C, S)$	$P(C, \bar{S})$	$P(C)$
B	$P(B, S)$	$P(B, \bar{S})$	$P(B)$
	$P(S)$	$P(\bar{S})$	1

The columns labeled S and $\bar{S}$ indicate one partition, the rows C and B another. Entries in the table, such as $P(C, S)$, indicate the joint probability that both C and S occur, that is, it is a sunny day following a cloudy forecast. Those probabilities summed in the margin, such as $P(S)$, denote the *marginal probabilities* of it being a sunny day (i.e., regardless of whether C or B occurs; in fact without knowing about C's or B's occurrence), and so on. Both sets of marginal probabilities sum to 1 because they are valid probability distributions.

As you will recall, the numbers in the joint probability table can be derived in a number of ways, depending upon how the data are available. For our purposes of exposition here, let us suppose that you look at the past 100 sunny days and find that the weather forecast was cloudy for 20 of them. Thus, you could estimate the conditional probability $P(C|S)$ as 0.2. This probability of a cloudy forecast is a *conditional probability* because it was estimated from a restricted data base, namely, a set of sunny days. Similarly, let us suppose that an examination of 100 nonsunny days yielded a cloudy forecast on 90 occasions. Thus, the conditional probability $P(C|\bar{S}) = 0.9$. We can now find the joint probabilities by elementary manipulations of these assessments.

Recall that a joint probability can be written as the product of a marginal and a conditional probability, that is,

$$P(C, S) = P(C|S)P(S) = (0.2)(0.6) = 0.12$$
$$P(C, \bar{S}) = P(S|\bar{S})P(\bar{S}) = (0.9)(0.4) = 0.36$$

We also note that

$$P(B|S) = 1 - P(C|S) = 0.8$$
$$P(B|\bar{S}) = 1 - P(C|\bar{S}) = 0.1$$

since (B, C) is a partition. Thus, we additionally have

$$P(B, S) = P(B|S)P(S) = (0.8)(0.6) = 0.48$$

$$P(B, \bar{S}) = P(B|\bar{S})P(\bar{S}) = (0.1)(0.4) = 0.04$$

We can now fill in our table of joint probabilities, noting that the marginal probabilities do add up to 1 as a final check:

	S	$\bar{S}$	
C	0.12	0.36	0.48
B	0.48	0.04	0.52
	0.6	0.4	1

In our problem of thinking about tomorrow being sunny, having seen a cloudy forecast on television, we require the probability $P(S|C)$. This is a conditional probability because we wish to restrict our assessment to those situations for which a cloudy forecast had been obtained. Thus, we can write from the definition of a conditional probability

$$P(S|C) = \frac{P(S, C)}{P(C)}$$

$$= \frac{0.12}{0.48}$$

$$= 0.25$$

Notice how we have gone from an unconditional assessment $P(S) = 0.6$ to the conditional assessment $P(S|C) = 0.25$. That is the impact of the new information C. New information acts as a conditioning constraint upon a variable. It restricts attention to those circumstances associated with the occurrence of the information. In decision analysis we usually refer to this process as one of going from a *prior* probability $P(S)$ to a *posterior* probability $P(S|C)$. From the formula for conditional probability,

$$P(S|C) = \frac{P(S, C)}{P(C)}$$

We obtained $P(S, C)$ in the table from

$$P(S, C) = P(C|S)P(S)$$

Thus, we can write our formula for the posterior probability $P(S|C)$ as

$$P(S|C) = \frac{P(C|S)P(S)}{P(C)}$$

which emphasizes the role of the prior probability $P(S)$ in the numerator. The above equation is known as *Bayes' theorem*. As we have noted, its derivation follows from elementary joint probability reasoning. It essentially revolves around the fact that a joint probability $P(C, S)$ can be decomposed two ways in terms of conditional probabilities, namely,

$$P(C, S) = P(C|S)P(S)$$

or
$$P(C, S) = P(S|C)P(C)$$

[Note that $P(C, S)$ and $P(S, C)$ are logically equivalent.]

Thus, we can see that

$$P(S|C)P(C) = P(C|S)P(S)$$

and therefore

$$P(S|C) = \frac{P(C|S)P(S)}{P(C)}$$

Although the derivation of Bayes' theorem is quite trivial, there are two extremely noteworthy aspects of the formula:

1. *Prior to posterior probabilities.* We have noted how this formula allows us to go from the initial probability $P(S)$ (prior) to the more informative $P(S|C)$ (posterior).
2. *Reversal of conditionality.* We also observe, from the numerator, how we can go from $P(C|S)$ to $P(S|C)$, that is, we can reverse the "direction" of a conditional probability.

We can refer to the prior and posterior *distributions* on our variable of interest (in this case tomorrow's weather). Our prior distribution was

$$P(S) = 0.6$$
$$P(\bar{S}) = 0.4$$

and by Bayes' theorem, given the new information C, our posterior distribution becomes

$$P(S|C) = \frac{P(C|S)P(S)}{P(C)} = 0.25$$

$$P(\bar{S}|C) = \frac{P(C|\bar{S})P(\bar{S})}{P(C)} = 0.75$$

We observe that the denominator $P(C)$ is the same in both applications of Bayes' theorem. It is the least important part of the formula, serving only the "normalization" function of ensuring that the posterior probability distribution sums to 1. This becomes more apparent when we recall how $P(C)$ is actually derived. It is the marginal probability in the table of joint probabilities, obtained from the summation

$$P(C) = P(C, S) + P(C, \bar{S})$$

where the joint probabilities were themselves obtained from the conditional, that is,

$$P(C) = P(C|S)P(S) + P(C|\bar{S})P(\bar{S})$$

Evidently the denominator in Bayes' theorem is just the sum of the numerators and is really just serving as a scaling factor.

For this reason, Bayes' theorem is sometimes just expressed in proportionality terms, for example,

$$P(S|C) \propto P(C|S)P(S)$$

emphasizing the two important components of the equation, namely, the prior probability $P(S)$ and what is known as the *likelihood* of the new datum, $P(C|S)$, which is the probability of its occurrence conditional upon the assumption for the variable of interest (in this case that tomorrow is sunny). Thus we change our prior belief upon an event, or hypothesis, according to the strength of our prior beliefs and the likelihood of the data under this belief that the event, or hypothesis, holds.

Whenever the prior probability distribution is defined on more than two hypotheses, a particularly tidy way to pursue a bayesian analysis is by means of a simple table.

Suppose a brand manager has three hypothetical scenarios for a new product, namely, high, medium, and low, with prior probabilities 0.6, 0.1, and 0.3, respectively. A market research survey has the properties that an average result will occur 30 percent of the time when the true state is high, 50 percent of the time when the true state is medium, and 90 percent of the time when the true state is low. The posterior probability distribution can be computed in the following tabular way assuming the survey suggests an "average" response:

Data: average

Hypothesis	Prior probability	Likelihood of data	Joint probability of hypothesis and data	Posterior probability
H	0.6	0.3	0.18	0.36
M	0.1	0.5	0.5	0.1
L	0.3	0.9	0.27	0.54
Totals	1		0.5	1

Identify the hypotheses in the distribution in the first column and put the appropriate prior probabilities alongside in the second column. The likelihood of the data under each hypothesis is then multiplied by the prior probability to give the column of joint probabilities for the data and hypotheses. Summing these joint probabilities gives us the marginal probability of the data, and this is the denominator in Bayes' theorem. The final posterior distribution is obtained simply by dividing each of the joint probabilities by this sum. It is evident that the above table is just an elaboration and reorganization of the table of joint probabilities which we used to motivate our presentation in this section. Both tabular forms are common in practice.

The designations prior and posterior are relative to a particular piece of information. Thus, when evaluating a second item of data, the prior probability in that bayesian analysis would be the posterior probability derived from consideration of the first item. Thus, if you had access to a second weather forecast, which said tomorrow would be dull, then your posterior probability would be evaluated by Bayes' theorem as

$$P(S|D, C) \propto P(D|S, C)P(S|C)$$

and thus a whole series of data can be used to sequentially revise initial belief.

Example: Sequential bayesian analysis An oil company holds a lease on a small tract which has three possible drilling sites. The geological experts have assessed the probabilities of no reserves N, small reserves S, and large reserves L, under the tract to be 0.5, 0.3, and 0.2, respectively. On drilling at any of the three sites, the wells will be dry D, wet W, or gushing G. Each of the three drilling sites X, Y, and Z appears equally favorable, and therefore there is no reason to prefer one sequence of drilling to another a priori.

If there are large reserves, then drilling at any of X, Y, and Z will produce a gushing well. If there are no reserves, then all the wells will be dry. If there are small reserves under the tract, then a mixture of dry and wet wells could be found. However, once a wet well has been found, the tract will be determined as having small reserves. Hence, if the reserves are small, it has been assessed that there is a probability of 0.8 of finding one dry well (if just one hole is drilled), and 0.4 of finding two dry wells (if just two holes are drilled).

Since the order of drilling is immaterial, we will consider it to go XYZ. Thus, first of all let us consider setting up a table of joint probabilities for the outcomes and states of the tract for drilling at site X. We can set up this table quite readily, with D_X representing a dry hole at site X, and so on.

Joint probabilities for site X

	D_X	W_X	G_X	
N	0.5	0	0	0.5
S	0.24	0.06	0	0.3
L	0	0	0.2	0.2
Totals	0.74	0.06	0.2	1

The first and third rows are computed easily. Furthermore, we are told that

$$P(G_X|S) = 0$$

and
$$P(D_X|S) = 0.8$$

which is sufficient to compute the second row as

$$P(S, D_X) = P(D_X|S)P(S) = 0.24$$
$$P(S, W_X) = P(W_X|S)P(S) = 0.06$$
$$P(S, G_X) = P(G_X|S)P(S) = 0$$

and the marginal distribution on D_X, W_X, and G_X is summed in the bottom row.

If G_X or W_X occurs with probability 0.26, then exploratory drilling will stop. Otherwise, with a dry well at X, D_X, there is still the chance of small reserves, and thus site Y may be worth exploring. The table of joint probabilities for the Y outcomes will now be conditional upon D_X, that is,

**Joint probabilities
for site Y**

	D_Y	W_Y	
N	0.68	0	0.68
S	0.16	0.16	0.32
Totals	0.84	0.16	1

Note that we have only two states of the tract, N and S, and two outcomes, D_Y and W_Y. Our prior probabilities on N and S must now be conditional upon D_X, that is, the posterior probabilities from the X table. Thus,

$$P(N|D_X) = \frac{0.5}{0.74} = 0.68$$

$$P(S|D_X) = \frac{0.24}{0.74} = 0.32$$

Also, as before,

$$P(N, W_Y) = 0$$

and we are told that

$$P(D_Y, D_X|S) = 0.4$$

Thus,
$$P(D_Y|D_X, S) = \frac{P(D_Y, D_X|S)}{P(D_X|S)}$$

and since
$$P(D_X|S) = \frac{0.24}{0.3} = 0.8$$

then
$$P(D_Y|D_X, S) = \tfrac{1}{2}$$

and the table can be completed.

Evidently, if outcome W_Y occurs, then the state of the tract is definitely S, but if D_Y occurs, the situation is again equivocal. The posterior probabilities on N and S are now

$$P(N|D_Y, D_X) = \frac{0.68}{0.84} = 0.81$$

$$P(S|D_Y, D_X) = \frac{0.16}{0.84} = 0.19$$

and so there remains the prospect of drilling at site Z and finding small reserves for the tract.

Remember that drilling at the third site, Z, resolves finally the exact state of the tract. Hence, these posterior probabilities are also the marginal probabilities of the outcomes D_Z, W_Z. The corresponding table of joint probabilities for drilling at site Z is evidently of diagonal form:

**Joint probabilities
for site Z**

	D_Z	W_Z	
N	0.81	0	0.81
S	0	0.19	0.19
Totals	0.81	0.19	1

Note how the probability of no reserves has increased via a sequence of dry wells,

$$P(N) = 0.5$$

$$P(N|D_X) = 0.68$$

$$P(N|D_Y, D_X) = 0.81$$

$$P(N|D_Z, D_Y, D_X) = 1$$

and how the posterior probability of a state, such as N, with respect to an event, such as D_X, becomes the prior probability with respect to the subsequent events D_Y, and so on. The designations "prior" and "posterior" are only relative to a particular event or piece of information.

One final point on this sequential model which is worth stating concerns the assignment of zero prior probabilities. Evidently, once a zero prior probability has been assigned in bayesian inference, it can never be changed. Thus, unless one is absolutely certain that a hypothesis is impossible, a nonzero probability should be given in all cases, no matter how unlikely.

7.4 CONDITIONAL INDEPENDENCE

Two events, or hypotheses, are independent if their joint probability can be computed as the product of their separate marginal probabilities, that is,

$$P(A, B) = P(A)P(B)$$

This also implies that the conditional probabilities on each other equal the marginal probabilities,

$$P(A|B) = P(A)$$

$$P(B|A) = P(B)$$

That any two of the above follow from the third can be seen from applying Bayes' theorem. In bayesian terms, the posterior probability is the same as the prior. The occurrence of an independent event has not changed the initial belief at all. Of course, this makes sense, for we understand by independence the idea that the occurrence of one in no way affects the chances of the other occurring. Thus, we learn only from dependent events.

If we are applying three or more events or hypotheses, the situation can be more intricate. Events A and B can be dependent upon each other in the sense that

$$P(A, B) \neq P(A)P(B)$$

but this dependency is "explainable" by a third event or hypothesis C, such that conditional upon C,

$$P(A, B|C) = P(A|C)P(B|C)$$

In this case A and B are conditionally independent, given C. This is often a very useful condition in the bayesian analysis of a series of events, for it allows the valuable learning from multiple dependencies with the convenience of manipulating independent events.

Example: Slick betting Sammy Slick is a regular bettor at the Newmarket horse races. This particular afternoon he is especially interested in the young filly Wanda's Revenge running in the big race at 3:00. If the going is good, that is, the track is firm, then he thinks that Wanda's Revenge has a 90 percent chance of winning. However, if the going is not good, the track is soft, then he believes the chance of her winning is only 20 percent. When he first arrived at the racetrack at noon, he was uncertain as to the state of the track. He thought it looked rather soft and accordingly assessed the probability of it being good at only 0.3. However, the results of the two earlier races are now causing him to revise his assessment. Mrs. Whippy won the 1:30 and Aunt Jemima the 2:00. He felt that if the going were good, Mrs. Whippy and Aunt Jemima would have had probabilities 0.8 and 0.9, respectively, of winning, compared with probabilities 0.4 and 0.5 if the going were soft.

What should Sammy Slick's assessment of the probability of Wanda's Revenge winning the big race now become?

Let us denote

$$WR = \text{the event Wanda's Revenge wins}$$

$$MW = \text{the event Mrs. Whippy wins}$$

$$AJ = \text{the event Aunt Jemima wins}$$

Sammy Slick clearly requires the posterior probability of WR, given that MW and AJ have occurred, that is,

$$P(WR \,|\, MW, AJ)$$

Now the events WR, MW, and AJ are conditionally independent in that they do not really affect each other as such, but their occurrence allows us to change our probability of G, the good going, an event upon which they all depend. Thus,

$$P(WR \,|\, MW, AJ) = P(WR \,|\, G)P(G \,|\, MW, AJ) + P(WR \,|\, \bar{G})P(\bar{G} \,|\, MW, AJ)$$

and $\quad P(G \,|\, MW, AJ) \propto P(MW, AJ \,|\, G)P(G)$

$$\propto P(MW \,|\, G)P(AJ \,|\, G)P(G)$$

$$\propto 0.216$$

$$P(\bar{G} \,|\, MW, AJ) \propto P(MW, AJ \,|\, \bar{G})P(\bar{G})$$

$$\propto P(MW \,|\, \bar{G})P(AJ \,|\, \bar{G})P(\bar{G})$$

$$\propto 0.4(0.5)(0.7)$$

$$\propto 0.14$$

Hence, by normalizing,

$$P(G \,|\, MW, AJ) = \frac{0.216}{0.356} = 0.61$$

$$P(\bar{G} \,|\, MW, AJ) = \frac{0.14}{0.356} = 0.39$$

giving, by substitution,

$$P(WR \,|\, MW, AJ) = 0.9(0.61) + 0.2(0.39) = 0.63$$

Thus, by indicating the underlying "cause" (a good or a soft going) we have quite easily been able to compute a posterior probability for events whose dependence might have been difficult to assess directly. Looking for instances of conditional independence is one of the modeling skills of decision analysis. It renders the assessments and calculations easier and provides a greater understanding of the way the uncertainty unfolds. It is a prime example of the decomposition principle. Further examples will appear in subsequent sections, particularly that on hierarchical inference.

7.5 BAYESIAN UPDATING WITH FUNCTIONAL LIKELIHOODS

The likelihood in Bayes' theorem gives the probability of the new data, conditional upon some assumptions. Often the data will be considered generated according to some particular distribution, such as binomial, normal, etc., and the focus of attention will be upon how new data modify prior assumptions on the parameter(s) of this distribution. This problem lends itself quite nicely to bayesian analysis. In this section, we shall consider bayesian updating of parameter uncertainty according to (1) binomial and (2) normal models of the data.

Binomial Likelihoods

Recall the following structural assumptions of the binomial model:

1. We are concerned with dichotomous data. An item is either defective or not, a person either buys the product or does not, etc.
2. A sequence of such dichotomous outcomes is envisaged. A series of items will be tested for defects, many people will have an opportunity to buy the product, etc.
3. There is a constant probability p of one of the outcomes (defective, purchaser, etc.) throughout the sequence of trials.
4. Each trial through the sequence is conditionally independent in the sense that given p, the probability of one of the outcomes is independent of the previous history of outcomes in the sequence.
5. We are interested in the total number, out of a sequence of n trials, of outcomes of one sort (defective, purchasers, etc.); in fact, those outcomes that each have the probability p.

Under these assumptions the probability of obtaining a total number of r outcomes out of n trials, each of which has a probability p, is given by the following formula:

$$f_{\text{bin}}(r \mid n, p) = \binom{n}{p} p^r (1 - p)^{n-r}$$

where
$$\binom{n}{r}$$

is the combinatorial notation for

$$\frac{n!}{r!(n-r)!}$$

Tables are available (Appendix, Table 1) for evaluating binomial probabilities so that we do not often have to use the above formula. Note, however, that the expression $f_{\mathrm{bin}}(r|n, p)$ emphasizes the conditional nature of the probability. The parameter n is usually selected by statistical design, being part of the topic of optimal sample size. The parameter p is usually the focus of bayesian analysis. For example, suppose that a marketing manager is interested in the market share p that a new product will obtain. Evidently p is also the probability that a randomly selected potential customer will buy the product. If n potential customers are independently sampled in a test market and r of them buy it, then the likelihood of this datum is evidently $f_{\mathrm{bin}}(r|n, p)$. The application of Bayes' theorem could quite easily revise any prior probability that the manager had upon p, that is,

$$P(p|r, n) \propto f_{\mathrm{bin}}(r|n, p)P(p)$$

For a numerical example let us suppose that the manager had three actual hypotheses, namely, high ($p = 0.25$), medium ($p = 0.1$), and low ($p = 0.05$), and that his prior probabilities for these were 0.2, 0.3, and 0.5, respectively. On taking a random sample of five consumers, he found that only one of them was a purchaser of our product. The posterior probabilities can now be computed in the usual tabular way:

Hypothesis	Prior probability	Likelihood	Joint probability	Posterior probability
$p = 0.05$	0.5	0.2036	0.1018	0.3645
$p = 0.1$	0.3	0.3281	0.0984	0.3523
$p = 0.25$	0.2	0.3955	0.0791	0.2832
Totals	1		0.2793	1

This is exactly analogous to the examples considered in previous sections, except that the likelihoods were derived from Table 1 in the Appendix under the binomial assumption. Sequential inference can proceed similarly. Thus, suppose that our manager in the above example thought that his new posterior probabilities did not discriminate sufficiently between the three hypotheses and so he sampled a further five consumers, finding this time that two of them purchase our product. New posterior probabilities are now evaluated:

Hypothesis	Prior probability	Likelihood	Joint probability	Posterior probability
$p = 0.05$	0.3645	0.0214	0.0078	0.0721
$p = 0.1$	0.3523	0.0729	0.0257	0.2375
$p = 0.25$	0.2832	0.2637	0.0747	0.6904
Totals	1		0.1082	1

Normal Likelihoods

The normal distribution is the most common model for data assumed to be drawn from a symmetric distribution. It assumes the variable to be continuous, although it is frequently used to approximate discrete data. The normal probability density function $f_N(y|\mu, \sigma)$ for a random variable y has the mathematical form

$$f_N(y|\mu, \sigma) = \frac{\exp\{-\frac{1}{2}[(y - \mu)/\sigma]^2\}}{(2\pi\sigma^2)^{1/2}}$$

although we rarely have to make explicit use of the formula. Both $f_N(y|\mu, \sigma)$ and $F_N(y|\mu, \sigma)$ are well tabulated (see Tables 2 and 3 in the Appendix). The conditioning parameters are the mean μ and the standard deviation σ. Bayesian updating of these parameters can proceed individually (if one is known or assumed) or simultaneously, that is,

$$P(\mu|y, \sigma) \propto f_N(y|\mu, \sigma)P(\mu|\sigma)$$

or

$$P(\sigma|y, \mu) \propto f_N(y|\mu, \sigma)P(\sigma|\mu)$$

or

$$P(\mu, \sigma|y) \propto f_N(y|\mu, \sigma)P(\mu, \sigma)$$

Example: Mean uncertainty Stickywicket Enterprises manufactures bottles of glue. One of the machines that squirts glue into bottles has a setting that occasionally slips. The machine is designed to deliver an average of 8.2 oz, but sometimes slips to give an average of only 7.9 oz. The intrinsic variability is the same on either setting, namely, a standard deviation of 0.1 oz. The quality control manager believes there to be a 50:50 chance that the machine has slipped. He examines one bottle and finds it contains exactly 8.0 oz. What is the posterior probability of the machine having slipped?

The likelihood of observing 8.0 oz if $\mu = 8.2$ is given by $f_{SN}(z)$, the standard normal density function evaluated by

$$z = \frac{8.0 - 8.2}{0.1}$$

$$= -2$$

which, from Table 2 in the Appendix, equals 0.0540. Similarly, $f_{SN}(z)$ for

$$z = \frac{8.0 - 7.9}{0.1}$$

$$= 1$$

gives a likelihood of 0.2420 if $\mu = 7.9$.

Thus, we set up the simple table for bayesian analysis:

Data: 8.0 oz

Hypothesis	Prior probability	Likelihood	Joint probability	Posterior probability
$\mu = 7.9$	0.5	0.2420	0.1210	0.82
$\mu = 8.2$	0.5	0.0540	0.0270	0.18
Totals	1		0.1480	1

There are a couple of noteworthy points concerned with the above example. First, we note that we have evaluated the likelihood of the event, 8.0 oz, as the value of the normal probability density function at this point. But we cannot say that, for example, 0.2420 is the probability of observing an 8.0-oz bottle if the mean is 7.9 oz. We are dealing with a density function for a continuous random variable. The values of the density function just give *relative* probabilities for tiny ε-width outcome intervals around outcome points. Since we are dealing with a continuous variable and we only require relative probabilities anyway, as we normalize the posterior probability distribution by the fourth-column total, this is a reasonable procedure in the above example. However, if the normal distribution is being used as an approximation to a discrete distribution, then the correct procedure is to evaluate interval probabilities for the likelihoods. For example, suppose the number of customers in a marketing example were modeled by the normal approximation. Then the likelihood of, say, 35 customers would be computed as

$$P(35 | \mu, \sigma) = F_N(35.5 | \mu, \sigma) - F_N(34.5 | \mu, \sigma)$$

(see Exercise 7.12). This correction for discretization may or may not be important, according to the precision required in the analysis.

The second point to note is that we could again conduct a sequential analysis to obtain the posterior probability after two, three, or more bottle examinations. Alternatively, if a batch of four bottles had been tested, we could revise the prior probabilities in one single stage, once having computed the joint likelihoods of these data. For example, suppose the four values were 8.0, 8.0, 8.1, and 7.9. We require joint likelihoods

$$P(8.0, 8.0, 8.1, 7.9 | \mu = 7.9, \sigma = 0.1)$$

$$P(8.0, 8.0, 8.1, 7.9 | \mu = 8.2, \sigma = 0.1)$$

If we assume that these weights are independent, given the true mean and the standard deviation, then we can evaluate the above likelihoods by multiplication:

$P(8.0, 8.0, 8.1, 7.9 | \mu = 7.9, \sigma = 0.1)$

$$= f_N(8.0 | \mu = 7.9, \sigma = 0.1)^2 \, f_N(8.1 | \mu = 7.9, \sigma = 0.1) \, f_N(7.9 | \mu = 7.9, \sigma = 0.1)$$

Note the role of conditional independence here. Thus, we have

$$P(8.0, 8.0, 8.1, 7.9 | \mu = 7.9, \sigma = 0.1) = (0.242)^2(0.054)(0.3989) = 0.0012614$$

and

$$P(8.0, 8.0\ 8.1, 7.9 | \mu = 8.2, \sigma = 0.1) = (0.054)^2(0.242)(0.0044) = 0.0000031$$

The bayesian updating table is now as follows:

Data: 8.0, 8.0, 8.1, 7.9

Hypothesis	Prior probability	Likelihood	Joint probability	Posterior probability
$\mu = 7.9$	0.5	0.0012614	0.0006307	0.997
$\mu = 8.2$	0.5	0.0000031	0.0000015	0.003
Totals	1		0.0006322	1

7.6 BAYESIAN UPDATING WITH CONTINUOUS PRIOR DISTRIBUTIONS

It is apparent that the tabular nature of the bayesian analyses undertaken in the previous section allowed prior belief only to be encoded as a discrete distribution. However, in the marketing research example, instead of conceiving of a set of discrete possible scenarios for the new product's market performance, that is, high (25 percent), medium (10 percent), and low (5 percent), and attaching subjective probabilities to each of these, we may wish to undertake an analysis based more realistically on the fact that the potential market share is a continuous variable between 0 and 100 percent. Let us denote this market share variable by p, where $0 \leq p \leq 1$, and the subjective articulation of our state of uncertainty on p by means of a probability density function $f(p)$. Thus, $f(p)$ is a continuous subjective probability distribution.

Consider now how we might update $f(p)$ in light of some additional information in the form of market research data. Suppose that a random sample of size n had been undertaken and r of them said they would buy the new product. If we knew the actual propensity p of an individual, selected at random, to purchase the product, then the probability of getting r out of n would be a simple binomial probability,

$$f_{\text{bin}}(r | n, p)$$

which we recognize as the likelihood of the data (that is, r) under the hypothesis (that is, p). Thus the posterior probability density function $f(p|r, n)$ is given in an exactly analogous way to the discrete case by the continuous version of Bayes' formula:

$$f(p|r, n) = \frac{f_{\text{bin}}(r|n, p)f(p)}{\int_0^1 f_{\text{bin}}(r|n, p)f(p)\, dp}$$

where the normalization (the denominator) must now be done by integration rather than summation. Thus, we realize that the solution of the above expression for an arbitrary prior density function $f(p)$ will not in general be easy analytically, and resort may have to be made to simulation or numerical approximation methods.

A very easy analytical solution to the above problem can, however, be achieved if the prior density function can be constrained to a particular distribution. For a given likelihood function of the data, a prior distribution can be found such that the associated posterior distribution has also the same distributional form, except with a change in the parameters to reflect the new information. Such a prior density function is known as a *natural conjugate* for the given likelihood function. Remember that the likelihood function reflects the model of the way in which the new data are generated (such as binomial) and that the prior density function is defined on one or more of the parameters of this data-generating process (such as the binomial parameter p).

Thus, if it is found appropriate to model the prior density function $f(p)$ in terms of a natural conjugate, all that we need to be concerned with are the prior and the posterior distribution parameters rather than the equations of the distributions. The prior and posterior distributions will be of the same functional form, and we can update the prior distribution just by following the appropriate rule or rules for updating the parameters. We will consider the conjugate prior distributions for (1) binomial and (2) normal data.

Conjugate Prior Distribution for Binomial Data

If the data are binomial, then the conjugate prior distribution is the beta distribution $f_{\text{bet}}(p|r', n')$. This is defined by two parameters r' and n' (where the primes indicate that the parameters are prior). Thus, if we can fit a beta prior distribution to the uncertainty of the decision maker on p and thereby derive either directly or indirectly the prior parameters r' and n', we do not have to evaluate the full bayesian equation to define the posterior density function. We know that the posterior density function will also be beta (since we are using a natural conjugate), and all that we require is the rule for deriving the posterior parameters, which is very simple, namely,

$$r'' = r' + r$$

$$n'' = n' + n$$

We are using double primes to identify posterior parameters.

Example Suppose that a brand manager's prior belief on the future market share p that a new product might obtain can be described by a beta distribution with parameters $r' = 3$ and $n' = 10$. If the manager conducted some research by interviewing 100 (n) randomly selected potential buyers from this target population and found that 35 (r) would genuinely buy the product, then the posterior belief would also be represented by a beta distribution with parameters $r'' = 38$ and $n'' = 110$.

Although we rarely make explicit use of the functional equation for the beta probability distribution, some of the more mathematically inquiring readers may like to see it:

$$f_{\text{bet}}(p) = B^{-1}(r', n')p^{r'-1}(1 - p)^{n'-r'-1} \qquad \text{for } 0 < p < 1, \quad r', n' > 0$$

where $B(r', n')$ is the *beta function*,

$$B(r', n') = \frac{\Gamma(r')\Gamma(n' - r')}{\Gamma(n')}$$

with the gamma function $\Gamma(n')$ being equivalent to the factorial notation $(n' - 1)!$ for integer n', that is,

$$\Gamma(n') = (n' - 1)(n' - 2)\cdots[n' - (n' - 1)]$$

but more generally defined upon noninteger values as well.

$$\text{Mean} = \frac{r'}{n'}$$

$$\text{Mode} = \frac{r' - 1}{n' - 2}$$

$$\text{Variance} = \frac{r'(n' - r')}{(n')^2(n' + 1)}$$

In order that notation for the parameters in the beta distribution may not become too cumbersome, the superscripts on r and n will be utilized only when it is necessary to distinguish explicitly between prior and posterior states of knowledge.

The beta density function is an extremely flexible probability distribution for representing uncertainty on the parameter of a binomial data process. Figure 7.1 demonstrates some of the possible forms that can be taken according to the choice for r and n. In practice, given the richness of this distribution, there is usually no difficulty in fitting a beta density function to a decision maker's assessed subjective probability distribution on the parameter p.

It is also clear from Figure 7.1 that the beta distribution becomes more informative and "tighter" as n increases, with the variance as given in the above formula becoming smaller accordingly. Thus, in a general sense n measures the information base inherent in a particular beta distribution, and for this reason is sometimes referred to as the *hypothetical prior sample*.

On many occasions, a bayesian style of analysis is desired insofar as it allows a probability distribution to be defined upon a population parameter p (in contradistinction to most nonbayesian methods which treat p as a fixed constant),

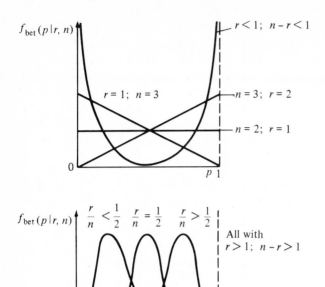

Figure 7.1 Shapes of some beta density functions

but without the incorporation of subjective belief. This requires the use of an "uninformative" prior distribution, which will subsequently be updated with empirical observations to form a purely data-based posterior distribution. Such an uninformative prior density function is usually taken as the straight-line form with $r = 1$ and $n = 2$. It clearly gives the same weight to all admissible values of p. Note, however, that if this is used as the uninformative prior distribution, then the sample content of any posterior distribution subsequently derived is strictly $n - 2$, and not n as in the previous paragraph.

An alternative uninformative beta prior distribution is sometimes taken to be the U-shaped form with $r = 0$ and $n = 0$. This retains the interpretation of n being the real or hypothetical sample content in any particular beta distribution, depending upon whether it was derived empirically or subjectively. It does, however, have the disadvantage that this U shape is often intuitively an unacceptable reflection of a decision maker's absence of opinion on the parameter p. Furthermore, the reader will recall that the beta distribution is not strictly defined for r and n equal to zero. Its use results in an *improper* distribution, where the area under the curve does not integrate out to 1. Thus, it is not a valid distribution to use in its own right, but it is nevertheless often used as a *notional* distribution for the initialization of the bayesian analysis of subsequent data. Hence, if a decision maker has to make a decision with no knowledge at all on p he or she will generally use the uniform prior distribution with $r = 1$ and $n = 2$. If, however, he or she wants to evaluate a posterior distribution on p which reflects no subjective opinion but just the sample data, he or she may well use the U-shaped prior form to facilitate this.

It is often useful in practice to note the relationship of the beta distribution to the binomial distribution. If r and n are integers, then the probability that p is less than a particular value p^* is the cumulative beta distribution with parameters r and n, that is,

$$\text{Prob}\,(p \leq p^*|r, n) = F_{\text{bet}}(p^*|r, n)$$

This probability is also equal to the cumulative binomial probability of obtaining more than $r - 1$ events out of $n - 1$, where the individual probability of each event is p^*, that is,

$$F_{\text{bet}}(p^*|r, n) = 1 - F_{\text{bin}}(r - 1|p^*, n - 1)$$

It also follows that for integers r and n, the beta density function can be expressed as

$$f_{\text{bet}}(p|r, n) = (n - 1)f_{\text{bin}}(r - 1|n - 2, p)$$

Thus, beta probabilities can be derived from binomial probability tables. Furthermore, when n gets larger (say, > 20), the normal approximation becomes increasingly useful.

Example Given a beta distribution for p with $r = 5$ and $n = 10$, what is the probability that p is less than 0.4?

Using the binomial equivalence relationship,

$$F_{\text{bet}}(0.4|5, 10) = 1 - F_{\text{bin}}(4|0.4, 9)$$

Hence, from Table 1 in the Appendix,

$$F_{\text{bet}}(0.4|5, 10) = 1 - 0.7334$$

$$= 0.2666$$

Suppose that the beta distribution for p is $r = 25$ and $n = 50$. What is the probability that p is again less than 0.4?

Since the binomial tables do not extend to $n = 50$, we must use the normal approximation:

$$\text{Mean} = \frac{r}{n} = 0.5$$

$$\text{Variance} = \frac{r(n - r)}{n^2(n + 1)} = 0.005$$

$$z = \frac{0.4 - 0.5}{0.07} = -1.42$$

From Table 3 in the Appendix, the probability that a standard normal deviate is less than -1.42 is given as 0.0778, which is thus the probability that p is less than 0.4.

Discussion in this section has so far been concerned with inferences upon the parameter p of a binomial data-generating process. Suppose, however, that a decision maker is interested in the number of failures r in the *next* sample of size n, where the data are again determined by a binomial process, parameter p. Thus, the decision maker requires what is known as the predictive distribution for a set of data. He or she is not directly interested in the parameter p, but in the actual data r. For a particular value of p, the *conditional* predictive distribution for r is the usual binomial function

$$f_{bin}(r\,|\,n, p) = \binom{n}{p} p^r (1 - p)^{n-r}$$

If, however, the decision maker does not know or wish to assume a value for p, but desires to incorporate his or her belief in terms of a beta prior distribution, parameters r' and n', then the *unconditional* predictive distribution for r is given by

$$f_{bb}(r\,|\,r', n', n) = \int_0^1 f_{bin}(r\,|\,n, p) f_{bet}(p\,|\,r', n')\,dp$$

where $f_{bb}(r\,|\,r', n', n)$ is the *beta binomial* distribution,

$$f_{bb}(r\,|\,r', n', n) = \frac{\Gamma(r + r')\Gamma(n + n' - r - r')\Gamma(n')\Gamma(n + 1)}{\Gamma(n' - r')\Gamma(n + n')\Gamma(r')\Gamma(r + 1)\Gamma(n - r + 1)}$$

for $r = 0, 1, 2, \ldots, n$. Then

$$\text{Mean} \qquad E(r) = \frac{nr'}{n'}$$

$$\text{Variance} \qquad V(r) = \frac{n(n + n')r'(n' - r')}{(n')^2(n' + 1)}$$

Example If the decision maker's prior distribution for the proportion of failures p is beta ($r' = 1$, $n' = 20$), what are the mean, the variance, and the probability of getting less than two failures in a binomial sample of size 5?

$$\text{Mean} \qquad E(r) = \frac{5(1)}{20} = 0.25$$

$$\text{Variance} \qquad V(r) = \frac{5(25)(1)(19)}{400(21)} = 0.283$$

$$\text{Probability} \qquad P(r \le 1) = f_{bb}(0\,|\,n, r', n') + f_{bb}(1\,|\,n, r', n')$$

$$= \frac{19}{24} + \frac{19(5)}{24(23)}$$

$$= 0.9638$$

Note that by means of this predictive distribution, the beta binomial distribution, we considered for the first time the uncertainty in predicting the next items of data, rather than encoding parameter uncertainty. If $f(y|m)$ is a general form for a predictive distribution conditional upon parameter m, and $f(m)$ is the prior probability distribution on m, then the general evaluation of the predictive distribution is given by

$$f(y) = \int_m f(y|m)f(m)\, dm$$

if m is continuous, or

$$f(y) = \sum_m f(y|m)f(m)$$

if m is discrete. We shall make further use of predictive distributions where the focus of attention in decision analysis is upon subsequent items of data rather than parameter.

Conjugate Prior Distribution for Normal Data

Datum x, which is generated according to the normal probability density function depends upon two parameters, μ and σ^2, the mean and the variance,

$$f_N(x|\mu, \sigma^2) = \frac{1}{\sqrt{2\pi\sigma^2}} \exp\left[-\frac{1}{2}\left(\frac{x-\mu}{\sigma}\right)^2\right]$$

In considering the appropriate natural conjugate prior distributions for these two parameters, three special cases should be identified: (1) μ unknown and σ^2 known; (2) μ known and σ^2 unknown; and (3) μ and σ^2 unknown.

Case 1: Conjugate prior distribution for μ; σ^2 known If σ^2 is known, the natural conjugate prior density function upon μ is the normal $f_N(\mu|m', \sigma^2/n')$, where m' and n' are the prior parameters representing the mean and the prior sample size, respectively. The prior sample size n' can represent a real sample or a hypothetical sample base equivalent to prior subjective opinion.

Thus, if a sample of size n is taken from a normal distribution with $f_N(\mu|m', \sigma^2/n')$ encoding the prior belief in the mean μ, and the sample mean $\bar{x}$ results, then the posterior distribution on the population mean μ is also normal (because the natural conjugate prior was used) with density function $f_N(\mu|m'', \sigma^2/n'')$. The posterior parameters m'' and n'' are given by

$$n'' = n' + n$$

$$m'' = \frac{n\bar{x} + n'm'}{n''}$$

As a numerical example, suppose that a machine fills containers with a constant standard deviation of 2 and a varying mean. The quality control inspector assesses a prior distribution for the mean setting of the process which is normal, mean 100, and standard deviation 1. Of 20 containers sampled, the mean is found to be 98.

Since $\sigma^2 = 4$ and the variance of the prior distribution on the mean was assessed as 1, we can infer that the hypothetical information base n' is given by $1 = 4/n'$, that is, $n' = 4$.

Note that this concept of a hypothetical sample being represented in a prior parameter is exactly analogous to the n' of the prior beta distribution in the conjugate analysis of binomial data, which we considered earlier.

In the above example, it now follows that the posterior distribution on the mean is also normal, $f_N(\mu|m'', \sigma^2/n'')$, with

$$n'' = n' + n = 4 + 20 = 24$$

$$m'' = \frac{4 \times 100 + 98 \times 20}{24} = 98\tfrac{1}{3}$$

Evidently, the posterior mean is just the linear combination of the prior and sample means, weighted by the sample base of each. It is also clear that were a further sample to be taken, the prior distribution on the mean would now be normal with parameters m'' and n'' as above. If a purely data-based posterior distribution is required, then the appropriate uninformative prior parameters are $m' = n' = 0$.

Note that such an uninformative prior distribution implies infinite variance for a normal distribution and is clearly improper. Like the improper U-shaped prior distribution for the binomial parameter p considered previously, it should not be used as a distribution in its own right, but can, arguably, be used as a notional distribution to derive data-based posterior distributions.

If we are interested in the predictive distribution for the mean $\bar{x}$ of a future sample of size n, then this distribution would also be normal with mean $= m''$ and with variance equal to the sum of the sampling variance of the mean, that is, σ^2/n, and the variance of the parameter μ, that is, σ^2/n''. Thus,

$$V(\bar{x}) = \frac{\sigma^2(n'' + n)}{n''n}$$

You will recall that this follows from one of the basic properties of variance, namely that the variance of a random variable about some point A can be decomposed as the sum of the variance of the random variable about another point B and the variance of B about A. In our terminology, A would be m'' and B would be μ.

Continuing with our above example, the predictive distribution for the mean of a further sample of size 20 would therefore be given as normal,

$$\text{Mean} = 98.33$$

$$\text{Variance} = \frac{4(44)}{20(24)}$$

$$= 0.37$$

Then, if we required the probability of this mean being less than 100, using standard normal tables,

$$z = (100 - 98.33)(0.37)^{-1/2} = 2.78$$

The probability of a standardized normal variate being less than 2.78 is 0.9973, and this is also the required probability of $\bar{x}$ being less than 100.

Case 2: Conjugate prior distribution for σ^2; μ known If a sample of size n is taken from a normal probability distribution with known mean, then the sample estimate s^2 of the unknown population σ^2 is given by

$$s^2 = \sum_{i=1}^{n} \frac{(x_i - \mu)^2}{n}$$

The natural conjugate prior density function for the unknown variance σ^2 of normal data with known μ is the inverse gamma, $f_{i\gamma}(\sigma^2 | \psi', v')$, with prior parameters ψ' and v', both of which should be positive:

$$f_{i\gamma}(\sigma^2 | \psi', v') = \frac{2 \exp(-v'\psi'/2\sigma^2)(v'\psi'/2\sigma^2)^{(1/2)v'+1}}{v'\psi'\Gamma(v'/2)}$$

The mean and the variance are given by

$$E(\sigma^2) = \frac{v'\psi'}{v' - 2}$$

$$V(\sigma^2) = \frac{2(v'\psi')^2}{(v' - 2)^2(v' - 4)}$$

Figure 7.2 shows the richness of this density function in representing prior belief on σ^2. An uninformative prior distribution would be one with $v' = \psi' = 0$. This again is an improper prior distribution and therefore subject to the same caveat as before.

After observing the sample statistic s^2 based upon n new observations, the posterior density function for σ^2 will also be inverse gamma, $f_{i\gamma}(\sigma^2 | \psi'', v'')$,

$$v'' = v' + n$$

$$\psi'' = \frac{v'\psi' + ns^2}{v''}$$

which again is clearly a linear combination of prior and sample estimates weighted by the information base of each.

The situation of having an unknown variance but known mean is quite rare in practice. Because of this, presentation of the predictive distribution for a future sample variance s^2 which involves a new distribution, namely, the inverse beta, will not be undertaken here. The interested reader is referred to Lavalle (1970).

Let us consider the example of an accurate balance producing readings which are distributed normally about the true weight of an object with unknown variance

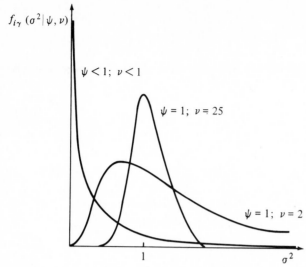

Figure 7.2 Shapes of some inverse gamma density functions

σ^2. Ten independent readings of a 10-kg weight gave the statistic $s^2 = 0.2$. The prior density function for σ^2 was assessed as $f_{i\gamma}(\sigma^2 | \psi', v')$ with prior parameters $\psi' = 0.1$ and $v' = 5$. With this new information, the posterior density function should be $f_{i\gamma}(\sigma^2 | \psi'', v'')$, with posterior parameters

$$v'' = v' + n = 15$$

$$\psi'' = \frac{v'\psi' + ns^2}{v''} = \frac{5 \times 0.1 + 10 \times 0.2}{15} = 0.17$$

Case 3: Joint conjugate prior distribution for μ, σ^2 If we are sampling normal data for which neither the mean nor the variance is known, then with a sample size n, the statistics $\bar{x}$ and s^2 can be computed as estimates of μ and σ^2, respectively:

$$\bar{x} = \sum_{i=1}^{n} \frac{x_i}{n}$$

$$s^2 = \sum_{i=1}^{n} \frac{(x_i - \bar{x})^2}{n - 1} \qquad \text{(defined as 0 if } n = 1)$$

The natural conjugate prior density function assessed jointly on μ and σ^2 is commonly known as the normal-inverse gamma, $f_{Ni\gamma}(\mu, \sigma^2 | m', n', \psi', v')$. A great simplification of this bivariate distribution, due to the independence of μ and σ^2 in the normal case, is that it can be decomposed as the product

$$f_{Ni\gamma}(\mu, \sigma^2 | m', n', \psi', v') = f_N(\mu | m', \sigma^2/n') f_{i\gamma}(\sigma^2 | \psi', v')$$

for ψ', n', and v' all positive.

Observing the new sample information of size n, the posterior density function on μ and σ^2 is also normal-inverse gamma, $f_{Ni\gamma}(\mu, \sigma^2 | m'', n'', \psi'', v'')$, with the posterior parameters

$$n'' = n' + n$$
$$v'' = v' + n - \delta(n')$$

$$m'' = \frac{n'm' + n\bar{x}}{n''}$$

$$\psi'' = \frac{v'\psi' + (n - 1)s^2 + (\bar{x} - m'')^2 n''/nn'}{v''}$$

where
$$\delta(n') = \begin{cases} 1 & \text{if } n' = 0 \\ 0 & \text{if } n' > 0 \end{cases}$$

This distribution is not nearly as complicated to work with as might at first seem to be the case. The revision of the prior mean m' to the posterior mean m'' is the same as before when the variance was known, since it is just the weighted average of prior and sample means. The parameter ψ'' is a point estimate of the unknown variance, as before. The denominator v'' in its formula represents the number of independent observations involved in its estimation, the *degrees of freedom* as it is often called. If there is no prior knowledge on the mean ($n' = 0$), then a degree of freedom will be used up in estimating the mean from which the variance estimate is to be computed, hence, the $\delta(n')$ term. The numerator computes recursively the sum of squared deviations of the observations about the posterior mean m''. It does this via three terms. The first, $v'\psi'$, is the sum of squared deviations of the prior observation base about the prior mean m'. The second, $(n - 1)s^2$, is the sum of squared deviations of the new sample about the sample mean $\bar{x}$. The third term, $(\bar{x} - m'')^2 n''/nn'$, corrects both previous terms to be deviations about the posterior mean m'', as required. This "correction" requires some mathematical manipulation to be obvious, but the basic point of what this formula is doing should be intuitive. Compare it with the revision formula for ψ'' when μ is known. The parameters n'' and v'' are the observation bases (real or hypothetical) for the mean and the variance, respectively.

The marginal density function on σ^2 is $f_{i\gamma}(\sigma^2 | \psi'', v'')$, and on μ the marginal density function is Student's t, $f_s(\mu | m'', \psi''/n'', v'')$, also with v'' degrees of freedom.

Readers will recall that Student's t distribution is the sampling distribution for the mean of a normal data process when the variance is unknown. It takes into account the extra uncertainty that is introduced through having to use an estimated variance. As a consequence, it is relatively "fatter" that the normal distribution of the same mean and variance, depending upon the number of observations used to estimate the variance (that is, the degrees of freedom). Thus when we replace the unknown σ^2 in the formula $f_N(\mu | m'', \sigma^2/n'')$ by its estimate ψ'', the distribution becomes $f_s(\mu | m'', \psi''/n'', v'')$. Table 5 in the Appendix tabulates some of the fractiles of the standardized Student's t distribution for various degrees of freedom. Note that the Student's t distribution standardizes with zero mean and unit variance in exactly the same way as the normal distribution standardizes to z values. Thus, if we require $P(\mu \leq w)$, we convert w to a standardized value,

$$t_w = (w - m'') \left(\frac{\psi''}{n''}\right)^{-1/2}$$

which would be analogous to z_w if σ^2 were known. We then look up $F_{ss}(t_w | v'')$, the cumulative standardized Student's probability that $t \leq t_w$ with v'' degrees of freedom.

Thus, if the normal-inverse gamma prior distribution is being assessed separately by considering the inverse gamma distribution for the variance and the Student's t distribution for the mean, then care must be taken to ensure that they both have the same number of degrees of freedom v'. This implies that first the variance should be assessed in order to fix v' and then the Student's distribution should be assessed according to this v'.

For example, suppose a decision maker articulates his or her state of uncertainty on the mean of a normal data-generating process. If the degrees of freedom were fixed at 10 from the assessment of the variance of the process and the decision maker reported that 50 was the most likely estimate for the mean, all that is then required is a fractile estimate. Let us suppose that the decision maker reported a 90 percent chance that the mean would be less than 60.

From Table 5 in the Appendix, the value of the standardized Student's t distribution for this fractile with 10 degrees of freedom is 1.372. Since

$$t = (60 - 50) \, v^{-1/2}$$

the variance v of the distribution is now given as

$$v = \left(\frac{10}{1.372}\right)^2 = 53.12$$

In assessing the Student's distribution for the mean of a normal data process, it is often difficult in practice to encourage the decision maker to focus attention upon the mean rather than the actual variable. For example, a production control manager may well feel more comfortable (and therefore give more reliable estimates) in assessing directly a distribution for tomorrow's output x, rather than a distribution for the mean of x and a distribution for the variance of x. If it is required to assess, for decision analysis purposes, the normal-inverse gamma probability density function for the parameters of x, assumed normally distributed, it is a great simplification if n' and v' can be assumed to follow

$$v' = n' - 1$$

in the joint probability density function $f_{Ni\gamma}(\mu, \sigma^2 | \psi', v', m', n')$. This is not unreasonable in view of the fact that they both represent the hypothetical prior sample base and would therefore follow the above equivalence in a purely data-based prior normal-inverse gamma distribution. Given this assumption, the prior distribution for μ and σ^2 can be derived from the decision maker's predictive distribution for x.

Let us suppose that our production manager's predictive distribution for x was such that 50 was the most likely, 55 was the 60 percent fractile, and 76 was the 90 percent fractile. In fitting a Student's t distribution with an unknown number of degrees of freedom to this distribution, we note that

$$t_{0.6} = (55 - 50)v^{-1/2}$$

and where v is the variance of the predictive distribution,

$$t_{0.9} = (76 - 50)v^{-1/2}$$

Thus, the ratio

$$\frac{t_{0.9}}{t_{0.6}} = \frac{26}{5} = 5.2$$

Searching through the fractiles in Table 5 in the Appendix, we find that this ratio is achieved for approximately 15 degrees of freedom. Thus, we assume that $v' = 15$ and $n' = 16$. Now we can evaluate v, as before,

$$v = \left(\frac{26}{1.341}\right)^2 = 376$$

The predictive distribution for the mean of a future sample of size n is also Student's t, with

$$\text{Degrees of freedom} = v'$$

$$\text{Mean} = m'$$

$$\text{Variance } v = \frac{\psi'(n' + n)}{nn'}$$

Thus, in our example we have, for $n = 1$,

$$\text{Mean} \qquad m' = 50$$

$$\text{Degrees of freedom} \qquad v' = 15$$

$$\text{Variance} \qquad v = \frac{\psi'(n' + 1)}{n'} = 376$$

Since $n' = 16$,

$$\psi' = \frac{376(16)}{17} = 354$$

Hence, the complete normal-inverse gamma distribution for the parameters of a normal process has been assessed by means of encoding only the predictive distribution for the next observation in the form of a Student's distribution.

The uninformative improper prior distribution would again have $v' = n' = 0$. As emphasized previously, this prior distribution should be used for notional convenience only. In more advanced applications of bayesian inference than have been considered here, its use as a distribution in its own right can give rise to incoherence.

Example It is well known that the scores on an IQ test are normally distributed about some mean μ and with a variance of σ^2. A decision maker has expressed prior opinion on σ^2 in terms of the parameters ψ' and v' being 100 and 4, respectively, and on μ in terms of m' and n' being 110 and 8, respectively. Thus, effectively the conjugate prior distribution $f_{Ni\gamma}(\mu, \sigma^2 | m', n', \psi', v')$ has been assessed. Let us suppose that a sample of 10 individuals has been taken randomly from the group under consideration with $\bar{x} = 115$ and $s^2 = 90$. Thus, the posterior joint distribution of μ and σ^2 is $f_{Ni\gamma}(\mu, \sigma^2 | m'', n'', \psi'', v'')$ with

$$n'' = n + n' = 18$$

$$v'' = n + v' = 10 + 4 = 14$$

$$m'' = \frac{n'm' + n\bar{x}}{n''} = \frac{8 \times 110 + 10 \times 115}{18} = 112.78$$

$$\psi'' = \frac{v'\psi' + (n-1)s^2 + (\bar{x} - m')^2 n''/nn'}{v''}$$

$$= \frac{4 \times 100 + 9 \times 90 + (115 - 110)^2 18/80}{14}$$

$$= 86.8$$

Thus, the posterior expected value of the mean and the variance of the IQ of this group is 112.78 and

$$86.8 \frac{v''}{v'' - 2} = 101.3$$

The marginal posterior distribution of the mean is, of course, Student with an estimated mean of 112.78 and 14 degrees of freedom. The standard deviation of this mean is $(\psi''/n'')^{1/2}$, that is, 2.2.

The predictive distribution for the mean of a future sample of size 10 is also Student with mean 112.78 and 14 degrees of freedom, but the standard deviation is $[\psi'(n'' + n)/nn'']^{1/2}$, that is, 2.95.

Thus, if we require the predictive probability that the mean of the next 10 observations be less than 115, we first set the value of t, the standardized Student's value, analogous to the standardized normal value z. Thus,

$$t = \frac{115 - 112.78}{2.95} = 0.75$$

From Table 5 in the Appendix the probability that this value will not be exceeded has to be interpolated between 0.70 and 0.80 because of the abbreviated nature of the table. If our estimate is 0.77, then this is also the probability of $\bar{x}$, being less than 115 in the future sample of 10.

Note that the predictive distribution for the mean of a sample of size 1 is clearly just the predictive distribution for the next observation. The predictive distribution for the next observation is thus Student with mean m'', v'' degrees of freedom, and variance $\psi''(n'' + 1)/n''$.

The bayesian analysis of normal data is therefore quite intricate and very different from the nonbayesian sampling theory methods with which the reader may already be familiar. It may seem much more complicated, but then it does many more things for the decision maker in a style that nonbayesian reasoning cannot match.

7.7 SUMMARY COMMENTS

The special qualities of bayesian inference are not due to Bayes' theorem per se, which is a simple logical result common to all schools of probability, but lie in its two main features of interpretation: (1) the revision of subjective probabilities with new information and (2) the treatment of parameter uncertainty by means of a probability distribution.

The typical bayesian inferential model is therefore that of an individual expressing a subjective prior distribution upon some hypothesis (e.g., "success" of a new product) or parameter (e.g., mean of normal data), revising this according to the likelihood of observed data conditional upon the hypothesis, or a parameter value, to give a posterior distribution. It thus provides the facility to encode uncertainty upon such hypotheses or parameters, recognizing that from the perspective of the decision maker these are important uncertain outcomes which are going to affect his or her payoff. This facility is in contradistinction to most nonbayesian methods of inference which treat such hypotheses or parameters as having fixed but unknown values, and thereby precluding the treatment of them in terms of random variables. Nonbayesian methods would therefore not allow the representation of these uncertainties as probabilities, nor the use of the expected utility criterion to derive their certainty equivalents. It is for this reason, therefore, that bayesian inference has become so closely related to decision analysis as to become one of its characteristic features. The other important aspect is, of course, that through the bayesian revision process of incorporating new information to upgrade a prior probability distribution into a posterior probability distribution which incorporates all available information, and particularly subjective belief, the bayesian style of inference is directed to fulfilling the principle of coherence in decision making, which is so fundamental to rational decision analysis.

For further reading on the topic of bayesian inference, the texts by Lavalle (1970), Winkler (1972), and Zellner (1971) are suggested. In pursuing this topic, the reader will find a rapidly expanding and already enormous literature on bayesian statistics, which may often appear a long way from the pragmatic issues of applied decision analysis.

EXERCISES

7.1 Assess a subjective probability distribution to represent your belief on tomorrow's maximum temperature.

7.2 How would you question a brand manager in order to derive his or her subjective belief on a product's market share in terms of a beta distribution?

7.3 *Constructing a Probability Table.* The social composition of the television audience for the three channels XTV, YTV, and ZTV was sampled one evening and categorized as *A, B, C,* or *D.* Overall, the proportions of the sample in social groups *A, B, C,* and *D* were found to be 0.2, 0.2, 0.3, and 0.3, respectively. It was also found that individuals in social group *B* were equally likely to be watching channels YTV and ZTV, but twice as likely to be watching XTV as YTV. The audience for channel YTV was found to be independent of social grouping, and the audience for channel ZTV was found to consist only of individuals in social groups *A* and *B* with equal probabilities. Construct the table of joint and marginal probabilities for the television audience categorized according to channel viewing and social grouping.

7.4 *Interpreting a Probability Table.* A particular geographical region can receive three television channels XTV, YTV, and ZTV. A sample of 1000 households was taken in the region one evening to investigate peak-time channel switching. Each channel featured hour-length programs starting at 8:00 P.M. and 9:00 P.M. The households were asked which channels they were predominantly watching between 8–9 P.M. and 9–10 P.M. The totals are summarized in the following table:

| | | Households watching 9–10 | | | |
		XTV	YTV	ZTV	No TV
	XTV	40	45	60	35
Households	YTV	60	50	165	25
watching 8–9	ZTV	140	90	160	10
	No TV	10	15	15	80

(*a*) What is the probability distribution for television channel viewing from 8 to 9 P.M?

(*b*) What is the probability distribution for the origin of the viewers for ZTV from 9 to 10 P.M. in terms of what they were doing during the previous hour?

(*c*) Which channel has the least chance of retaining its audience of 8 to 9 P.M. for the next hour?

(*d*) Are the events, watching ZTV from 8 to 9 P.M. and ZTV from 9 to 10 P.M. independent? Justify your answer.

7.5 *Bertrand's Box.* Each of three boxes has two drawers. In box 1 each drawer contains one gold coin, and each drawer of box 2 contains one silver coin, while in box 3 one drawer contains a gold coin, the other a silver coin. A box is chosen at random; one drawer is opened and is found to contain a gold coin. What is the probability that the coin in the other drawer of that box is also gold? One possible answer is the following: The box we picked must be either 1 or 3. If it is 1, the unopened drawer contains a gold coin; if it is 3, a silver coin. Since it was just as likely that we would pick box 1 as that we would pick box 3, the probability of finding a gold coin in the unopened drawer must be 50 percent. Do you agree with this answer?

7.6 Suppose it is believed that the market share which a new product will obtain is 0.2, 0.25, or 0.3, with prior subjective probabilities of 0.4, 0.3, and 0.3, respectively. A sample of 20 potential customers is taken, and six of them buy the new product. What are the posterior probabilities for the market share?

7.7 A doctor believes the probability of a randomly selected individual catching a disease, if exposed to it, is 0.1, 0.15, 0.2, or 0.25, with a prior subjective probability distribution of 0.2, 0.4, 0.3, and 0.1. An experiment exposes 12 individuals to the disease, and two people catch it. What should the posterior probability distribution be?

7.8 In a binomial sampling experiment, the decision maker has two hypotheses for the proportion of defectives, namely, $H_1 : p = 0.3$, $H_2 : p = 0.4$. The prior probabilities are $P(H_1) = P(H_2) = 0.5$. A random sample of size 10 will be taken. What is the decision maker's probability of finding exactly five defectives?

Later, having found five such defectives in the sample of 10, the decision maker is considering repeating the experiment with a further 10 random investigations. What is now the probability of finding five defectives? Is your answer consistent with the assumption that the two samples are random and independent?

7.9 *Cyclo Dividend.* Whether the Cyclo Corporation raises its dividend, keeps it unchanged, or lowers it at the end of this year depends upon whether or not the economy is generally considered to be in a recession. The current probability of a recession is estimated by a particular shareholder at 0.7. If there is a recession, there is no chance of a higher dividend and a 0.4 chance of the dividend being reduced. Alternatively, if there is no recession, the dividend will either be increased or stay the same with equal probabilities.

A popular columnist in the financial press, G. Ru, is about to profess his latest foresight. Our shareholder believes that if there really is going to be a recession, Ru has an 80 percent probability of saying so correctly. Similarly, Ru has a 70 percent probability of forecasting no recession if there really is to be no recession. Furthermore, our shareholder believes that Ru's forecast will have no effect upon Cyclo's dividend policy in the sense that, conditional upon there being a recession, Ru's forecast and Cyclo's policy are independent. Likewise, if there is no recession, this "conditional independence" of Ru and Cyclo again holds.

If Ru does say that there will be a recession, how should our shareholder assess his probability distribution on Cyclo's dividend policy?

7.10 If two events are mutually exclusive, are they also independent?

7.11 *Reliable Source.* The satiric magazine *Reliable Source* publishes embarrassing stories concerning the private lives of eminent politicians. A rumor concerning the activities of Senator N. O. Scruples has reached the editorial office. If they publish the story, they will make an extra $200,000 through increased sales, but they could be sued for damages. The probability of being sued depends on whether the rumor is true. The editor currently assesses the rumor to have a probability of 0.7 of being true. If it is true, the senator will sue with probability 0.3, if not he will sue with probability 0.9. The chances of *Reliable Source* losing the case in court are assessed as 0.3 if the rumor is true and at 0.8 if it is false. If they do lose, it may ultimately cost them $0.5 million.

The editor has a couple of days before the weekly deadline to decide whether to go ahead with the story. He considers it worth hiring a private investigator, C. Shave, for two days' work on the rumor. The editor knows that Shave revels in a scandal and that, therefore, his opinion will be less than perfectly diagnostic. In fact, the editor assesses that Shave will say the rumor is true with probability 1 if it is really true and with probability 0.4 if it is false.

A couple of days later, just prior to the deadline editorial meeting, Shave arrives and asserts that the rumor is true. Also in the meantime, one of the respectable daily newspapers had reported part of the rumor. The editor's opinion is that if the rumor is true, that daily would certainly print the report, but it is only likely to do so with probability 0.4 if the rumor is false. The editor also believes that conditional upon the truth or falsity of the rumor, Shave's opinion and the newspaper report constitute independent evidence.

Should the editor go ahead with the story? The appropriate utility function is shown in Figure 7.3.

7.12 A market research manager believes that a new product will receive a market value of either 30 percent or 10 percent with equal chances. The manager therefore commisions a small test with 25 potential customers, randomly selected. Six of these said they would buy the product. Use the normal approximation to compute the posterior probability distribution on market share. What role does conditional independence play in the analysis? [Recall that the mean of a binomial distribution is np and the variance $np(1 - p)$.]

7.13 A new product could either be a success (S) or a disaster (D), to which the brand manager attaches the prior subjective probabilities $P(S) = 0.3$ and $P(D) = 0.7$. If the product is marketed

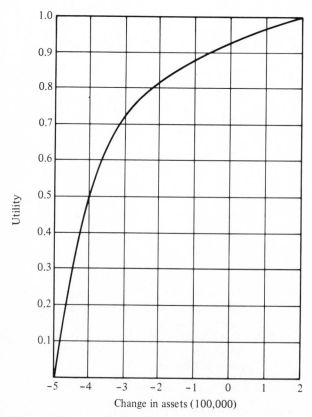

Figure 7.3 Editor's utility function

and results in a success, the company gains 500 compared with a loss of 300 if it results in a failure. The company is considering two independent separate surveys offered by the same agency. The cost of survey I is 20, that of survey II is 30, and the cost of both (which must be decided in advance) is 40. It is also possible to order survey I and thereafter decide to use survey II, but not vice versa. The surveys result in either a favorable (F) or an unfavorable (U) indication with the following reliabilities.

$$\text{For I} \quad P(F|S) = 0.6 \quad P(F|D) = 0.1$$
$$\text{For II} \quad P(F|S) = 0.8 \quad P(F|D) = 0.1$$

What course of action should the manager take?

7.14 A decision maker knows that the variance of a normal process is 80, but is unsure of whether the mean is 100 or 120. Equal prior probabilities are assigned to these two means. A sample of 5 yields data 103, 101, 111, 121, and 116. What are the posterior probabilities for the mean?

7.15 A quality control manager assesses a beta prior distribution with parameters $r' = 3$ and $n' = 20$ for the rate of defectives produced in a manufacturing process. The manager observes two defectives in a sample of 10. What should the posterior distribution be defined as?

7.16 Assume you know nothing about the probability of a complex piece of equipment failing. You then examine one and find it is a failure. What is your probability of the next one also being a failure?

7.17 (a) Given a beta distribution p with parameters $r = 6$ and $n = 14$, what is the probability that p is less than 0.5?

(b) Given a beta distribution on p with parameters $r = 60$ and $n = 80$, what is the probability that p is less than 0.7?

7.18 A production manager is interested in the mean setting for a filling machine. The machine fills cans with a weight of material which is normally distributed with a variance of 4 and a mean that drifts. The manager assesses a prior distribution for the mean, which is normal, as 50 with a variance of 0.4. The manager then samples five items and finds the mean weight of the contents to be 53. What is now the posterior distribution on the mean setting?

7.19 Given the normal-inverse gamma prior distribution for a normally distributed data process x with parameters $\psi' = 100$, $v' = 10$, $m' = 50$, and $n' = 12$, estimate the probability that the mean of the next 10 observations will be less than 45.

7.20 A decision maker knows that a series of data is generated according to a normal process with variance 4, but has no knowledge at all on the mean. The decision maker takes a sample of size 1, measuring the datum at 33. What is the posterior distribution for the mean of this process and what is her distribution for the next item of data?

7.21 A decision maker knows that a series of data is generated according to a normal process with mean 1, but knows nothing at all about the variance. The decision maker takes a sample of size 1 and measures the outcome at 5. What is the posterior distribution for the variance?

7.22 Show that the predictive distribution for the mean of a sample of size n approaches the prior distribution for the mean as n becomes large, where the data are generated according to a normal process.

7.23 A decision maker assumes some data to be generated by a normal process with unknown mean and variance. The decision maker observes a sample of 1, whose value is 7. What are now the posterior distributions of the mean and the variance, their expected values, and the predictive distribution of the next observation? The next observation is 8. What are now the posterior distributions of the mean and the variance, their expected values, and the predictive distribution for the next observation? The third observation is 7. Compute the same posterior measures again. Also compute these measures assuming that the three values 7, 8, and 7 were not taken sequentially as above, but as an initial sample of size 3.

7.24 It is sometimes argued that a discussion of uninformative prior distributions for the normal process is irrelevant. If the decision maker knows enough about the data to assert their normality and possibly also the exact value of one of their parameters, then he or she will not be totally uninformed with respect to the unknown parameter(s). What is your view on this?

7.25 The number of customers entering a store on Saturday is normally distributed with unknown mean and variance. The store manager feels that the uncertainty on the variance can be represented by the inverse gamma distribution with parameters $\psi' = 4$ and $v' = 20$. Likewise, the uncertainty on the mean could be represented by the Student's t distribution fixing the degrees of freedom v' at 20 with a mean of 10 and variance 1. Over the next 10 Saturdays, the following customer counts were taken: 8, 9, 12, 13, 10, 11, 8, 15, 14, and 10. How should the belief on the Saturday customers now be represented?

7.26 Consider a normal distribution for which the value of the mean μ is unknown and the variance is 4, and suppose that the prior distribution for μ is normal with a variance of 9. How large a random sample from the given distribution must be taken in order to be able to specify an interval of width 1 unit such that the probability of μ being in this interval is at least 0.95.

7.27 A quality control manager believes defectives to be generated according to a binomial process with an expected value of the rate p being 0.2. You ask the manager to consider that if the next 10 inspections reveal five defectives, what the expectation for p would become. Let us suppose the assessment is revised upward to 0.3. What are the manager's prior parameters for the conjugate beta distribution representing prior belief on the defective rate?

7.28 Explain how you would assess the parameters of the appropriate natural conjugate prior probability density function for a normal data process with unknown mean and variance.

7.29 If the mean and the variance of a beta distribution are 0.6 and 0.1, respectively, what are the prior parameters?

7.30 If the mean and the mode of a beta distribution are 0.35 and 0.2, respectively, estimate the prior parameters.

7.31 In a tertile assessment procedure for a normal prior distribution, the points 70 and 100 were given. Estimate the prior parameters.

7.32 You are trying to assess the prior distribution for the mean of a normal process with known variance. The 25 percent and 75 percent fractiles have been assessed as 160 and 180, respectively. What are the prior parameters?

7.33 In assessing the prior distribution for the parameters of a normal process, the decision maker assessed the predictive distribution. The most likely value was assessed to be 150, with the 60 percent and 95 percent fractiles being 160 and 220, respectively. What do you estimate the parameters of the normal-inverse gamma prior distribution to be? Justify any assumptions that you make.

7.34 In assessing the inverse gamma prior distribution for the variance of normal data with a known mean of 100, the predictive distribution for the next observation was elicited. This was found to have 60 percent and 90 percent fractiles of 110 and 155, respectively. What are the prior parameters?

7.35 The use of the next observation predictive distribution for the estimation of the normal-inverse gamma prior parameters requires extremely precise assessment of the Student's distribution. Construct examples to demonstrate the sensitivity of the imputed degrees of freedom and other parameters to estimation errors in the elicitation of the Student's predictive

probability distribution function for a variable x prior to the variable's realization, then when the outcome of the variable becomes known, define ζ as

$$\zeta = F_x(x)$$

that is, that fractile of the distribution function which was actually realized. Thus, in a repetitive forecasting context, a whole sequence of ζ values would be obtained. Clearly, ζ is a random variable taking values between 0 and 1. If the estimator were perfectly calibrated, then for a particular value ζ^* the probability would be

$$P(\zeta \leq \zeta^*) = \zeta^*$$

This implies that ζ should have the uniform probability density function in the ideal situation of perfect calibration. Thus, the cumulative form $F_\zeta(\zeta)$ will in this case describe the straight line $F_\zeta(\zeta) = \zeta$.

Now in the realistic situation of imperfect calibration, suppose a set of n values of ζ are available from the track record of the estimator, and they are arranged in the order $\zeta_1, \zeta_2, \ldots, \zeta_n$ of increasing value. We can then estimate $F_\zeta(\zeta)$ from these data. Thus, since $(\zeta_1, \zeta_2, \ldots, \zeta_n)$ is a random sample, we can form the estimated cumulative distribution in the usual way as

$$F_\zeta(\zeta_j) = \frac{j}{n} \qquad \text{for } j = 1, 2, \ldots, n$$

Hence, for a perfectly calibrated estimator $F_\zeta(\zeta)$ should approach the straight line as the sample base n increases. Alternatively, as an example of systematic bias, anchoring is a common form in subjective probability distributions, causing the assessed distribution to be too "tight" about its median. In this case we would expect a large number of high and low values of ζ to occur, giving rise to a calibration function, as illustrated Figure 8.4. Furthermore, an estimator who tends to overestimate the tail probabilities would show the type of calibration function shown in Figure 8.5.

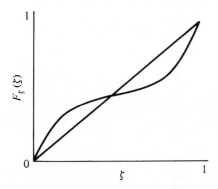

Figure 8.4 Anchoring bias in a calibration function

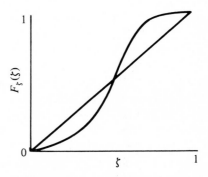

Figure 8.5 Overestimation of tail probabilities in a calibration function

If a mathematical equation can be fitted to the calibration function, then debiasing of the estimator can be easily undertaken as

$$F'_x(x) = F_\zeta(F_x(x))$$

where $F'_x(x)$ is the corrected form of $F_x(x)$. If a convenient form of the curve $F_\zeta(\zeta)$ cannot be estimated, then the above procedure must be done numerically.

Example On 10 recent occasions, a technical expert assessed normal probability distributions on the performance index x_i of a series of research experiments. The results are shown in the table below:

Experiment i	1	2	3	4	5	6	7	8	9	10
Mean μ_i	20	21	24	22	20	21	23	22	20	21
Variance σ_i^2	4	1	1	4	1	1	1	4	1	4
Actual value x_i	23	24	23	19.5	20	23	21	18.7	21	29
ζ_i	0.93	0.99	0.16	0.1	0.5	0.97	0.03	0.05	0.84	0.99+

The first two rows represent the prior subjective assessments of the normal predictive distribution $f_N(x_i|\mu_i, \sigma_i^2)$. The actual value x_i, which was realized, is given in the third row. The value of ζ_i in the fourth row is computed from the cumulative form of the predictive distribution,

$$\zeta_i = F_N(x_i|\mu_i, \sigma_i^2)$$

using standard cumulative normal tables.

The set of 10 ζ values is now arranged in ascending order to give (0.03, 0.05, 0.1, 0.16, 0.5, 0.84, 0.93, 0.97, 0.99, 0.99+), which is reindexed through j. The calibration function $F_\zeta(\zeta)$ is now estimated for each of these points. Thus, for $j = 1$, $\zeta = 0.03$ and $F_\zeta(0.03) = 0.1$, and so on. Hence the calibration function shown in Figure 8.6 is constructed from these nine points.

Now suppose that this estimator assessed the distribution shown in Figure 8.7 for an eleventh experiment. Then, using the calibration function $F_\zeta(\zeta)$, a corrected, debiased distribution can be reevaluated as shown in the same figure. This has been done by correcting the 10, 25, 50, 75, and 90 percent fractiles of the assessed distribution $F_N(x_{11}|\mu_{11}, \sigma_{11}^2)$, namely, $\zeta_{0.1}, \zeta_{0.25}, \zeta_{0.5}, \zeta_{0.75}$, and $\zeta_{0.9}$, by means of the estimated calibration function $F_\zeta(\zeta_j)$. This procedure can be seen to be intuitively reasonable. The calibration function of Figure 8.6 shows that when the estimator has given a value of an uncertain quantity x for which he or she estimates a 10 percent probability that it will not be exceeded, that is, $F_x(x) = \zeta = 0.1$, it was in fact not exceeded 30 percent of the time, that is, $F_\zeta(0.1) = 0.3$. Thus, in debiasing the estimator, the next time he or she gives $F_x(x) = 0.1$, it should be corrected to $F'_x(x) = 0.3$. It can clearly be seen that this has been done in Figure 8.7 for the entire distribution $F_x(x)$.

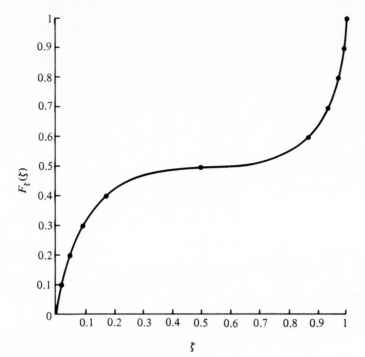

Figure 8.6 Experimenter's calibration function

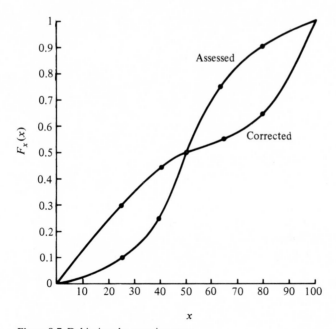

Figure 8.7 Debiasing the experimenter

The issue of systematic bias and the need for explicit calibration are not confined to the repetitive forecasting situation. In a single estimation task, which for greater precision has been decomposed into a sequence of several components, each requiring separate probability estimates, the need to model systematic assessment bias is not conspicuously evident and can often be missed. In particular, systematic bias can often render the usual independence assumptions invalid (see Harrison, 1977).

Example Suppose that a project consists of 10 independent tasks indexed through i, each with its completion time t_i assessed by the distribution $f_i(t_i)$. The final eleventh task can be completed by the usual process with an assessed distribution $f_{11}(t_{11})$, or a faster more expensive process with an assessed distribution $f^*_{11}(t_{11})$. With an overall deadline to meet, an optimal decision rule can be identified for selection of the eleventh task, given the various costs involved. In evaluating the overall expected value of the project, it may be assumed that all eleven tasks are completely independent in the sense that the time to complete any one of them does not influence the completion time of any other. Thus, if the $f_i(t_i)$ were logically correct probability distributions, then

$$f_{11}(t_{11}|t_1, t_2, \ldots, t_{10}) = f_{11}(t_{11})$$

and so on. However, because the probabilities are subjectively assessed and subject to systematic bias, the above equation will not generally hold.

Thus, in evaluating the above project, the calibrated form

$$F'_{11}(t_{11}) = F_\zeta(F_{11}(t_{11})|t_1, \ldots, t_{10})$$

should be used where the calibration function $F_\zeta(\zeta|t_1, \ldots, t_{10})$ is clearly conditional on all the previous 10 values obtained for t_i. This may be constructed as in the previous example. A more complicated issue concerns how much data is required to construct a reliable calibration function. Clearly one would not wish to change subsequent assessments on the basis of a calibration function drawn through only three or four points.

Nevertheless, it is important to keep in mind the implications of systematic bias and the need for calibration whenever decompositions of subjective probability distributions are being utilized. Even though distributions on totally different and clearly independent variables may be involved, they will not generally be independent if assessed subjectively because of systematic bias. Such dependencies are introduced as a feature of the assessment process rather than of the variables under consideration. It may well be better practice, therefore, to include always a calibration function alongside assessments in a multiple-stage decision analysis. In most cases, with little or no previous information having been realized, these calibration functions will just take on the form of a degenerate one-to-one transformation. However, in some cases this practice will result in identifying a need for an informative calibration of subsequent assessment which may otherwise have escaped notice.

It is important to remain aware that good calibration by itself is not a sufficient condition for making a valuable estimator. A weather forecaster who knows that the long-term average rate of rainfall for a certain region is 183 days per year could be very well calibrated in the long run by making the forecast a 50 percent chance of rain every day. Thus, a well-calibrated estimator is far more valuable when giving estimates near 0.9, etc., rather than around 0.5. Therefore, a more thorough form of estimator evaluation may sometimes be required, especially if a reward system is to be based upon it. We will now consider some mathematical evaluation schemes called *scoring rules*, which seek to provide indices of good assessments.

8.3 EVALUATION THROUGH SCORING RULES

At first it might seem that a convenient way of evaluation would be to have a penalty function reflecting how far an assessor differs from the estimates that a perfect predictor would make. Thus, if a weather forecaster assessed a 0.7 probability to the occurrence of rain on the next day, and it did in fact rain, then he or she would be penalized with a value of 0.3, since a perfect predictor would have assessed a probability of 1. If it had not rained, then he or she would have been penalized by 0.7, since the perfect predictor would have assessed a zero probability.

Such a system of scoring is known as a linear scoring rule. It is also known as an improper scoring rule because an assessor can continue to obtain a higher score by giving probability estimates which do not reflect his or her "true" state of opinion. In the above example, the weather forecaster's expected penalty $S(0.7)$ is given simply as

$$S(0.7) = 0.3 \times 0.7 + 0.7 \times 0.3 = 0.42$$

Suppose, however, that the weather forecaster had reported a probability of 1 for rain on the next day, even though he or she really believed it still to be 0.7. If it rained he or she, would receive a penalty of 0 compared with a penalty of 1 if it did not rain. Thus the expected penalty $E[S(1)]$ is given as

$$E[S(1)] = 0 \times 0.7 + 1 \times 0.3 = 0.3$$

which is clearly less than the 0.42 for being truthful. Thus, penalizing an individual by this absolute deviation from the ideal encourages untruthful responses. Whenever an individual believes the chances to be greater than one-half, it would pay to pretend certainty.

In order to formalize this situation, let us suppose than an estimator's true state of knowledge on an uncertain event is represented by the probability p, but when asked to reveal this probability, he or she responds with a value r. The scoring rule $S(r)$ gives the payoff

$S_1(r)$ if the event occurs

$S_2(r)$ if the event does not occur

Thus, the individual's expected payoff is

$$E[S(r)] = S_1(r)p + S_2(r)(1 - p)$$

A scoring rule is said to be strictly proper if

$$E[S(p)] > E[S(r)] \qquad \text{for all } r \neq p$$

and thus the estimator maximizes his or her score by giving the most truthful opinion. (Note the conventional change from minimizing expected penalty to maximizing expected score.)

It is a simple extension to go from the dichotomous event situation as above to the general discrete distribution. Let us suppose that the outcome space is partitioned into n events, with the estimator's true probability mass function being $p_1, p_2, \ldots, p_n$. The scoring rule $S(r_1, r_2, \ldots, r_n)$ gives the payoff $S_j(r_1, r_2, \ldots, r_n)$ if event j occurs, and so on. Thus the expected score is given as

$$E[S(r_1, r_2, \ldots, r_n)] = \sum_{i=1}^{n} p_i S_i(r_1, r_2, \ldots, r_n)$$

and the scoring rule is strictly proper if

$$E[S(p_1, p_2, \ldots, p_n)] > E[S(r_1, r_2, \ldots, r_n)]$$

for $r_i \neq p_i$.

The three most commonly encountered proper scoring rules are the quadratic, logarithmic, and spherical rules, namely,

$$S_j(r_1, r_2, \ldots, r_n) = 2r_j - \sum_{i=1}^{n} r_i^2$$

$$S_j(r_1, r_2, \ldots, r_n) = \log(r_j)$$

$$S_j(r_1, r_2, \ldots, r_n) = \frac{r_j}{(\sum_{i=1}^{n} r_i^2)^{1/2}}$$

These can be extended to the continuous case by limiting arguments. If x is the revealed value and $r(x)$ the previously assigned density function on the random variable, then the above rules become

$$S(r(x)) = 2r(x) - \int_{-\infty}^{+\infty} r^2(x)\, dx$$

$$S(r(x)) = \log r(x)$$

$$S(r(x)) = \frac{r(x)}{[\int_{-\infty}^{+\infty} r^2(x)\, dx]^{1/2}}$$

Example Using the previous example with the quadratic scoring rule, our weather forecaster's expected score is

$$E[S(0.7, 0.3)] = 0.7(1.4 - 0.49 - 0.09) + 0.3(0.6 - 0.49 - 0.09) = 0.58$$

If he or she had reported a probability of 1 for rain the next day, the expected score would have been

$$E[S(1, 0)] = 0.7(2 - 1) + 0.3(0 - 1) = 0.4$$

which is now less than 0.58, unlike the improper linear scoring rule before, which would give a higher score (lower penalty) to the devious response of certainty.

This shows how the use of proper scoring rules can encourage estimators to give careful and truthful responses by providing motivation in the correct direction. The exprerience with weather forecasters in the United States, (e.g., Murphy and Winkler, 1977) has shown that the use of such scoring rules seems to improve the estimating performance quite significantly and can help reduce the various assessment biases resulting when the estimators are in an unmotivated situation, as discussed previously. Some psychologists are, however, sceptical about their real value, doubting whether individuals have the cognitive capacity to determine their "optimal" responses. Also, it is usually the case that scoring rules are relatively insensitive to small departures from the "optimal" response. However, even if they are not directly effective in improving the quality of assessments, through their feedback of performance scores they do provide a way of evaluation and may counter other organizational pressures to bias assessments.

EXERCISES

8.1 A project engineer gives success probabilities a priori to various research and development programs. The past three probabilities and their outcomes S or F were:

Project	1	2	3
Outcome	S	S	F
Probability	0.8	0.7	0.5

What are the accumulated total scores using the quadratic, logarithmic, and spherical scoring rules?

8.2 Estimators are often evaluated according to the probability which was previously assigned to the value actually realized. Show that this is an improper scoring rule.

8.3 Show analytically how the linear scoring rule is improper.

8.4 Criticize the scoring rule approach to estimator evaluation from the point of view of rational expected utility decision making.

8.5 To what extent are individuals in large organizations rewarded according to "proper" or "improper" scoring rules in their behavior? To what extent do you think scoring rules should provide a basis for financial incentive?

8.6 Explain why anchoring bias in $F_x(x)$ produces an assessed distribution that could be described as "too steep," but in $F_\zeta(\zeta)$ we have called it "too flat."

8.7 An individual has produced maximum temperature forecasts in the form of normal distributions for the past 10 days. The mean and the variance of the predictive distribution, together with the actual realized values, are shown below:

Day	1	2	3	4	5	6	7	8	9	10
Mean	12	10	14	11	11	12	9	10	9	10
Variance	4	4	5	4	4	3	4	3	3	4
Actual	10	11	12	9	10	11	10	10	11	11

For the eleventh day, the mean and the variance given by the individual were 12 and 4, respectively. What would you as a decision maker use as the predictive distribution for the maximum temperature on the eleventh day based only upon this individual's advice and record?

8.8 Two forecasters assessed discrete distributions over x partitioned into five categories,

$$f_1(x) = (0.1, 0.2, 0.3, 0.3, 0.1)$$

$$f_2(x) = (0.3, 0.1, 0.1, 0.3, 0.2)$$

If the fourth event in this partition actually occurred (i.e., the one to which they both assessed 0.3), what are their respective scores using the quadratic, logarithmic, and spherical scoring rules? How do these results compare with your intuitive feeling for the better performance?

8.9 A weather bureau issues forecasts of rain one day ahead. Each forecast is expressed in terms of probability in increments of 0.10. Below are the past five-month record of such forecasts (fcst.) and the actual observations (obs.) for the periods of the forecasts, where P denotes that measurable precipitation was observed and NP that none was observed.

Suppose you have a decision in which the presence of precipitation tomorrow plays an important role. If the forecast is a 0.60 probability of precipitation tomorrow, what probability would you use in analyzing your problem?

Day	May		June		July		August		September	
	fcst.	obs.	fcst.	obs.	fcst.	obs.	fcst.	obs.	fcst.	obs.
1	0.60	P	0.30	NP	0.10	NP	0.10	NP	0.30	NP
2	0.70	P	0.10	NP	0.30	NP	0.50	NP	0.70	P
3	0.50	P	0.40	P	0.30	NP	0.30	NP	0.20	NP
4	0.20	NP	0.10	NP	0.10	P	0.00	NP	0.10	NP
5	0.10	NP	0.10	NP	0.60	NP	0.00	NP	0.00	NP
6	0.30	NP	0.40	P	0.00	NP	0.20	P	0.00	NP
7	0.20	P	0.40	P	0.00	NP	0.40	NP	0.10	NP
8	1.00	P	0.80	P	0.10	NP	0.50	P	0.60	P
9	0.20	NP	0.20	P	0.30	NP	0.20	NP	0.00	NP
10	0.00	P	0.00	NP	0.20	NP	0.00	NP	0.00	NP
11	0.20	NP	0.10	NP	0.10	NP	0.20	NP	0.20	NP
12	0.00	NP	0.10	NP	0.20	P	0.30	NP	0.50	NP
13	0.40	P	0.40	NP	0.50	NP	0.10	P	0.30	P
14	0.50	P	0.50	NP	0.30	NP	0.20	NP	0.10	NP

	May		June		July		August		September	
Day	fcst.	obs.	fcst.	obs.	fcst.	obs.	fcst.	obs.	fcst.	obs.
15	0.50	NP	0.50	P	0.40	NP	0.00	NP	0.30	NP
16	0.30	NP	0.20	P	0.40	NP	0.10	NP	0.10	NP
17	0.20	NP	0.20	NP	0.30	NP	0.70	NP	0.20	NP
18	0.10	NP	0.50	P	0.00	NP	0.10	NP	0.50	NP
19	0.70	P	0.40	NP	0.20	NP	0.00	NP	0.10	NP
20	0.80	NP	0.80	NP	0.30	NP	0.00	NP	0.20	NP
21	0.10	NP	0.80	P	0.10	NP	0.10	NP	0.60	NP
22	0.00	NP	0.40	P	0.20	P	0.20	NP	0.60	NP
23	0.00	NP	0.70	NP	0.40	P	0.30	NP	0.20	NP
24	0.00	NP	0.40	NP	0.30	NP	0.30	NP	0.20	NP
25	0.00	NP	0.40	NP	0.20	NP	0.30	P	0.20	NP
26	0.00	NP	0.30	NP	0.10	NP	0.40	P	0.40	NP
27	0.00	NP	0.10	NP	0.10	NP	0.60	P	0.10	NP
28	0.00	NP	0.40	NP	0.10	NP	0.60	NP	0.40	P
29	0.00	NP	0.80	P	0.10	P	0.40	NP	0.40	P
30	0.60	P	0.40	NP	0.20	NP	0.40	P	0.10	NP
31	0.90	P			0.30	P	0.50	P		

8.10 A subjective probability forecaster makes assessments every day with daily feedback, such as the weather forecasting situation in Exercise 8.9. Such a forecaster is considering *self*-calibrating his or her own assessments daily. If each day's assessment is a coherent forecast, to what extent would the self-imposition of a calibration function be incoherent?

8.11 Some decision scientists argue that calibration is not relevant in repetitive forecasting situations because feedback should automatically ensure coherence, and that it is not relevant across different assessments because their contexts are not the same. What is your view on this? When is calibration relevant?

REFERENCES

√ Harrison, J. M. (1977): "Independence and Calibration in Decision Analysis," *Management Science*, vol. 24, no. 3, pp. 320–328.

√ Murphy, A. H., and R. L. Winkler (1977): "Reliability of Subjective Probability Forecasts of Precipitation and Temperature," *Applied Statistics*, vol. 26, no. 1, pp. 41–47.

Winkler, R. L., and A. H. Murphy (1968): "Good Probability Assessors," *Journal of Applied Meteorology*, vol. 7, pp. 751–758.

NINE

DECOMPOSITIONS OF PROBABILITY ASSESSMENT

9.1 INTRODUCTION

The decision analysis principle of decomposition has been reiterated many times in this text. The more an individual's reasoning can be explicated on paper, the more tests of coherence can be applied, the better he or she is able to communicate the analysis, and the more comfortable the individual is likely to be with his or her understanding of the problem. Thus, the more a probability assessment can be split up into a sequence of interrelated factors and causal links, the more effective becomes the analysis in decision analytic terms. Recall, however, one caveat: there is a limit to the extent of clarification obtained by decomposition. An overdecomposed model may confuse more than it clarifies. We discussed this in Section 1.3 under requisite modeling, and will come back to it again in Chapter 12. In the next two sections, we present two applied studies of separate decomposition approaches to probability assessment. The first is the hierarchical approach as exemplified particularly by the work of Decisions and Designs Incorporated in the early 1970s on behalf of the U.S. Advanced Projects Research Agency. The second is the fault tree approach as exemplified in the Rasmussen report on reactor safety, to which we have already referred (in Chapter 6.)

9.2 AN EXAMPLE OF HIERARCHICAL INFERENCE

The example used here is based upon one by Barclay et al. (1977), which was concerned with estimating the probability that a country intends to develop a nuclear weapons capability within the next five years. Figure 9.1 indicates how this task was decomposed as a hierarchy of precursive indications.

Notice how, first of all, the proposition H under consideration was clearly identified alongside its complement $\bar{H}$. We then have a set of precursive data (labeled D^i) or indicators (labeled I^i) comprising the first hierarchy. These are

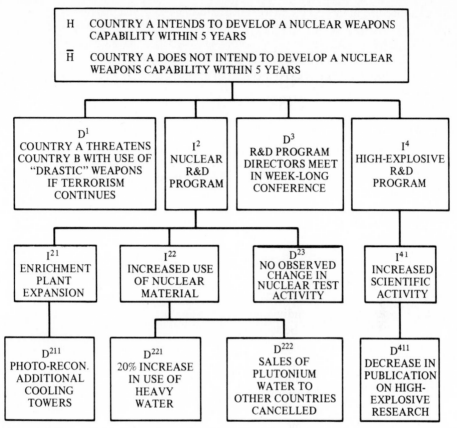

Figure 9.1 Hierarchical structure for nuclear weapons development program (*Adapted from Barclay et al., 1977.*)

further decomposed into a second hierarchy, which is again decomposed into a third. Notice particularly how these are indexed. Clearly, the number of superscripts indicates the level of the hierarchy where a particular datum or indicator functions.

One of the great benefits of such a hierarchical decomposition in social, political, and technological forecasting is that different experts can give their assessments at the appropriate places. This is in contrast to many other methods of combining forecasts where each expert gives just an overall forecast of the variable under consideration, such as H, and may, to a large extent, be making judgments over areas for which he or she has no substantive expertise at all.

Another powerful feature of the bayesian analysis of hierarchical decompositions can be the use of likelihoods in the analysis. The more conventional bayesian approach to forecasting is to work from the predictive distributions conditioned upon certain indicators, and then form a linear expectation. This is because we intuitively focus upon H as our uncertain quantity, and on factors such as D^1, I^2,

D^3, I^4 as useful conditioning states of information from which to assess the separate predictors, namely, $P(H|D^1)$, $P(H|I^2)$, $P(H|D^3)$, $P(H|I^4)$, $P(H|\bar{D}^1)$, $P(H|\bar{I}^2)$, $P(H|\bar{D}^3)$, $P(H|\bar{I}^4)$, where D^1 is the occurrence of D^1 and $\bar{D}^1$ its complement (just as H and $\bar{H}$ are complementary).

Thus, if we denote $P(H)$ as the marginal probability of H with respect to evaluation factor D^1, then

$$P(H) = P(H|D^1)P(D^1) + P(H|\bar{D}^1)P(\bar{D}^1)$$

where $P(D^1)$ is the estimated probability of factor D^1. In this way, a set of predictors based upon each factor is obtained as $P_j(H)$ for $j = 1, 2, 3,$ and 4 in this example. With the conventional or synthetic approach, these four predictors $P_j(H)$ are treated just like a set of expert opinions or forecasts from different models and are combined with the linear weights w_j to give the composite forecast

$$P_{1234}(H) = \sum_{j=1}^{4} w_j P_j(H)$$

where
$$1 = \sum_{j=1}^{4} w_j \qquad 0 \le w_j \le 1$$

Apart from the difficulty of assigning the importance weights w_j, a crucial problem in practice is assessing such predictors as $P(H|D^1)$, which is supposed to be an estimate of the probability of H based upon considering D^1 *alone*. It is a very difficult cognitive task for an individual to isolate his or her opinion on the variable which is important to him or her, namely, H, in terms of being determined by one factor. It also strains the patience of an assessor who may not really understand why each predictor should be kept separate.

The use of likelihoods in analyzing the decompositions works in exactly the opposite way to the more intuitive synthetic approach and can often be a more convenient method of assessment. Rather than focusing upon the predictor $P(H|D^1)$, we instead deduce the likelihood $P(D^1|H)$ by postulating the situation where it is actually true that country A plans to go nuclear in five years, and conceiving how likely it would be that this country would use such a threat D^1 now. In some cases this deductive method of analysis has been found to be more feasible than the inductive estimates required by the synthetic approach.

Furthermore, rather than assessing the probability of a given datum $P(D^j|H)$, which might be very small, it is often simpler just to assess the likelihood ratio

$$\frac{P(D^j|H)}{P(D^j|\bar{H})}$$

This is most practicable in hierarchical decompositions involving data which have already been observed, and therefore $P(D^j) = 1$, and so on.

In the example being considered here, all factors labeled D^j are data that have been observed, and some of them have been more easily estimated in terms of likelihood ratios. For example, D^1 was considered twice as likely to have happened if H were true than if $\bar{H}$ were true. Thus the matrix

	H	$\bar{H}$
D^1	2	1

was assessed.

The factors labeled I^j are not known with certainty at the time of analysis, and therefore a matrix of probabilities has to be assessed:

	H	$\bar{H}$
I^2	0.9	0.8
$\bar{I}^2$	0.1	0.2

Estimating the likelihoods in this deductive fashion gives the assessments shown in Figure 9.2. Having obtained these probabilities, it is easy to revert to the inductive reasoning required for forecasting by means of Bayes' theorem.

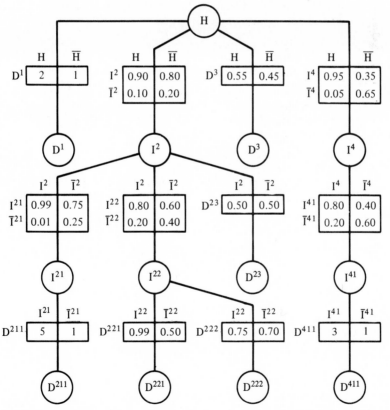

Figure 9.2 Deductive hierarchical structure for nuclear weapons development program (*Adapted from Barclay et al., 1977.*)

In order to commence a bayesian inferential process, prior probabilities of the hypotheses H and $\bar{H}$ are required and must be based only upon information not included in the hierarchical decomposition. If a full hierarchical decomposition has been obtained to the best knowledge of the decision analyst, then it contains all the information, and the prior probabilities must be uninformative. Thus, it is most usual to assign a likelihood ratio of unity to the hypotheses being so decomposed,

$$\frac{P(H)}{P(\bar{H})} = 1$$

Ultimately, what we are aiming for is the ratio

$$\frac{P(D|H)}{P(D|\bar{H})}$$

where D represents all of the data included in the hierarchical decomposition. Note that the decomposition is a tree with each branch eventually ending in some diagnostic datum. Having obtained the above ratio, we can compute the posterior probabilities of H and $\bar{H}$ from Bayes' theorem in ratio form as

$$\frac{P(H|D)}{P(\bar{H}|D)} = \frac{P(D|H)P(H)}{P(D|\bar{H})P(\bar{H})}$$

$$= \frac{P(D|H)}{P(D|\bar{H})}$$

In order to arrive at this point, we must work up through the tree, essentially performing two types of operation.

For each indicator in the tree we must obtain the likelihood of all data upon which it is contingent, that is, those data that are below it. Thus, for I^{22} two pieces of data, D^{221} and D^{222}, are contingent. If these are conditionally independent, that is, independent given a value of I^{22}, then their joint likelihood is simply obtained as their product,

$$P(D^{221}, D^{222}|I^{22}) = P(D^{221}|I^{22})P(D^{222}|I^{22})$$

$$= 0.99(0.75) = 0.74$$

$$P(D^{221}, D^{222}|\bar{I}^{22}) = P(D^{221}|\bar{I}^{22})P(D^{222}|\bar{I}^{22})$$

$$= 0.5(0.7) = 0.35$$

Thus, we now have the little matrix

	I^{22}	$\bar{I}^{22}$
D	0.74	0.35

which can be placed at the I^{22} point in the tree, as shown in Figure 9.3. Note that D is used for brevity to denote all data below a certain point on a branch, and thus in

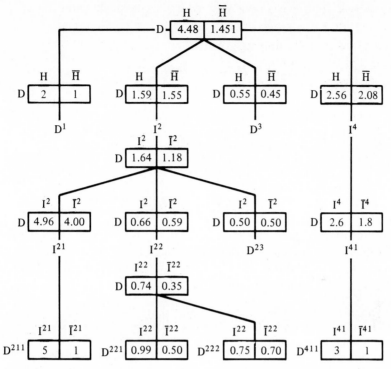

Figure 9.3 Inductive hierarchical structure for nuclear weapons development program (*Adapted from Barclay et al., 1977.*)

this case it implies D^{221} and D^{222}. At the top of the tree, for H and $\bar{H}$, D implies all of the data, as before.

In order to relate D^{221} and D^{222} to I^2, this must be done through the matrix of likelihoods assessed in Figure 9.2. Thus,

$$P(D|I^2) = P(D|I^{22})P(I^{22}|I^2) + P(D|\bar{I}^{22})P(\bar{I}^{22}|I^2)$$

$$= 0.74(0.80) + 0.35(0.2) = 0.66$$

$$P(D|\bar{I}^2) = P(D|\bar{I}^{22})P(I^{22}|\bar{I}^2) + P(D|\bar{I}^{22})P(\bar{I}^{22}|\bar{I}^2)$$

$$= 0.74(0.60) + 0.35(0.40) = 0.59$$

giving the little matrix

	I^2	$\bar{I}^2$
D	0.66	0.59

as in Figure 9.3.

Proceeding back up the tree in this way resulted in the likelihood ratio

$$\frac{P(D|H)}{P(D|\overline{H})} = \frac{4.48}{1.451}$$

and thus the posterior probability of H was assessed as about 0.75.

Such an analysis of a hierarchical decomposition therefore avoids the two problems of assessing predictive probabilities based upon isolated indications and attaching importance weights to them for the purpose of forming the composite forecast. It may also be easier for an assessor to think deductively in terms of assessing likelihoods than inductively for the predictive distribution.

9.3 AN EXAMPLE OF FAULT TREE ANALYSIS

The following is extracted from "Reactor Safety Study," U.S. Nuclear Regulatory Commission (1975).

4.1 INTRODUCTION

This study has divided the work into a number of tasks whose results were combined to produce the overall risk assessment. The detailed technical work of each task is reported in the appendices of this report. This chapter describes the methods used in each task and the way the results of each were combined to produce the final result. This discussion is brief; however, Addendum I to this report provides a detailed overview of the entire methodology used.

The risk determination was divided into the three major tasks shown in Figure 4-1.

Task I includes the identification of potential accidents and the quantification of both the probability and magnitude of the associated radioactive releases to the environment. The major part of the work of the study was devoted to this task. The organization of the work and the methodology used are discussed in section 4.2.

Task II uses the radioactive source term defined in Task I and calculates how the radioactivity is distributed in the environment and what effects it has on public health and property. The methodology used is described in section 4.3.

Task III combines the consequences calculated in Task II, weighted by their respective probabilities to produce the overall risk from potential nuclear accidents. To give some perspective to these results, they are compared to a variety of non-nuclear risks. The task is described in section 4.4.

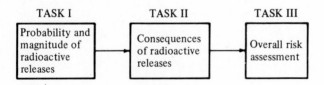

FIGURE 4-1 Major tasks of study

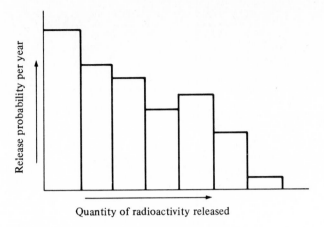

FIGURE 4-2 Illustrative release probability
versus release magnitude histogram

4.2 QUANTIFICATION OF RADIOACTIVE RELEASES

The objective of this task is to generate a histogram, of the form shown in Figure 4-2, which shows the probability and magnitude of the various accidental radioactive releases. The isotopic composition,[1] elevation of the release point above ground level and the timing and energy content associated with the release must also be determined to permit the calculation of consequences due to the releases.

This histogram could be determined for a single type of accident (such as a loss of coolant accident). By combining many accidents one can obtain a composite histogram for all important contributors. Since the histogram could be different for the various isotopes released, a full characterization of all accidents could involve a large number of such histograms. A significant effort was devoted to combining all isotopes and accidents into a single histogram for each reactor. This work is described in Appendix V.

To generate a composite histogram of the type shown in Figure 4-2, the methodology employed must in principle be able to identify the accidents that can produce significant releases and determine their probability. To do this for all accidents in a system as complicated as a nuclear power plant is a formidable task because of the very large number of accidents that can be imagined. The problem becomes more manageable, however, when it is realized that, of this large number of potential events, many have trivial releases, many are illogical (i.e., violate known physical conditions) and others have very small probabilities compared to accidents which result in essentially the same release magnitude. To ensure that unnecessary analyses are not pursued, the methods used must provide a way for logically eliminating accidents that do not significantly contribute to the radioactive source term.

The characterization of the radioactive releases was divided into the subtasks shown in Figure 4-3, which also indicates the report appendix applicable to each subtask. The

---

[1] Tasks I and II consider 54 isotopes in calculating releases and consequences as indicated in Appendix VI.

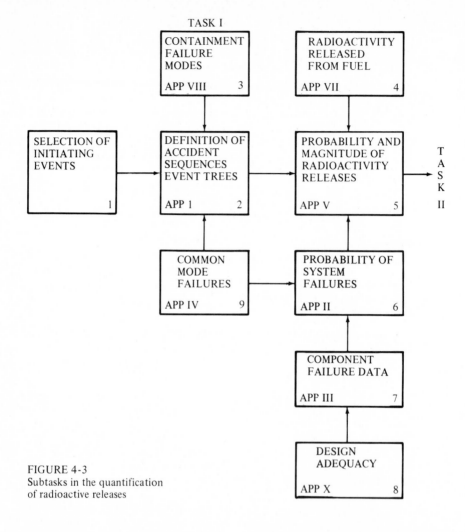

TASK I

CONTAINMENT
FAILURE
MODES

APP VIII   3

RADIOACTIVITY
RELEASED
FROM FUEL

APP VII   4

SELECTION OF
INITIATING
EVENTS

1

DEFINITION OF
ACCIDENT
SEQUENCES
EVENT TREES

APP 1   2

PROBABILITY AND
MAGNITUDE OF
RADIOACTIVITY
RELEASES

APP V   5

T
A
S
K
II

COMMON
MODE
FAILURES

APP IV   9

PROBABILITY OF
SYSTEM
FAILURES

APP II   6

COMPONENT
FAILURE DATA

APP III   7

DESIGN
ADEQUACY

APP X   8

FIGURE 4-3
Subtasks in the quantification
of radioactive releases

logic for selecting the initiating events is discussed in Chapter 3. A logic diagram called an event tree was developed for those initiating events that involved complex interactions.[2] The event tree defined the possible sequences of events subsequent to the initiating event and resulted in the definition of a number of possible accident sequences, many of which produce core melt. These systematically defined core melt sequences provided a basis for analyzing the physical processes occurring during core melt and for determining the containment failure modes and the timing of various other events (Appendix VIII). This information allowed completion of the definition of accident sequences. These completed sequence definitions then permitted, on the basis of experimental data, estimates of the amount of radioactivity that would be released from the fuel (Appendix

[2] Event trees will be described further herein. They are also described in considerable detail in Appendix I.

VII). These releases, the containment failure modes, and the timing of various events provided input to a computer code called CORRAL which calculates the amounts of the various types of radioactivity released to the environment (Appendices V and VII).

To obtain the probability of a given release, it was necessary to determine the probabilities of various accident sequences identified in the event trees. These probabilities were generally obtained through the use of fault tree analysis (discussed herein and in Appendix II). Fault tree analysis produces a logic diagram to which failure rates, appropriate time intervals, and other values can be assigned and combined to derive system failure probabilities. Since the failure rate assigned to system components usually assumed that the equipment was properly designed and qualified for those aspects of nuclear service that are unique, a check was made on a selected number of components, systems, and structures to verify that such requirements had been adequately met.[3] This effort was called the design adequacy task and is described in Appendix X.

A key step in the development of system failure probabilities is gaining an understanding of any dependencies between failures. Such dependencies, known as common mode failures, are known to exist in and between the systems modeled in the fault trees and the event trees. Considerable effort was expended in identifying such dependencies and accounting for their effects.

It should be recognized that the steps indicated in Figure 4-3 do not flow as simply as implied by the sketch. For example, it was often not obvious which accident sequences were important and which made only negligible contributions to risk. Thus, many sequences were analyzed under a set of pessimistic, simplifying assumptions. Those that showed up as significant contributors were then reanalyzed using more detailed, realistic methods. A number of such iterations were often necessary to determine the accident sequences that were the dominant contributors to the probability of occurrence of various consequences.

The event tree and fault tree methods described below are used to show relationships between component and system failure probabilities as well as interactions between various systems. The implementation of these methods often requires knowledge about the details of plant construction. Thus, for that part of the analysis requiring this detailed information, the study has used, as indicated in Chapter 1, a particular PWR and a particular BWR as typical of each of these classes of plants.

4.2.1 Definition of Accident Sequences—Event Trees

A major element in the characterization of the radioactive releases associated with potential nuclear power plant accidents is the identification of the accident sequences that can potentially influence the public's risk from such accidents. The study employed event tree methodology as the principal means for identification of the significant accident sequences.

An event tree is a logic method for identifying the various possible outcomes of a given event which is called the initiating event. The number of possible final outcomes depends upon the various options that are applicable following the initiating event. This technique has been used widely in business where the initiating event is a particular business decision and the various outcomes depend upon subsequent decisions. In business applications the trees are known as decision trees.

---

[3] Component failure rates were also modified when the components experienced accident environments, which is described in Appendix III.

In the application to reactor safety studies the initiating event is generally a system failure, and the subsequent events are, for the most part, determined by system characteristics and engineering data. In this study the trees are called event trees, and a particular sequence from the initiating event to a final outcome is termed an accident sequence.

In this study the application of event trees was limited to the analysis of potential accidents involving the reactor core. For this purpose it was found convenient to separate the event trees into two types of trees. The first was used to determine how potential accidents were affected by failures in major systems, particularly the engineered safety systems. They cover the significant LOCA[4] and transient initiating events.

These trees were supplemented with a second type of tree, the containment event tree, to provide combined accident sequences from the initiating event to release of radioactivity from the containment. This procedure is described briefly below and in greater detail in Appendix I and Addendum I to this report. It produced a list of systematically defined sequences leading to the release of radioactivity to the environment. The list of these accident sequences is found in Appendix V. The starting point for the development of an event tree is the event (failure) that initiates a potential accident situation. The initiating event is basically either a reactor coolant system rupture that results in a LOCA or any of a number of reactor transients. The initiating events of particular significance have been discussed briefly in the Chapter 3 sections treating LOCAs and reactor transients. Appendix I provides more detailed information on the selection of initiating events for the development of the system event trees and on the development of event trees for use in the study.

The application of event trees in determining system operability effects on potential accident sequences is illustrated by the following simplified example in which the initiating event is a large pipe break in the primary system of a reactor. The first step in developing this event tree is to determine which systems might affect the subsequent course of events. In this example these are station electric power, the emergency core cooling system, the radioactivity removal system, and the containment system. Through a knowledge of these systems it is possible to order them in the time sequence in which they influence the course of events. They are ordered in this way across the top of Figure 4-4 which shows event trees in which the upper branch represents success and the lower branch represents failure of the system to fulfill its function. In the absence of other constraints there are $2^{(n-1)}$ accident sequences, where n is the number of headings (functions, systems, etc.) included on the tree. However, there are known relationships (constraints) between system functions. For example, if station electric power fails, none of the other systems can operate because they depend upon power. In addition to such functional relations there may also be hardware common to more than one system. Once these functional and hardware relationships are incorporated, many of the chains shown in the upper tree of Figure 4-4 can be eliminated because they represent illogical sequences. Such sequences are eliminated in the lower tree shown in Figure 4-4. Note that elimination of the choices following failure of electric power reduces the number of sequences by about half.

The probability of failure of each system is indicated by the P values noted in Figure 4-4. The probability of success is $(1 - P)$ since it is assumed that a system operates successfully if it does not not fail. If the events (failures, successes) are independent then the probability of occurrence of a given sequence is the product of the probabilities of the

---

[4] Loss of coolant accident.

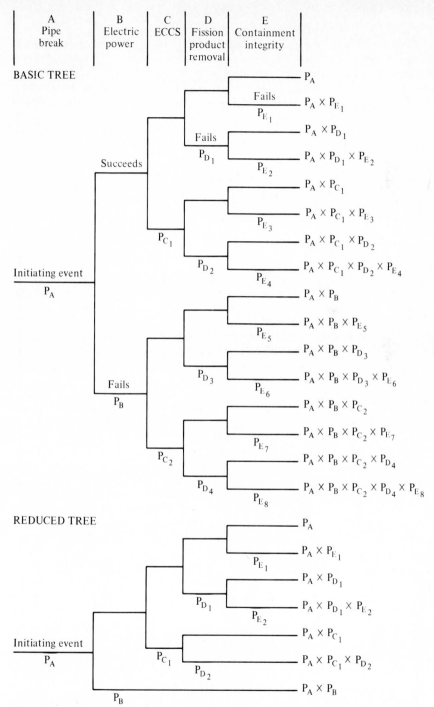

A Pipe break	B Electric power	C ECCS	D Fission product removal	E Containment integrity

BASIC TREE

P_A

$P_A \times P_{E_1}$

Fails
P_{E_1}

$P_A \times P_{D_1}$

Fails
P_{D_1}

$P_A \times P_{D_1} \times P_{E_2}$

P_{E_2}

Succeeds

$P_A \times P_{C_1}$

$P_A \times P_{C_1} \times P_{E_3}$

P_{E_3}

$P_A \times P_{C_1} \times P_{D_2}$

P_{C_1}

P_{D_2}

$P_A \times P_{C_1} \times P_{D_2} \times P_{E_4}$

P_{E_4}

Initiating event
P_A

$P_A \times P_B$

$P_A \times P_B \times P_{E_5}$

P_{E_5}

$P_A \times P_B \times P_{D_3}$

P_{D_3}

$P_A \times P_B \times P_{D_3} \times P_{E_6}$

P_{E_6}

Fails
P_B

$P_A \times P_B \times P_{C_2}$

$P_A \times P_B \times P_{C_2} \times P_{E_7}$

P_{E_7}

$P_A \times P_B \times P_{C_2} \times P_{D_4}$

P_{C_2}

P_{D_4}

$P_A \times P_B \times P_{C_2} \times P_{D_4} \times P_{E_8}$

P_{E_8}

REDUCED TREE

P_A

$P_A \times P_{E_1}$

P_{E_1}

$P_A \times P_{D_1}$

P_{D_1}

$P_A \times P_{D_1} \times P_{E_2}$

P_{E_2}

Initiating event
P_A

$P_A \times P_{C_1}$

P_{C_1}

$P_A \times P_{C_1} \times P_{D_2}$

P_{D_2}

$P_A \times P_B$

P_B

Note: Since the probability of failure, P, is generally less than 0.1, the probability of success $(1-P)$ is always close to 1. Thus, the probability associated with the upper (success) branches in the tree is assumed to be 1.

FIGURE 4-4 Simplified event trees for a large LOCA

individual events in that sequence, as indicated in Figure 4-4. Since the failure probabilities are almost always 0.1 or less it is common practice to approximate $(1 - P) \approx 1$, as shown in Figure 4-4. The probability of occurrence of each system failure is shown to be different in each accident sequence in which it appears. This is done to account for the differences in system failure probabilities that may occur due to the differing dependencies in each accident sequence.

It should be noted that as indicated by Figure 4-4, the study developed event trees in which each branch point provides only two options, system success or system failure. No consideration is given to the fact that partial system success may occur within an accident sequence. Thus, an accident sequence is conservatively assumed to lead only to total core melt or no core melt, but never to partial core melt. This has been done because uncertainties in the calculational methods preclude predictions of the detailed conditions that lead to a partial core melt. Similarly, because of the difficulty in calculating, with reasonable certainty, the effects of partial system failure, the study has treated all such questionable cases of system operability as complete system failures. Since most applicable systems involve considerable redundancy, the basic procedure involved determination of the fraction of the redundant equipment that must be operable to assure successful function of a particular system. The probability of failure of the system is the probability that the system is in a condition with less than this fraction of the equipment operating. This success/failure treatment can significantly affect the overall risk assessment only through accident sequences which are important contributors to risk. Since a large fraction of the sequences analyzed were found to have an insignificant effect on the risk, the fact that their analysis was done conservatively has a negligible effect on the magnitude of the total estimated risk. Those accident sequences that were found to contribute importantly to the risk were subjected to further analysis in an attempt to remove any unwarranted conservatisms.

If the event tree has been constructed with detailed information, the series of events in each accident sequence would be well enough defined so that it is possible to calculate the consequences for that particular series of events. For example, the bottom sequence in Figure 4-4, where no core cooling would be available, can be shown to result in melting of the core, and the fraction of core radioactivity that would be released can be calculated. Since, as pointed out in Chapter 3, the molten core would violate the containment, the accident could produce a release of radioactivity outside of the containment. The mode of containment failure would affect the overall probability of the sequences as well as the magnitude of the release. The event tree therefore provides a definition of the possible accident sequences from which the radioactive releases to the environment can be calculated and, if the failure probabilities are known, the probability of each release can also be calculated. Again, it should be noted that this example is greatly simplified for illustrative purposes; the actual event trees for this and other cases are discussed in great detail in Appendix I.

In summary, the event trees were the principal vehicles, supplemented by additional analyses, utilized for achieving a systematic determination of the radioactive release magnitudes and probabilities associated with potential nuclear power plant accidents. They first were utilized to identify the many possible significant accident sequences. Then, through an iterative process involving successive improvements in the definition of failure probabilities, the incorporation of system interactions and the resolution of physical process descriptions, they provided for the identification of those accident sequences that are important to the achievement of a realistic risk assessment. These selected accident sequences served as the basis for determining the magnitude of applicable radioactive releases (Section 4.2.3). They also served as the vehicle for combining the initiating event probabilities, system failure probabilities, and containment failure probabilities into the composite probabilities applicable to the radioactive releases. With respect to system failure probabilities, the event trees were the principal means of identifying the various system failure definitions needed in the fault trees that were used for determining system failure probabilities.

4.2.2 Probability of Releases

As noted previously, there were a large number of iterations in various parts of the risk assessment cycle described in this chapter. These iterations were necessary in order to determine the dominant accident sequences for use in the final overall risk assessment. The methods described below were utilized in this iterative process and aided in the selection of the dominant accident sequences. However, such iterations and other exploratory analyses are neglected in the following discussion, which is generally concerned with the determination of the radioactive release probabilities for the final overall risk assessment.

The final risk assessment is based on a number of different release categories. Each of these release categories is associated with a specific type and magnitude of release (see Section 4.2.3 and Appendix V). The final risk assessment requires the probability applicable to each of these release categories. In general a specific release category applies to many accident sequences but, because of the wide range in probability of occurrence of these sequences, it is found that only a few sequences determine the probability of occurrence of a particular category. Thus, the determination of the release probability associated with each release category required the determination and summation of the probability of occurrence of each of the dominant accident sequences in the category.

The probability of occurrence of an accident sequence is composed of the initiating event probability, the failure probabilities of systems included in the sequence, and the containment failure probability. The probabilities for LOCA initiating events such as pipe breaks, vessel ruptures, transients, etc., were determined by deriving appropriate failure rates from available failure rate data. The large majority of the system failure probabilities were determined with the aid of the fault tree technique. This technique, discussed in the next section, is suited for analysis of failures of complex systems. To account for probable dependencies in failures of components and systems involved in the fault trees and event tree accident sequences, many special analyses were performed for the purpose of determining significant common mode failures. These analyses are discussed in Section 4.2.2.3. The applicable containment failure modes are largely determined by the accident sequences and the various physical processes that can result from the accident sequences. The basis for the likelihood of containment failure modes was determined by fault trees and by the analysis performed in Appendix VIII, which analyzed the applicable physical processes.

4.2.2.1 Fault trees As noted in Section 4.2.1 the event trees define certain system failures whose probabilities are needed to determine the risk. In this study the fault tree method has been used to estimate the majority of these failure probabilities. The method uses a logic that is essentially the reverse of that used in event trees. Given a particular failure, the fault tree method is used to identify the various combinations and sequences of other failures that lead to the given failure. The technique is particularly suited to the analysis of the failure of complex systems. The effective utilization of this logic requires that the

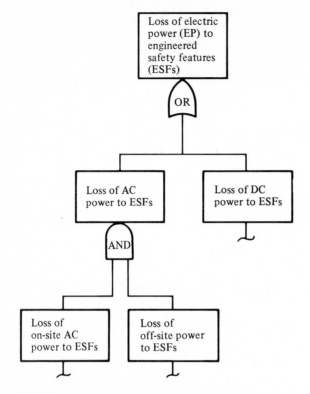

FIGURE 4-5 Illustration of fault tree development

analyst have a thorough understanding of the system components and their functions. This section gives a general discussion of the fault tree method. A more detailed discussion is provided in Appendix II and Addendum I to this report.

The fault tree method is illustrated in Figure 4-5 which shows the first few steps of a fault tree concerning loss of electric power to all engineered safety features (ESFs). In this case it is known that the electric power to ESFs would require both alternating current (AC) power and direct current (DC) power. The AC provides the energy needed but the DC is required by the control systems which turn on the AC. Thus, failure of each of these systems appears in the first level and they are coupled to the top event by an OR gate. This symbol signifies that either one failure or the other (or both) can cause the top event and that the probability of the top event is, to a close approximation, the sum of the probabilities of the two events in the first level. Thus, if $P_{AC} = 0.001$ and $P_{DC} = 0.001$, then $P_{EP} = 0.002$. The EP failure probability can be computed in this way if there are sufficient failure data to determine P_{AC} and P_{DC} directly. However, in general, such failures have not occurred often enough to provide meaningful statistical data and therefore, the analysis must proceed to lower failure levels. The next level is developed only for loss of AC power. In this case it is known that either off-site power (the electrical grid) or on-site power (the station diesel generators) can supply the needed energy. Failures of these systems are therefore coupled by an AND gate, indicating that both would have to fail in order to produce the failure above.

The above basic method is used to develop the trees until they have identified failures for which statistical data exist to determine their probability. In developing the tree, consideration is given to intrinsic component failures, human factors and test and maintenance. Detailed discussions of this point are provided in Appendices II and III. The probabilities of the failures are then assigned to the appropriate elements of the tree and the probability of the top event is calculated. For complex trees, such as those involved in this study, the aid of a computer program is utilized for computing the top event probability. In general the individual probabilities are obtained from a limited amount of experience data so they have an appreciable uncertainty associated with them. A computer code used in the study propagated these uncertainties using a standard statistical procedure and determined an uncertainty for the system failure probability.

Fault trees were developed for almost all the major individual systems represented in the event trees. These systems include the various ESFs and some of the normally operating plant systems. In some cases several different versions of a given system fault tree were required, depending upon the accident conditions prevailing at the time the system failure is postulated. For example, the probability of failure of the ECCS may be different depending upon whether the containment spray system operates or fails. Such differences have been accounted for in the study.

There are a number of limitations in applying fault trees to a risk assessment of nuclear power plant accidents. The most important drawback is probably that detailed fault trees for complex systems are very time consuming to develop. Furthermore, there are different ways in which the logic can be developed. Thus two different analysts are likely to produce different trees for the same system. Although both trees may be logically correct and produce the same system failure probability, the fact that they appear to be considerably different can be misleading.

As with event trees, serious errors can be made if it is assumed that all failures are independent. A substantial amount of the effort in this study has been expended on the search for common mode failures. The fault trees and event trees have been extremely useful in helping define those common mode failures that can contribute to the overall risk.

As with event trees, there is no way of proving that a complex fault tree includes all the significant paths to failure. Generally, at some point in the analysis, the analyst must truncate his fault tree by assuming certain events are not significant. Thus, the accuracy of the tree depends appreciably upon the skill and experience of the analyst. Any modeling, of course, depends upon the skill of the analyst, however it is particularly important for fault trees where few explicit rules and guidelines exist. However, a good check on the logical adequacy and completeness of a fault tree is obtained when it is quantified and subjected to sensitivity studies. In general all the trees constructed in this study were found to go into more detail than was needed.

4.2.2.2 Failure rate data The study utilized failure rate data in two principal ways. They were used directly to establish the probabilities of major events (failures) for which fault trees were not constructed. Such uses included the determinations of the probabilities of initiating events such as pipe breaks and reactor vessel ruptures. However, the majority of failure data was utilized as input to the fault trees so that the probabilities of the system failures could be determined. This failure data included estimates of component failures, human errors, and testing and maintenance contributions.

The accuracy of the fault tree method is highest when component failure rates are based on data obtained from failures in systems identical to the one under analysis. In the case of reactors the experience of a few hundred reactor-years is not sufficient by itself to provide statistically meaningful probabilities for most of the required component failure rates. It has therefore been necessary to also use data from a much broader base of industrial experience.

In this study extensive searches have been made for sources of failure rate data. These are discussed in detail in Appendix III. Each source has been investigated to determine its appropriateness for application to nuclear plants. The conditions of service of most of the components in reactors are similar to conditions in many other applications, such as those in fossil-fueled plants and chemical processing plants. The compilations of such industrial experience are the basic source of most of the failure rate data used in the study.

Certain components of nuclear systems may be subjected to rather unique environments, particularly during serious accidents. Foremost among these environmental factors are radiation and high temperature steam. In the process of determining applicable failure rates, the study employed specialists in component reliability to assess the effect of such conditions on system components. Based on their assessments, component failure rates and their uncertainties were increased for the extreme environments.

The design specifications of the components of the ESFs require that they be qualified to operate under a variety of accident conditions. It is, of course, possible that certain components may fail to meet these special design conditions. To ascertain how likely such design errors may be, this study carefully reviewed the components in a selected number of important safety systems to determine how well the design specifications had, in fact, been satisfied. A detailed report of this effort is provided in Appendix X. Based on these assessments, component failure rates were modified to account for the deficiencies found.

A common criticism of the fault tree method is that the system failure probabilities are not meaningful because of uncertainties in the knowledge of applicable failure rates. In general, the failure rates used in this study have uncertainties of a factor of 10 or 100 (± 3 or ± 10). In a few cases the uncertainty is a factor of 1000 (± 30). Based on these uncertainties, a Monte Carlo technique (see Appendix II) was used to calculate the uncertainty of the overall system failure probability. The study has used a log-normal distribution for all the uncertainties assigned to component failure rates. The log-normal distributions were combined in a statistical manner to account for the error contributions from different component failure rates.[5] It was found that even with the larger component failure rate uncertainties that were used, the system failure probabilities were sufficiently accurate to obtain meaningful values for risk evaluation.

4.2.2.3 Common mode failures[6] Common mode failures are multiple failures that result from a single event or failure. Thus, the probabilities associated with the multiple failures become, in reality, dependent probabilities. The single event can be any one of a number of possibilities; a common property, process, environment, or external event. The resulting multiple failures can likewise encompass a spectrum of possibilities including, for example, system failures caused by a common external event, multiple component

---

[5] Studies indicated that, with the wide ranges of uncertainties used herein for component failure rate data, the exact form of the distribution used had little effect on the results obtained.

[6] A more specific discussion of the treatment of common mode failure is contained in Addendum I to this report.

failures caused by a common defective manufacturing process, and a sequence of failures caused by a common human operator.

Because common mode failures entail a wide spectrum of possibilities and enter into all areas of modeling and analysis, common mode failures cannot be isolated as separate study, but instead must be considered throughout all the modeling and quantification steps involved in the risk assessment. In the study, common mode and dependency considerations were incorporated in the following stages of analyses:

- Event tree construction
- Fault tree construction
- Fault tree quantification
- Event tree quantification
- Special engineering investigations

In the event tree development, common mode failures were first treated in the detailed modeling of system interactions. If failure of one system caused other systems to fail or be ineffective these dependencies were explicitly modeled in the event trees. The systems rendered failed or ineffective by the single system failure were treated in the subsequent analysis as having failed with probability of one and the analysis concerned itself only with the critical single system failure. The changes produced in event trees by these relationships often produced significant increases in predicted accident sequence probabilities since a product of system failure probabilities was replaced by a single system failure probability. The development of the containment event tree that relates various modes of containment failure to system operability states and the physical processes associated with core melt, as discussed in detail in Appendix I, also accounted for dependencies which were due to the initiating event.

The event trees also defined the conditions for which the individual fault trees were constructed. Particular system failures, i.e., the top events of the fault trees, were defined as occurring under specific accident conditions that frequently included the prior failure of other systems. The fault trees were thus coupled to other systems in the accident sequence, as well as to the particular, common, accident environments that existed. The fault trees were drawn to a level such that all relevant common hardware in the systems was identified. This depth of analysis permitted identification of single failures that cause multiple effects or dependencies. These included single failures that cause several systems to fail or be degraded, or cause redundancies to be negated. The failure causes modeled in the fault tree analysis include not only hardware failures, but also include failures caused by human intervention, test and maintenance actions, and environmental effects. Thus, a spectrum of potential dependencies is incorporated in the fault trees. In many cases these additional causes, usually due to human or test and maintenance interfaces, have higher probability contributions to system failure than the hardware causes. In a number of cases these non-hardware actions result in failure probabilities (essentially single failure probabilities) that are high enough to dominate the system failure probability.

The fault tree quantification stage, in which system probabilities were numerically computed, incorporated dependency and common mode considerations throughout the calculations. The failure rate for a particular component included not only contributions from pure hardware failure (sometimes called the random failure rate), but also included applicable contributions from test or maintenance errors, human causes, and environmental causes. Human errors were investigated to identify causes of dependent failures if, for instance, the same operator could perform all the acts. Testing or maintenance activities were examined for causes of dependent failures, for example, when several components would be scheduled for simultaneous testing or maintenance. Components were examined for potential dependent failures that may arise as a result of the environments created by accidents. The quantification formulas treated both hardware and non-hardware contributions with their relevant dependencies. The quantification process included determinations of the maximum possible impacts from common mode failures which might exist but were not previously included in the analyses. These determinations indicated whether additional common mode failures could have significant impact on the computed accident probabilities. The applicable systems and/or components were reexamined to identify the ways, if any, in which such significant common mode failures could occur.

After the fault trees were quantified, the event tree quantification stage combined the individual fault tree probabilities to obtain accident sequence probabilities. Since a sequence in the event trees can be viewed in terms of fault tree logic, the same quantification techniques were used on the accident sequences as were used on the individual fault trees. Since multiple systems were analyzed, the couplings now included dependencies across systems.

As a final check on possible dependencies and common mode effects, special engineering investigations were performed to complement the modeling and mathematical techniques which had been used throughout the study. Those event tree accident sequences which dominate the probability of occurrence of the categories were carefully reexamined for any specific dependencies which may have been overlooked.

The probability versus consequence calculations involve several inputs which have no significant common mode failure contributions. The accident probabilities, the weather, and the population distributions used in the calculation of consequences are essentially independent of one another (see Section 4.3).

4.2.3 Magnitude of Releases

This section discusses the manner in which the magnitude of the radioactivity release from the plant to the environment was determined. The release magnitude is influenced by three major factors; the amount and isotopic composition of radioactivity released from the core, the amount of radioactivity removed within the containment, and the containment failure mode. All of these are time dependent factors which influence the radioactive release magnitude. Thus, the accident sequences defined by the event trees were of particular value in establishing the release magnitudes applicable to each of the release categories noted previously.

As already noted, only those potential reactor accidents that lead to core melting affect the risk significantly. Thus, for the most part, the determination of the release of radioactivity from the reactor core involved the estimation of the fractions of significant radioactive isotopes that are released from cores melting under various conditions. The various conditions and timing of core melting were defined by appropriate analysis of the applicable accident sequences in event trees. A variety of experiments reported in the literature provides information on the radioactivity released from fuel under various conditions. Such information was used in the determination of the applicable release fractions. These determinations are described in detail in Appendix VII. This work resulted from the deliberations of a group of specialists, who have been conducting work in this area at National Laboratories. In general, the experiments on which these results are based were carried out with relatively small samples of fuel. It is believed that, because of the large surface to volume ratio in such experiments compared to that which would exist in a molten core, the release fractions used in the study tend to overpredict the fraction released from a core. However, since no large scale experiments have been conducted, there is no experimental verification that reductions in the release fractions will in fact be observed. For this reason such potential effects were not taken into account in establishing the release fractions applicable to the various release categories.

Radioactivity released from the core is subjected to a variety of physical processes that reduce the amount of radioactivity available for release to the environment. These processes include wash out by the fission product removal systems, natural plate out and deposition processes on surfaces within the containment, radioactive decay, and the effects of filters. These processes, coupled with the fuel release and the mode and timing of containment failure, are the major determinants of the magnitude of radioactive release to the environment. To account for all these effects a computer code called CORRAL was developed. It is described in detail in Appendixes V and VII. The various parameters used in the code are based on recent investigations, conducted at National Laboratories, of the transport of radioactive materials within containments. The CORRAL code output is the quantity of each of 54 biologically significant isotopes released to the environment as a result of a given accident sequence, as indicated in Appendix VI.

Many of the accident sequences involve similarity in core melting, similarity in radioactivity removal processes, and the same containment failure mode. This permitted classification of accident sequences into a number of different types called release categories. Thus, the releases produced by core melt are characterized by several different categories, each involving a particular composition, timing and release point.

The work outlined above provided the information for composite histograms of the type shown in Figure 4-2, that represent the probability and magnitude of the radioactive releases associated with each consequence category.

EXERCISES

9.1 Suppose in the hierarchical example of Figure 9.1 we were given a new item of data D^{412}, equally as diagnostic about I^{41} as D^{411}. How does this new evidence change the assessed probability of H?

9.2 The logarithm of the likelihood ratio has many attractions in bayesian decision analysis. Suggest some of these and criticize its deficiencies.

9.3 The following deductive branch of a hierarchical analysis was assessed:

	H_1	H_2	H_3
I^1	0.55	0.95	0.15
$\bar{I}^1$	0.45	0.05	0.85

	I^1	$\bar{I}^1$
I^{11}	0.5	0.15
$\bar{I}^{11}$	0.5	0.85

	I^{11}	$\bar{I}^{11}$
D^{111}	10	7

The prior probabilities for the three hypotheses were 0.1, 0.1, and 0.8. What are their posterior probabilities after the hierarchical analysis of this branch?

9.4 A person may or may not suffer from disease D. There are three common symptoms for D, namely, S_1, S_2, and S_3. The likelihoods of these symptoms are:

	D	$\bar{D}$
S_1	0.6	0.2
S_2	0.3	0.15
S_3	0.1	0.65

Each of these symptoms can be observed by three tests, namely, blood, urine, and radiology. Let B_i, U_i, and R_i denote the event of positive indication of symptom i on each of these. The likelihoods of these tests are:

	S_1	S_2	S_3
B_1	0.95	0.05	0.05
B_2	0.01	0.90	0.01
B_3	0.02	0.01	0.90
U_1	0.70	0.05	0.05
U_2	0.05	0.70	0.20
U_3	0.10	0.10	0.60
R_1	0.80	0.05	0.05
R_2	0.05	0.80	0.20
R_3	0.10	0.10	0.65

Which is the most diagnostic test? If the prior probability of D is 0.001 and all three tests indicated that only symptom 1 was present, what is the posterior probability of D?

9.5 Compare and contrast the hierarchical and fault tree decompositions. What are the essential similarities and differences?

9.6 Criticize the fault tree decomposition in the reactor safety study from the point of view of calibration.

9.7 The following two paragraphs have been extracted from the *Executive Summary* to the reactor safety study referenced above.

These results showed that the probability of an accident resulting in 10 or more fatalities is predicted to be about 1 in 3,000,000 per plant per year. The probability of 100 or more fatalities is predicted to be about 1 in 10,000,000, and for 1000 or more 1 in 100,000,000. The largest value reported in the study was 3300 fatalities, with a probability of about one in a billion.

If a group of 100 similar plants are considered, then the chance of an accident causing 10 or more fatalities is 1 in 30,000 per year. For accidents involving 1000 or more fatalities the number is 1 in 1,000,000 per year. Interestingly, this value coincides with the probability that a meteor would strike a U.S. population center and cause 1000 fatalities. [p. 9]

Discuss the statistical assumptions involved in the calculations of the second paragraph in relation to those of the first. Is the second paragraph a reasonable conclusion?

9.8 Discuss the use of tree representations and models as a convenient form of decomposition and compare it with any other style of modeling that you can think of.

REFERENCES

Barclay, S., et al. (1977): *Handbook for Decision Analysis*, Defence Advanced Research Projects Agency, 1400 Wilson Blvd., Arlington, Va. 22209.

U.S. Nuclear Regulatory Commission (1975): "Reactor Safety Study," WASH-1400 NUREG-75/014.

ANALYSIS OF MULTIPLE-STAGE PROBLEMS

10.1 DECISION TREE STRUCTURE

A large number of complex decision problems do not fit nicely into the single-stage model. Often it is not sufficient to analyze a problem solely in terms of the currently available set of actions and their *immediate* consequences. In the longer term, actions taken now may preclude or initiate other opportunities or restrictions in the future. Thus, many important strategic analyses require us not only to analyze now their immediate consequences, but also to anticipate their implications for future options, tactical flexibility, and the incorporation of more information. The best course of action may be the one which, in a more myopic analysis, appears to take a short-term loss. Essentially, our decision analysis must now incorporate a sequence of decisions and outcomes. Clearly, the single-stage payoff matrix does not capture this multiple-stage feature at all. A diagrammatic procedure that models the multiple-stage feature very effectively is the *decision tree*. This has been an important technique in decision analysis, possibly surpassing the expected utility criterion and bayesian inference as the most salient characteristic. To many people, decision analysis is the decision tree model.

We have seen a treelike decomposition in the previous section on hierarchical inference. There we observed a branching representation of causal factors associated with inference upon a particular variable (a country's nuclear capability). In decision tree analysis we again have a branching representation, but here it represents the chronological sequence of the various decision-outcome developments that can be foreseen. Decision trees are built up as a connection of essentially two fundamental entities, decision nodes and outcome nodes.

Decision nodes, Figure 10.1, are conventionally represented by a square box and indicate that subsequent nodes connected to this box can be reached according

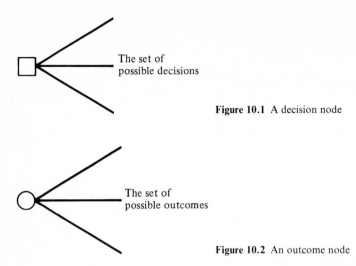

The set of
possible decisions

Figure 10.1 A decision node

The set of
possible outcomes

Figure 10.2 An outcome node

to a deterministic choice on the part of the decision maker at this point. The set of branches or paths emanating from a decision node indicate the distinct courses of action open to the decision maker at this point. Each of these branches leads to an uncertain prospect (an outcome node), a further decision (a decision node), or a certain payoff (a terminal value). The branches should represent mutually exclusive and collectively exhaustive courses of action at that point. This ensures that the decision node represents the complete set of distinctly different options available.

Outcome nodes, Figure 10.2, are conventionally represented by circles and indicate that the set of subsequent nodes connected to this circle will be reached according to some probabilistic process over which the decision maker has no control (although there will typically be some belief upon which are more or less likely than others). This set of subsequent nodes will thus represent the set of possible outcomes and will be either future decisions or outcomes, or a final terminal payoff. Again, the branches should be mutually exclusive and collectively exhaustive, this time to ensure that a valid subjective probability distribution can be assigned upon them.

The general decision model will consist of alternating decisions and outcomes, finally terminating in a net payoff evaluation for each possible path through the tree. To see how a research and development decision process can be represented in terms of connected decision and outcome nodes, consider the case of a textile company faced in 1963 with the decision whether or not to develop a polyester suitable for reinforcing automobile tires. Figure 10.3 displays a decision tree for this problem.

Any sensible decision problem will start with a decision node. (Otherwise there is no pressing need for a decision.) If the company decides to go ahead with developing a polyester reinforcement for automobile tires, the crucial issue is whether or not the safety image of the polyester will be superior or inferior to that

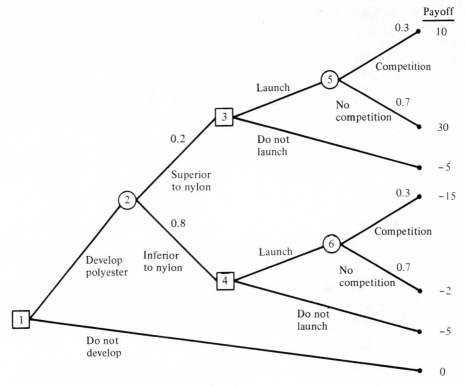

Figure 10.3 Decision tree for the polyester tire decision

of the existing nylon reinforcement. These are the two uncertain outcomes of interest which are shown emanating from outcome node 2. Associated with these two outcomes are subjectively assessed probabilities of 0.2 and 0.8.

Having made the initial decision to develop the polyester, and dependent upon the uncertain outcome at node 2, the company will have to face the launch or scrap decision either at node 3 (if the product is better than nylon) or at node 4 (if the developed product is worse than nylon).

If the company goes ahead with the launch, its success in the market depends mainly upon whether research elsewhere on Nylon 44 will yield a marketable product before 1975. This would be a very strong competitor to the polyester reinforced tire, but the probability of such a breakthrough was assessed as 0.3. Nodes 5 and 6 take account of the different payoffs which would accrue dependent upon the appearance of the Nylon 44 competition.

The terminal net payoffs for each possible sequence of decisions and uncertain outcomes are grouped together in a column on the right-hand side. Thus, every path through the tree, which represents a distinctly different scenario, ends in a terminal evaluation. In a sense, therefore, the final column displays the set of ultimate scenarios which the decision maker envisages could evolve in the resolution of the situation.

The basic rules of the decision tree representation are thus quite intuitive:

1. A terminal evaluation date for the decision problem is selected.

Clearly, all strategies should be evaluated at the same point in time; otherwise the analysis would be ignoring the time value of money.

2. The causal sequence of decision and outcome nodes unfolds as a branching process in chronological order from a single decision node.

Conventionally the tree unfolds from left to right, although sometimes from top to bottom. Note that because the tree seeks to display all the distinctly different ways in which the situation could be resolved, branches should unfold in the strict sense of never coalescing. In other words, there must be only one branch entering any node. For example, in considering whether to take an umbrella to a picnic tomorrow, the decision tree representation should be as shown in Figure 10.4, not as in Figure 10.5. Even though in Figure 10.4 node 3 just duplicates node 2, the costs involved in reaching nodes 2 and 3 are different, and thus they give rise to ultimately different terminal payoffs. Therefore, they must be kept separate in the analysis.

The chronological aspect of the unfolding refers to the order in which the decision maker *learns* about the outcomes and must make decisions. This may not be the same as a more objective (scientific) index of their timing. For example, look at Figure 10.6. This is part of a decision tree to analyze an oil exploration decision. Node 1 represents the outcome of whether the seismic test is positive or negative, and in this branch the decision maker knows the outcome before

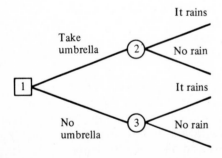

Figure 10.4 Correct tree for umbrella problem

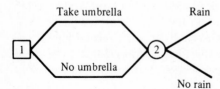

Figure 10.5 Incorrect tree for umbrella problem

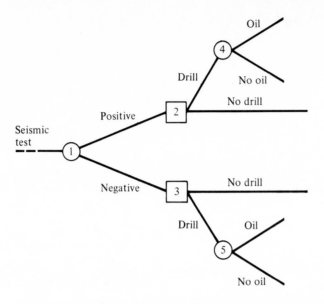

Figure 10.6 Branch of an oil exploration decision tree

making the drilling decision (nodes 2 and 3). Thereafter, the oil bearing status is ultimately revealed (nodes 4 and 5). This branch represents the decision maker's learning and decision sequence. However, a more scientific description would be to say that whether or not the geological structure is oil bearing determines to a large extent the seismic test result. A more accurate causal explanation of the situation would put an oil/no oil outcome node in front of node 1. But this would not represent the decision maker's perspective. Again we see a methodological distinction between the pragmatism of decision analysis and the verisimilitude of scientific explanation. It cannot be emphasized too much to beginners in decision tree analysis that *outcome nodes preceding a decision node represent uncertainties that will be resolved by the time of that decision.*

3. Branches emanating from either a decision or an outcome node must be mutually exclusive and collectively exhaustive.

We have discussed this already. It ensures that all probability distributions are valid and that the tree unfolds a complete and distinctly different set of paths by which the situation could be resolved.

A decision tree can always be represented in terms of alternating decision and chance nodes. Figure 10.7 shows how a sequence of decision nodes can be re-expressed using one decision node. Similarly, Figure 10.8 shows how a sequence of outcome nodes implies a set of outcomes from one chance node. However, sequences of decision nodes are often used in decision trees where it makes the logical pattern of decision, particularly over time, more evident. Similarly, and more often,

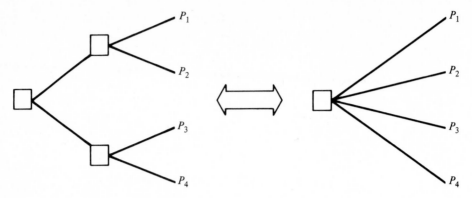

Figure 10.7 A series of decision nodes

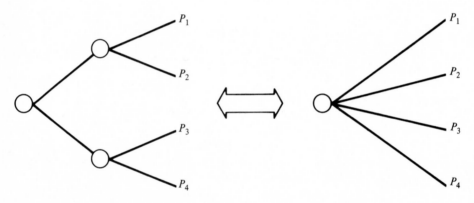

Figure 10.8 A series of outcome nodes

sequences of outcome nodes can exemplify the causal relationships between outcomes and can thereby aid the assessment of compound probabilities.

Note that where there is a sequence of adjacent outcome nodes, their actual order is sometimes arbitrary. Since no decision node intervenes in such a sequence, whether one outcome or another is conceived as occurring first makes no difference to the decision-making perspective. This flexibility to interchange adjacent outcome nodes sometimes facilitates the assessment of probabilities and checking for consistency.

10.2 DECISION TREE ANALYSIS

Recall Figure 10.3 and our polyester tire decision. The decision tree representation displays the nature of the problem in terms of the sequence of decisions and outcomes, the relevant probabilities, and the terminal payoff evaluations. Sometimes just this structural representation is a sufficient vehicle for clarifying the decision maker's reasoning without further analysis. If this is not the case, we should formally incorporate a decision-making criterion to choose the most preferable course of action at decision node 1. Thus, in analyzing the decision tree, we need to identify the branch of the highest certainty equivalent emanating from node 1. Note that this is the entire purpose of the decision tree: to identify the best decision now in anticipation of acting optimally in the future. It is not seeking to define an unalterable plan of future actions or to make commitments before necessary. Things may change by then; new information and options may become available. However, at this moment in time the decision maker, using the best current information, must anticipate future actions in order to decide what best to do now. Hence, in our decision tree the decision maker must anticipate what he or she will do at nodes 3 and 4 before being able to evaluate the certainty equivalent of taking the development option. Thus, the analysis of decision trees works backward from the future to the present.

Suppose that our decision maker is risk-neutral on this company decision. Then analyzing the polyester tire decision according to the expected money value criterion, we first replace nodes 5 and 6 by their certainty equivalents (EMVs):

$$\text{EMV(node 5)} = 0.3 \times 10 + 0.7 \times 30 = 24$$

$$\text{EMV(node 6)} = 0.3 \times (-15) + 0.7 \times (-2) = -5.9$$

For decision nodes 3 and 4, we select the maximum certainty equivalents, which are 24 and -5, respectively, and these become the effective payoffs for chance node 2:

$$\text{EMV(node 2)} = 0.2 \times 24 + 0.8 \times (-5) = 0.8$$

As the payoff for doing nothing has been evaluated at zero, on expected money value grounds, it would be preferable to go ahead with the development, but reserve the option to drop out if the developed product did not prove a technical success.

To summarize, we work backward from the terminal payoffs, replacing each outcome node by its certainty equivalent and each decision node by the maximum certainty equivalent that is open to choice at that stage. The options of lower certainty equivalents are dominated, and these branches are indicated closed by vertical "gates," effectively closing off various paths from further consideration. Figure 10.9 demonstrates this analysis.

If the company were not risk-neutral, then the expected money value criterion would be inappropriate, and an expected utility analysis would be necessary. Let us suppose that the utility function over the payoff domain had been obtained from the board of directors, as illustrated in Figure 10.10. This is clearly a risk-averse utility curve. Replacing the terminal payoff values in the decision tree of Figure 10.9 by the utilities, the expected utility analysis of the problem is shown in Figure 10.11. The optimal action is now not to launch because the risk aversion

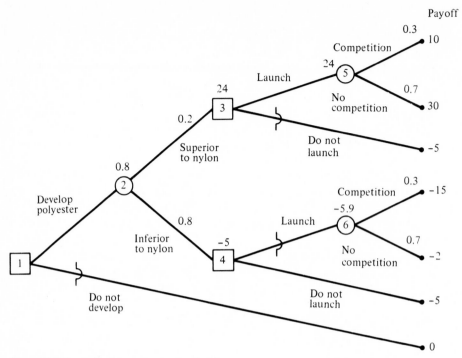

Figure 10.9 Analysis of the polyester tire decision

implicit in the utility function diminishes the certainty equivalent of the more risky launch option.

Clearly, the procedure of decision tree decomposition and analysis can be applied in a similar manner to far more complicated multiple-stage problems. Usually the analysis proceeds in an iterative and interactive process. The full tree should not be sought right from the outset, but simpler schematic trees should

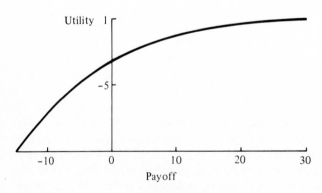

Figure 10.10 Utility function for tire company

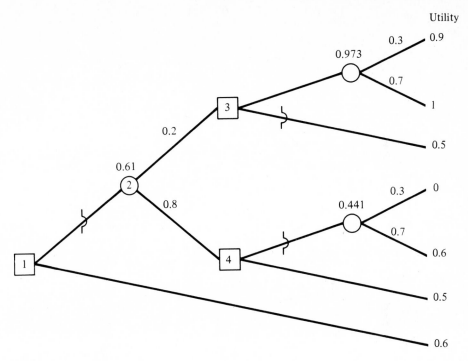

Utility

Figure 10.11 Expected utility analysis of polyester tire

gradually be embellished to the point at which a final tree captures the requisite amount of detail to provide reliable insights into the problem without becoming overly elaborated and confusing in its intricacy. Likewise, the interactive nature of decision tree analysis can render it useful as a strategic planning tool. Hypothetical considerations can readily be given to what might happen if particular outcome and decision nodes could be moved around. This can sometimes help suggest new options or strategic directions for change. As we have noted in the earliest chapters in this text, the analysis itself is important more as a means of investigating possibilities rather than to deduce the "correct" course of action. The generation of insights and the facility to communicate and open up the analysis of the problem to wider discussion are perhaps the greatest merits of the approach. To this end, tidy schematic forms of the decision tree, as in the following example, are common summary presentations of a decision analysis.

Example: An overseas investment decision Reproduced below is part of some promotional material from the Stanford Research Institute International decision analysis consulting group. It describes a case history of an application of the decision analysis approach to a foreign investment decision The author is grateful to Syed Shariq and SRI International for permission to use this material in its original form.

While each international risk-assessment analysis is different, we have found that there are often similarities in the structure and key parameters. A recently completed analysis exemplifies the application of decision analysis to a decision involving political uncertainties. Our client was contemplating a major ($200 million) new plant investment. Their business was resource-based; therefore, their profitability was heavily dependent on obtaining cheap, secure resource supplies. SRI was retained because the client's currently held contracts were due to expire, and new domestic contracts could only be obtained at much higher prices. The client was considering several options including renewing its domestic contracts, constructing a new plant in a foreign country, or divesting itself of that particular business area entirely. The domestic option was further complicated by uncertainty as to whether to construct new, more efficient plants or to continue operating the older facilities.

The foreign options were being seriously considered because raw materials in these areas were attractively priced. However, senior management was very concerned about these options because several of the options were perceived as being volatile, particularly with respect to long-term supply security. Assimilating the political uncertainty surrounding each of the foreign options was therefore essential.

Decision Analysis Process Overview

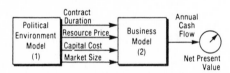

SRI's analysis proceeded incrementally. Working with the client's corporate staff and other SRI specialists, we developed a political and economic perspective for the regions in question. These perspectives were then translated into forecasts of business variables that were relevant to the venture.

Political Environment Model (1) Details

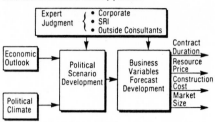

We then developed a simple model composed of the business variables, technical and financial factors to generate cash flows for each venture.

Business Model (2) Details

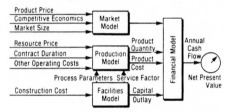

Using most likely values for all the variables, the model results below showed that one particular foreign option was more lucrative than the other alternatives:

Initial Net Present Value Calculations

Location Options	Net Present Value (Millions of Dollars)
Foreign Country 1	532
Foreign Country 2	430
Domestic Option	
• Buy resource at market price	150
• Become a resource producer	350

10.3 VALUE OF INFORMATION IN MULTIPLE-STAGE PROBLEMS

We have suggested that, for coherence, a decision maker should make use of all the information available and relevant to the problem in his or her decision analysis. Thus, if we have the simple decision prolem of either launching a test market of a new product or abandoning the project, as displayed in Figure 10.12, then the expected value of launching assumes that all the available information on the chance of success was embodied in the assessed probability of 0.3.

On expected value grounds, the decision analysis suggests that it would be

Sensitivity analyses were subsequently performed as an integral part of the analytical process and key variables identified. The uncertainty on the key factors was then evaluated and incorporated into the business model. Distributions on profit and loss were then calculated and displayed to give explicit representations of the business risk of each decision alternative:

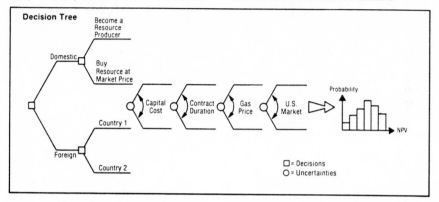

Decision Tree

This preliminary analysis showed that while Foreign Country 1 had large profit opportunities, it also posed a potential for significant loss. Unless some means for reducing the business risk could be found, the less attractive but safer alternative of Foreign Country 2 would be favored. Contrary to expectations, the domestic options were not as risk-free as the Foreign Country 2 option. This result was at first surprising, but proved to be a valuable insight.

Various risk reduction strategies were easily evaluated because the analytical framework was already developed. Scenarios resulting in negative profit outcomes were reexamined under each of the three generic risk-reduction strategies: **insurance, intelligence,** and **influence.**

The results of the analysis were presented to the Board of Directors, the assumptions made in the analysis were explicitly presented, and "What if" questions from the board were easily answered by the project team. After a considerable debate about the company's risk-return profile the company decided to locate the plant in Foreign Country 2, even though the expected profit levels were less than in Foreign Country 1.

The cost of SRI assistance was a small fraction of the total project investment proposed. ☐

Risk-return Trade-offs

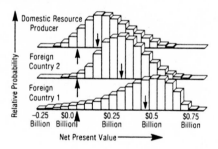

---

better to abandon the project. Before doing so, however, suppose it was suggested that it may be worth finding out more about the chance of success through the work of a market research agency.

In order to get first an upper bound on the value of additional information, it is worth evaluating the decision problem under the assumption that a perfect predictor were available. The decision tree for this hypothetical situation is shown in Figure 10.13.

If the perfect predictor indicates that the new product will be a success, then we will clearly launch, whereas if we know it will fail, the optimal decision is to abandon the project. Note that the probability of our perfect predictor indicating

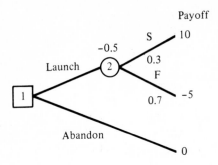

Figure 10.12 A new product decision

success is the same as our probability of the overall success of the product, that is, 0.3, since the two events are perfectly correlated. Thus, the optimal decision is to go ahead with using the perfect predictor, which has an expected value of 3.

The difference between the expected value with available information (EVWAI) and the expected value with a perfect predictor (EVWPP) is known as the expected value of a perfect predictor (EVOPP), that is,

$$EVOPP = EVWPP - EVWAI$$

which in this case equals 3.

Note that adopting a strategy of using a perfect predictor will result in a zero opportunity loss or regret, since the ideal decision will be taken for the indicated, and therefore actual, outcome. Thus, it is easy to see that for any decision strategy,

$$EVWPP = EV + EOL$$

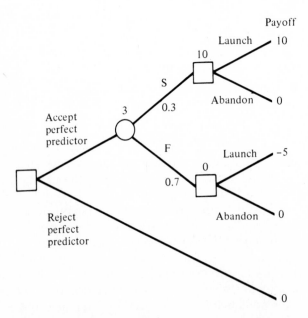

Figure 10.13 New product decision with a perfect predictor

Furthermore, the expected opportunity loss for the optimal strategy also equals EVOPP, that is,

$$EVOPP = \min_{a_i} \{EOL(a_i)\}$$

Thus, EVOPP is an upper bound on the value of information. No information can be better, and therefore can be worth more, than a perfect predictor. If the market research agency which is being considered to run a sample for estimating the new product's success, quotes a cost greater than 3, it can be dismissed at the outset for being not worthwhile. In practice, very rarely do we have access to a perfect predictor, but nevertheless the concept is very useful for providing an upper bound.

The expected value with imperfect predictor (EVWIP) and also the expected value of an imperfect predictor (EVOIP) are evaluated in an analogous way:

$$EVOIP = EVWIP - EVWAI$$

EVWIP could be evaluated from a decision tree, as in Figure 10.14, provided the appropriate probabilities are known. It is assumed, for simplicity of exposition, that the market research agency will give either a good or a bad indication and that it has made a charge of 2 for the service.

The decision to launch the new product will be made after knowing the market research report. Thus the probabilities of success or failure will be conditional probabilities, namely, $p(S|G)$ and $p(F|G)$ or $p(S|B)$. The actual probabilities of being in the position of having observed the data are also required, namely $p(G)$ and $p(B)$.

We have our original probabilities, prior to observing the market research data, of

$$p(S) = 0.3$$
$$p(F) = 0.7$$

Let us also suppose that the agency is willing to give reliability assessments on its estimates, which are in the form of

$$p(G|S) = 0.9$$
$$p(B|F) = 0.8$$

In other words, if the true state is S, then the market research agency has a probability of 0.9 of recording G. Likewise, if the true state is F, then there is a 0.8 probability of recording B.

Thus, from Bayes' theorem we have

$$p(S|G) = 0.659$$
$$p(S|B) = 0.051$$
$$p(F|G) = 0.341$$
$$p(F|B) = 0.949$$

and

$$p(G) = 0.41$$
$$p(B) = 0.59$$

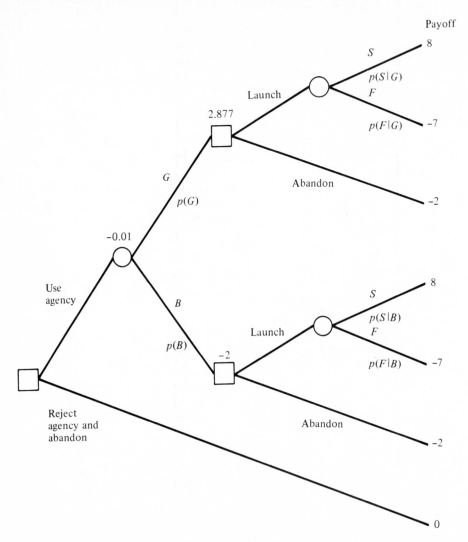

Figure 10.14 New product decision with an imperfect predictor

which are the required probabilities. Analysis of the decision tree with these probabilities gives us an EVWIP of -0.01, which is just slightly worse than abandoning. If the market research agency could reduce its fee by 1 percent, then it would be worthwhile on expected value grounds to go ahead with the market research.

Notice that if we have to use an expected utility analysis, the calculation of the value of information is not nearly so easy. We can compute an expected utility with available information (EUWAI) in the usual way, and it is also quite straightforward to compute the analogous EUWIP. The problem is that the difference EUWIP − EUWAI is the number in utility units which is not readily convertible back to money. Usually, when a value of information has to be computed and the decision maker is not risk-neutral, it has to be done by a trial and error search procedure. A value for the cost of information is assumed and subtracted from all the terminal values, and an EUWIP is computed. This assumed value is adjusted up or down until EUWIP = EUWAI. This is then the most that it is worth paying for the information, and therefore its value.

The value of information calculation is in any case somewhat contrived. It assumes in very formal terms that we are able to assess all that we might learn if we acquire new information. This is quite a modeling conceit. Information often provides many unanticipated qualitative insights which cannot be embodied in the type of calculations indicated above. Thus, in a sense the value of information calculations underestimates true value. On the other hand, the perfect predictor concept can often be a useful safeguard against spending needlessly too much upon new information.

10.4 DISCRETIZATION OF CONTINUOUS OUTCOME VARIABLES

It is quite common to have outcome variables modeled and assessed as continuous variables in a decision analysis. For example, in the new product decision of the previous section, we may choose not to model the market share as success or failure, as in Figure 10.12, but as a continuous variable s ($0 < s < 1$). Figure 10.15 demonstrates this; the notation used here for a continuous outcome node is quite common, though far from universal (compare the SRI example in Section 10.2). The outcome variable s may have been assessed subjectively as in Figure 10.16. While this seems to represent a more realistic model, it does pose a problem for decision tree analysis. The decision tree model, with its separate branches, is firmly designed to display all the distinctly different options and outcomes. But as soon as a continuous variable is introduced, in theory there is an infinite number of branches introduced to the model.

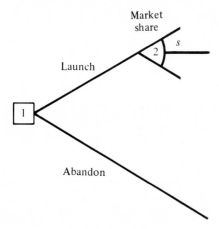

Figure 10.15 New product decision with continuous outcome

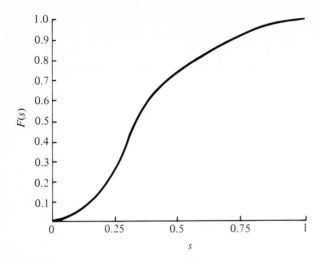

Figure 10.16 Cumulative distribution of s

In a few situations this can be handled analytically by calculus. Thus, if the continuous outcome node is the final node in a branch (as in Figure 10.15), its expected utility can be computed as

$$\text{EU(node 2)} = \int_0^1 U(s)f(s)\,ds$$

where $U(s)$ = utility function over s

$\quad\quad f(s)$ = probability density function over s

Unless $f(s)$ and $U(s)$ are convenient mathematical functions, the above integration will have to be done by an approximate numerical technique, in which case its results will be similar to that of *discretizing* the continuous variable from the outset. Thus, a more common general way of dealing with continuous nodes is to approximate them systematically by discrete outcome nodes. Figure 10.17 indicates a fourfold discretization of s. Clearly, the first problem is deciding upon the number of branches. A fourfold approximation may not be sufficiently precise for the analysis. On the other hand, if there are several such nodes, having more than four branches on each can quickly render the tree unmanageable in its total size.

The second, possibly more intricate, problem is to decide upon the values of s_1, s_2, s_3, and s_4, which are clearly point approximations to intervals on the s scale. One particularly convenient scheme, which is usually quite reliable, is to split the variable up into four equally likely intervals and take s_1, s_2, s_3, and s_4 to be the medians of each of these intervals. Thus, s_1 would be the 12.5 percent fractile, s_2 the 37.5 percent fractile, s_3 the 62.5 percent fractile, and s_4 the 87.5 percent fractile. Reading these off from Figure 10.16 gives us the discretized version of Figure 10.15, namely, Figure 10.18. Notice that this quartile method of

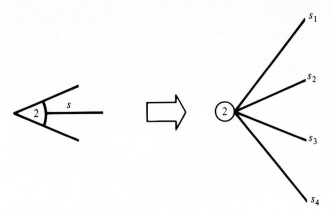

Figure 10.17 Fourfold discretization

discretization yields four branches of equal probability. This simplifies subsequent analysis and sometimes allows dominance reasoning to facilitate "pruning" of inferior options.

There are many other ways of discretization. All that is really required is a good histogram approximation to the continuous probability distribution. Of course, if a discrete assessment had been done in the first place, this particular technical problem would not have arisen. Nevertheless, continuous outcomes are

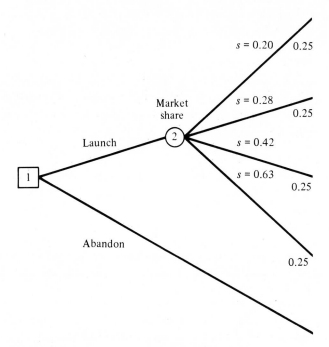

Figure 10.18 New product decision discretized

often modeled at the assessment stage because they may be more realistic and intuitive, and thereby provide more reliable and insightful assessments. Furthermore, they can be *simulated* quite readily in circumstances where simulation is an appropriate technique for analysis.

10.5 SIMULATION OF CHAINS OF OUTCOME NODES

Sometimes we find ourselves in the position of having to analyze quite large-scale decision models, which often involve very long chains of outcomes nodes. In such cases, the usual decision tree approach of enumerating all the discrete branches of the total tree can become enormously demanding in computation. For example, if we had just a sequence of eight outcome nodes, each with four branches, this would give a total of 2^{16} (approximately 65,000) distinct branches. Some decision trees have hundreds of nodes. There are three possible ways of analyzing chains of outcomes: (1) complete enumeration of all discrete branches, (2) mathematical analysis, and (3) simulation.

The first of these, complete enumeration, is usually quite feasible on high-powered computers, but can be very expensive. Mathematical analysis rarely works in large problems, although a few results (such as the sum of independent normally distributed variables being also normally distributed) can sometimes help to trim the size of the problem. Simulation, however, is very commonly used. In essence, what the simulation approach seeks to do is to generate from the decision model a random artificial statistical sample of values for the chain of outcomes. In other words, it seeks to simulate representative values for the way the process might occur. These are then treated as providing a frequency distribution of outcomes just like regular statistical sampling. Thus, when we wish to assess the voting behavior of an electorate, we do not enumerate every outcome (interview each person), but we estimate it reliably from a random sample. The same idea is applied to estimating the total effect of a large sequence of outcomes in a decision model. We estimate it by a random sampling procedure. Of course, the sampling must be done artificially because the real situation does not lend itself to experimentation. However, if our decision model is sufficiently realistic, it is a surrogate for the actual process and can therefore provide a basis for multiple experiments. Engineers take this type of approach regularly to perform experiments upon models which cannot be done in reality. The usefulness of such simulations depends upon the quality of the model and the number of experiments.

An example should make this clearer. Suppose that Figure 10.19 represents a decomposition of outcomes affecting the revenue of the new product launch decision that we have been considering in previous sections. Three variables, market sales, market share, and price, were assumed to be considered sufficient to determine revenue. Total market sales m was modeled continuously between 0 and 10,000, as illustrated in Figure 10.20. Market share s was modeled continuously, as shown earlier in Figure 10.16, and price p was modeled discretely into

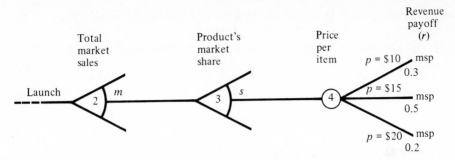

Figure 10.19 Outcome sequence for new product launch

three outcomes, namely, \$10, \$15, and \$20. Evidently total revenue r is just the product of these three variables, $r = msp$.

We could analyze the branch quite nicely, by discretization but for exposition here we shall simulate a frequency distribution for r. Let us suppose that we can sample randomly a representative value for m, call it m_1; similarly for s, namely, s_1, and also for p, namely, p_1. Then we would have one randomly selected value $r_1 (= m_1 s_1 p_1)$ from the distribution of r. If we repeat this 100 times, we will be able to estimate the true distribution of r by the frequency histogram constructed from the simulated sample $(r_1, r_2, \ldots, r_{100})$. The problem is in being able to sample random values of m, s, and p. Now recall what it means to sample properly a random variable. Your sample of values for m $(m_1, m_2, \ldots, m_{100})$ should be a sequence that could occur quite naturally by chance from a process with distribution function $F(m)$. Likewise for s and p. Therefore, we need procedures for gener-

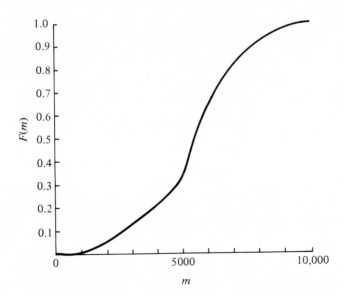

Figure 10.20 Cumulative distribution of m

ating random values from prespecified continuous and discrete probability distributions.

To do this, we make use of a table of random digits, such as, Table 4 in the Appendix. All of the major computing facilities have a subroutine that will generate sequences of random numbers. In Basic the function RND(1) will give a random number between 0 and 1. [Thus, INT*10*RND(1) will give a random digit from 0 to 9.] Repeated calling on a random number generator can give us a long sequence of random variables uniformly distributed between 0 and 1. Let us refer to such a random number as n.

Incidentally it is not a trivial algorithmic or even philosophical task to design a random number generator. Any process which generates a number according to some deterministic program can hardly be said to be random. In fact, most of the random number generators produce a sequence of numbers which behaves as if it were random, but after very many samplings will begin to repeat itself. Thus, these sequences are more accurately referred to as pseudo random numbers, although the cycle length is sufficiently large for nearly all practical purposes.

Thus, our problem now is to make use of the random sequence of a uniform variable, n, to produce random sequences of variables with arbitrary continuous and discrete probability distributions.

Sampling from a continuous distribution In general if we have a continuous random variable x with cumulative distribution $F(x)$, then a sequence of values of x $(x_1, x_2, \ldots, x_{100})$ will give a sequence of values $(F(x_1), F(x_2), \ldots, F(x_{100}))$. This latter sequence of fractiles will, in fact, be a random sequence of numbers between 0 and 1, that is, values of n. It is not difficult to see this. Thus, the 1 percent fractile $F_{0.01}(x) = 0.01$ implies that 1 percent of the values of $F(x)$ are below $F_{0.01}(x)$. Likewise, the 2 percent fractile $F_{0.02}(x) = 0.02$ implies that 2 percent of the values of $F(x)$ are below $F_{0.02}(x)$. Thus, again 1 percent of the values of $F(x)$ lie between $F_{0.01}(x)$ and $F_{0.02}(x)$. Extending this argument shows that values of $F(x)$ occur evenly throughout the interval between 0 and 1.

We can take advantage of this property in reverse to generate a random sample of x. Pick a random number n and treat this as being $F(x)$. Then, using the cumulative distribution function, as in Figure 10.21, find the corresponding value of x. Using a whole sequence of n can therefore generate the appropriate representative random sequence of x.

Sampling from a discrete distribution This is more straightforward. For example, if we have assessed the probabilities 0.2, 0.5, and 0.3 to a three-outcome node giving outcomes A, B, and C, respectively, then given a random number n, we can simulate an outcome from this distribution simply by specifying that if

$$0 < n \leq 0.2 \qquad \text{then } A \text{ has occurred}$$
$$0.2 < n \leq 0.7 \qquad \text{then } B \text{ has occurred}$$
$$0.7 < n \leq 1 \qquad \text{then } C \text{ has occurred}$$

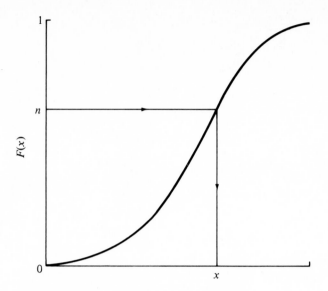

Figure 10.21 Sampling from a continuous distribution

Evidently, all that we are doing is to work from sections of the cumulative distribution function. This principle can be applied to any discrete distribution.

Having developed a way of sampling from outcome nodes, we can now sample whole chains of outcome nodes to estimate their composite distribution. Let us return to our new product launch decision and illustrate this procedure in full.

Simulation 1

$n_1 = 0.2271$ (Table 4) $m_1 = 3900$ (Figure 10.20)

$n_2 = 0.3025$ (Table 4) $s_1 = 0.26$ (Figure 10.16)

$n_3 = 0.3382$ (Table 4) $p_1 = \$15$ (Figure 10.19)

                                       $r_1 = \$15,210$

Simulation 2

$n_4 = 0.7870$ (Table 4) $m_2 = 6000$ (Figure 10.20)

$n_5 = 0.1697$ (Table 4) $s_2 = 0.20$ (Figure 10.16)

$n_6 = 0.3395$ (Table 4) $p_2 = \$15$ (Figure 10.19)

                                       $r_2 = \$18,000$

Simulation 3

$$n_7 = 0.6081 \text{ (Table 4)} \qquad m_3 = 5800 \text{ (Figure 10.20)}$$
$$n_8 = 0.3470 \text{ (Table 4)} \qquad s_3 = 0.27 \text{ (Figure 10.16)}$$
$$n_9 = 0.0432 \text{ (Table 4)} \qquad p_3 = \$15 \text{ (Figure 10.19)}$$
$$r_3 = \$23{,}490$$

Simulation 4

$$n_{10} = 0.4995 \text{ (Table 4)} \qquad m_4 = 5200 \text{ (Figure 10.20)}$$
$$n_{11} = 0.8246 \text{ (Table 4)} \qquad s_4 = 0.61 \text{ (Figure 10.16)}$$
$$n_{12} = 0.7825 \text{ (Table 4)} \qquad p_4 = \$15 \text{ (Figure 10.19)}$$
$$r_4 = \$47{,}580$$

Simulation 5

$$n_{13} = 0.6258 \text{ (Table 4)} \qquad m_5 = 5800 \text{ (Figure 10.20)}$$
$$n_{14} = 0.3235 \text{ (Table 4)} \qquad s_5 = 0.26 \text{ (Figure 10.16)}$$
$$n_{15} = 0.2525 \text{ (Table 4)} \qquad p_5 = \$10 \text{ (Figure 10.19)}$$
$$r_5 = \$15{,}080$$

We can continue on in this way. Five simulations is not many; 50 would probably be a minimum, and 500 ideal for this problem. However, based upon five simulations, we can estimate $\bar{r}$, the mean of r, as follows:

$$\bar{r} = \sum_{j=1}^{5} \frac{r_j}{5} = \$23{,}872$$

The cumulative frequency distribution can be constructed as shown in Figure 10.22. Again, in practice five points is too few, and this frequency distribution would become an increasingly better approximation to $F(r)$ the greater the number of simulations undertaken.

Simulation is thus a very convenient technique for analyzing chains of outcome nodes. It is easy to program on a computer, and its relative advantage over a full evaluation of all discrete branches in a tree generally becomes greater the larger the number of nodes in the problem. This is because the accuracy of a simulation is proportional to the number of complete simulations, whereas in the full enumeration, it depends upon the discretization at each node. Thus, adding a node does not increase the solution time of a simulation very much, but if the node is a fourfold discretization, it will increase the solution time of the enumerative method fourfold. Thus, simulation is a large-scale technique, and the larger the scale of the problem, relatively the more economical it becomes.

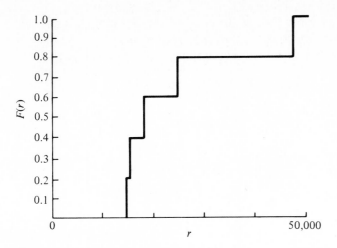

Figure 10.22 Cumulative frequency distribution of r

10.6 CLOSING COMMENTS

There are numerous variations on the decision tree representation of multiple-stage problems according to context. In some very well specified areas of application, such as production and quality control, a decision diagram may be closely interrelated with a planning flowchart for monitoring progress as well as making initial decisions. In less specified areas of personal decision making the decision diagram may be of a highly unconstrained form and appear more as a cognitive aid than a planning model. Some schematic representations of multiple-stage decisions obey few of the decision tree rules, yet have developed a usefulness in their own contexts.

That a decision tree is a model, and therefore a simplification of the real dimensions of the decision problem, should not be forgotten. In all but the most well specified circumstances, its purpose is to provide insights, not replace the personal responsibility of the decision maker. Mapping out *all* the causal links and implications of a multiple-stage decision problem can often transform the decision tree into a bushy labyrinth.

One of the main features of a good decision tree is the clarity of exposition it provides. Often several levels of the decision tree are constructed for analysis and communication. A highly detailed analysis may be undertaken on a computer, but presented in summary form as quite a simple decision tree. (Recall the SRI example given earlier.)

Even for the purposes of analysis, we try to work with the simplest tree possible. We prune dominated options and seek to model only to a "requisite" extent. Also, we often choose to model as events particular acts for which the decision maker does not wish to model more fully in terms of causality. Sometimes this "acts-as-events" feature creeps in almost unwittingly. For example, consider our previous new product decision, Figure 10.19, and look at the node reflecting price. Here we have chosen to model price as an uncertain outcome, even though it will be, at the time, set by our company in response to market considerations. Because whole scenarios of market conditions are not included in our model, we therefore treat price as a single outcome node. Brown (1975) gives a further discussion of this interconvertibility of acts and outcomes.

For further reading, exposition, and examples of decision trees, the texts by Brown et al. (1974), Holloway (1979), Lavalle (1978), Raiffa (1968), Schlaifer (1969), and Winkler (1972) are very useful. The studies included in the next chapter will provide further examples of the various structures that can be devised to model multiple-stage decision problems.

EXERCISES

Exercises 10.2 to 10.11 are reproduced from past Oxford University examination papers with permission.

10.1 Construct an example to show how it may be possible to completely analyze a decision tree decomposition of a problem using dominance criteria rather than decision criteria at the decision nodes.

10.2 A company has to decide whether or not to drill for oil in a particular place. There are three possible results of drilling: a high yield worth 10 units, a moderate yield worth 5 units, or no oil. The drilling operation costs 5 units. At similar places, 50, 30, and 20 percent of previous drillings have given high, moderate, or no yield, respectively. A seismic test is available which would indicate a good, fair, or bad prospect for the drilling. Past experience indicates the following probabilities for the results of the seismic test for the three different ultimate possible yields:

		Yield		
		High	Moderate	None
	Good	0.7	0.5	0.1
Results of test	Fair	0.2	0.2	0.3
	Bad	0.1	0.3	0.6

Find the best decision rule on the assumption that a test is made, and the maximum amount that it would be worth paying for such a test. If this is the actual cost of the test, what is the expected value of the potential well?

10.3 A company is deciding whether to launch or abandon a new product. The future profits if the product is a success amount to an estimated £10 million, compared with a loss of £5 million if it is a disaster. Abandoning the project at this moment in time has no implications for future cash flows, since all the costs have already been sunk in the project. The decision maker estimates that there is a 0.3 chance of the project being a success compared with 0.7 for a disaster. Should the decision maker launch or abandon the new product? What is the most he or she would pay for a perfect predictor?

Instead of launching the project nationally, a regional test market of the product could be undertaken. This would cost £1 million and would give some indication of the national market for the product. If the product were a success in the region, then £2 million would be recovered on the test, compared with nothing if it were a regional disaster. Past experience with this regional test market is such that there were regional successes 90 percent of those times in which the products were national successes and regional failures 80 percent of those times in which the national launches were failures. Should the decision maker go ahead with the test market?

10.4 A satirical magazine specializes in publishing embarrassing details of the private lives of eminent citizens. The editors are aware of a scandalous rumor about a prominent politician and wish to proceed with the story in a manner which maximizes expected net income. The risk of an expensive libel action cannot be ignored and the editors estimate that the effects of such an action will be a cost of £125,000 net if lost, taking into account possible fines, legal costs, effects on future sales, and so on, and zero if won. These costs, and the probability of losing, estimated to be 0.2, are, they believe, independent of whether or not the rumor is true. However, the probability of the politician suing does depend on whether the rumor is true, and they estimate that the probability of his taking legal action is 0.3 if the rumor is true and 0.9 if it is not. They currently estimate the probability of the rumor being true at 0.5.

They have three possible courses of action: (1) dropping the story, (2) publishing immediately, or (3) hiring a private detective to investigate the rumor further so that, after his report, they could take a decision on whether or not to publish. The private detective they have in mind would cost £10,000, and he is good but not infallible. The probability of his saying the rumor is true is 1.0 if indeed it is true and 0.2 if it is false. He will definitely answer in one direction or the other, but the probability of being sued depends only on whether the rumor is true or not.

They estimate extra net income (gross of any costs of legal activity) from increased circulation if they publish to be £50,000, and this would be independent of the truth of the story. What should they do? How much should they be prepared to pay for a report from an infallible private detective?

10.5 Manufacturers of a range of plastic components, pipes, guttering, etc., for the building industry estimate that they face a 20 percent drop in sales within three years unless they can expand or improve their current product line. Accordingly, the research manager has been given £12,000 extra in the annual budget and has ascertained that sales of piping can be greatly increased if a specified improvement in the strength and durability of current products can be achieved at reasonable cost. Research on piping is currently being undertaken by two teams whose approaches are entirely independent, with a view to achieving a definite result by the end of the current year.

The manager estimates the chances of success within the year as 50 percent for a group of chemists experimenting with a low-cost material which would improve the final product. His corresponding estimate for a group of engineers attempting to simplify an excessively costly production process by which piping of the required quality is already made is 60 percent.

With the extra funds the manager could expand the research teams. He can hire chemists at an additional cost (including nonsalary expenses) of £4000 per year and hire engineers for a similar cost of £6000 per year. He estimates that another chemist would reduce the chances of that team's failure to 40 percent, two extra would reduce it to 35 percent, and three extra to 30 percent. Another member of the engineering team would reduce that team's chance of failure to 30 percent, while two extra would reduce it to 25 percent.

Alternatively, he can second consultants from an associate company at an extra cost of £3000 per year each to explore fiber reinforcements of plastic pipes. A minimum-size team of two persons is estimated to have a 50 percent chance of success within the year, but this would be increased to 60 percent and 70 percent by a three or four person team.

Which new researchers should the manager hire, and what is the resulting chance of success? What is the expected value of perfect information?

10.6 The government has spent £1000 million on developing a new aircraft which is suitable for only one route. Unfortunately, the aircraft is rather noisy and is in danger of being refused landing rights on this route. There are two possible courses of action. The government can apply for rights now. Or it can commission further investment in an attempt to make the engines quieter before an application is submitted. There is no possibility of applying for rights more than once since if they are refused, the political situation will be such that the decision will not be reversed.

The research and development to make the engines quieter would cost £100 million, and the current estimate of the probability of success is 0.7.

Before embarking on this further project, the government would carry out a pilot project for £10 million. The report of the pilot project would indicate that, for £100 million, either the quiet engines are certain or they are unlikely. The engineers on the project are biased toward aircraft development, so the government estimates that even if the large project will fail to produce quieter engines, there is still a probability of 0.3 of the pilot project report saying that they are certain. If the larger project will in fact succeed, the pilot project is certain to indicate this. If the pilot project indicates that success is unlikely, then the government will not proceed with the main project and will apply for landing rights with the existing engines. If the pilot project report is favorable, the government will proceed with the larger project.

If quiet engines are successfully developed, landing rights are certain. If they are not developed, there is only a 50:50 chance of receiving rights. With either quiet or noisy engines the present value of operating profits on the route is £300 million.

What should the government do? What is the most it should pay to buy off the groups opposing granting of the rights so that the application with the noisy engines would be certain to succeed? What should the government pay (assuming that the opposition is not bought off) above the £10 million for a pilot project which would predict with complete accuracy what the outcome of the main project would be?

10.7 The marketing manager of a firm is considering the marketing of a newly developed product. He feels the current odds on its success are 4:1, and he has already commissioned a market survey at a cost of £90,000, which is currently in progress. If the product is ultimately to be a failure on the market, it is estimated that the survey will indicate this with probability $\frac{4}{5}$. However, there is an estimated $\frac{1}{10}$ chance of a spurious indication of nonmarketability. When the results of the first survey are available, he is considering a second smaller survey at a cost of £45,000, with a different statistical design, which has an estimated $\frac{2}{3}$ chance of correctly predicting nonmarketability when the first survey did, but an estimated $\frac{9}{10}$ chance when it did not. On the other hand, it has an estimated $\frac{1}{9}$ chance of spuriously indicating nonmarketability when the first survey did, but a $\frac{1}{12}$ chance when it did not. The company has invested £100,000 in the development of the product, and it is estimated that production and marketing costs will lead to a loss of £500,000 if the product is a failure. On the other hand, its success is thought to be worth £1 million in profit to the company. What policy should the marketing manager recommend to the directors on current information? Discuss briefly the usefulness of utilities in such situations.

10.8 The survey department of a ministry announces that a certain area of government land has property X. If the land does have property X, the probability of finding oil in marketable quantities is $\frac{9}{10}$, but if it does not, the probability is only $\frac{1}{10}$. This particular department has been wrong before, however, so the minister puts a probability of only $\frac{3}{4}$ on the survey department's announcement being correct.

The government has an immediate choice between three actions. It can sell the land for £300,000. It can drill itself at a cost of £400,000. It can commission a specialist consultant to do a test on the land at a cost of £20,000. The test can have two outcomes, positive or negative, and is such that the probability of a positive outcome is $\frac{9}{10}$ if X obtains and $\frac{3}{10}$ if X does not obtain. After the test the government will be able to drill or sell the land. The land can also be sold if drilling fails.

The selling price of the land if the government drills and fails is £100,000. The government knows that it cannot conceal the result of the specialist consultant's test and predicts that if the test is negative, the selling price will be only £100,000, but if the test is positive, the price will be £440,000.

The minister believes that the successful finding of oil is worth £1 million. What is the best policy if the government wishes to maximize expected monetary value? What is the most the government should pay for an envelope whose contents would reveal, to itself alone, whether or not the land had property X?

10.9 An electronic system consists of two principal components. Failure of either can cause failure of the system. An a priori estimate of their individual reliabilities is 0.5 and 0.6, respectively, as they come off the production line, but in assembly there is a 50 percent chance of causing a failure to either, independent of their individual reliabilities. Either component may be tested separately before assembly, at respective costs of £50 and £60, but there is then only a 0.6 and 0.8 chance, respectively, of finding a fault leading to system failure during a specified period of use. The assembled system can be tested at a cost of £120, and in this event any faults are detected with certainty. The system is installed in a piece of oceanographic equipment, and its subsequent failure during the period of use is estimated to cost £200 in data loss, inspection, and repair.

Use decision analysis to determine the optimal preinstallation testing procedure. How would a reestimate of failure cost at £300 modify your solution? (*Note*: "Reliability" is probability of working.)

10.10 A manufacturer is planning a production facility which involves the machining of rough castings. He intends to use a process which gives a probability of 0.9 that satisfactory results will be obtained from a perfect casting, but some of the castings contain flaws, and the probability of success from a flawed casting is only 0.2. A second, more expensive, process is also available for which the probabilities of producing satisfactory results are 0.95 and 0.3 for perfect and flawed castings, respectively. If the cost to the company of each scrap item produced is £15, how big must the difference in unit production costs be before the second process becomes uneconomic?

In order to try to reduce the cost of scrap, the castings may be inspected for flaws before machining. This process would cost £2.50 per unit inspected and is not perfect:

$$\begin{cases} \text{the probability of accepting a flawed casting is 0.10} \\ \text{the probability of rejecting a perfect casting is 0.02} \end{cases}$$

There are four options to consider — process 1 and process 2, each with and without preliminary inspection. For what values (if any) of P (the probability of a casting containing a flaw) is each option the most appropriate? You may wish to draw a graph.

(The unit cost of process 2 is £0.85 greater than that of process 1, and each casting rejected before machining costs £5.)

10.11 A company has an embryonic idea for a new type of aero engine. The successful development of the engine is much more likely if a recently developed substance has a certain property (call it property A). The managing director currently believes that the probability that this new substance has property A is $\frac{1}{2}$. He approaches the government for permission to go ahead with a project for developing the new engine. The government replies that permission will only be granted if the company's research department produces a positive test for property A. It costs £40 million to carry out this test. If the substance does have property A, the test will certainly be positive, but if it does not have property A, there is still a 1 in 5 chance that the test will be positive.

If the test result is positive, the managing director can send the idea to his main development department to turn it into an engine. The cost of this development program is estimated at £244 million. The test carried out by the research department is such that if the substance does not have property A but the test was positive, then the probability of successful development in the main department is $\frac{1}{10}$. On the other hand if property A does hold, the probability of successful development in this department is $\frac{9}{10}$. If development fails in the main department, the manager can send the idea for development to an expert problem-solving unit at an estimated cost of £180 million. If the main department failed to solve the problem, the expert unit has probability $\frac{1}{2}$ of solving it if A holds, but only $\frac{1}{20}$ if not.

If the estimated gain (excluding the costs described above) from successful development is £840 million and the firm wishes to maximize the expected money value (EMV), find its optimal strategy (assuming that it can give up at any stage without extra cost) and its expected money value.

10.12 A chemicals firm is considering the development of a new product. The major uncertainties are production cost C and market size X. C can be \$10, \$15, or \$20 per unit with probabilities 0.3, 0.3, and 0.4; X (in thousands) is assessed in Figure 10.23. If the firm develops this product, its net contribution N is given by

$$N = (40 - C)X - 100{,}000$$

Using a fivefold discrete approximation for X, construct the distribution function for N.

10.13 A new technology firm is attempting to evaluate the net contribution for a particular product according to the formula

$$C = M \cdot N - F$$

where C = net contribution

M = margin per unit sold

N = number of units sold

F = fixed costs for the product line

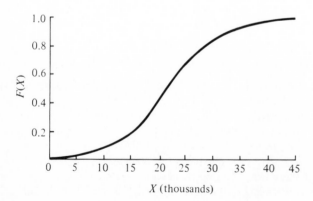

X (thousands)

Figure 10.23 Exercise 10.12

The distribution functions for F and M are given in Figures 10.24 and 10.25, respectively. The number of units sold depends upon whether a competitive product is launched upon the market next year. If this is the case, which management assesses to have a probability of 0.3, then N has the distribution function shown in Figure 10.26. Alternatively, if the firm keeps its monopoly, it will sell all that it can make, which is either 2000 or 3000 with probabilities 0.6 and 0.4, respectively. The random variables M, N, and F can be considered independent. Using Table 4 of the Appendix, simulate three Monte Carlo samplings of C and compute an estimate of their mean.

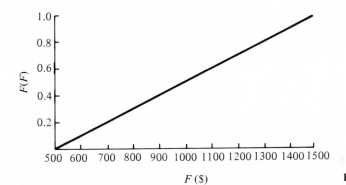

Figure 10.24 Exercise 10.13

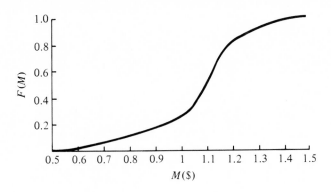

Figure 10.25 Exercise 10.13

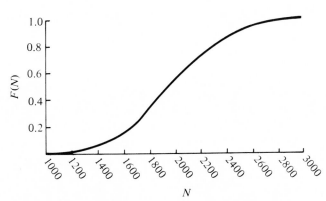

Figure 10.26 Exercise 10.13

10.14 You obtain the following information from a decision maker whom you are advising:

1. Given the choice

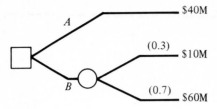

the decision maker *prefers A to B.*

2. Given the choice

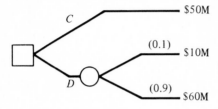

he is indifferent between *C* and *D.*

3. Given the choice

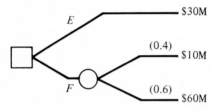

he is indifferent between *E* and *F.*

Use the information supplied to you by this decision maker to analyze the following decision tree with which he is faced. Indicate the best strategy for this decision maker to follow and his certainty equivalent for that strategy.

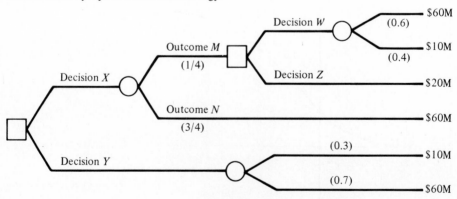

10.15 Consider again the bent coin wager (Exercise 1.2) and conduct a thorough decision analysis of the problem.

REFERENCES

Brown, R. V. (1975): "Modelling Subsequent Acts for Decision Analysis," Technical Report, Decisions and Designs, Inc., McLean, Va.

———, A. S. Kahr, and C. Peterson (1974): *Decision Analysis for the Manager*, Holt, Rinehart and Winston, New York.

Holloway, C. A. (1979): *Decision Making under Uncertainty*, Prentice-Hall, Englewood Cliffs, N.J.

Lavalle, I. H. (1978): *Fundamentals of Decision Analysis*, Holt, Rinehart and Winston, New York.

Raiffa, H. (1968): *Decision Analysis*, Addison-Wesley, Reading, Mass.

Schlaifer, R. O. (1969): *Analysis of Decision under Uncertainty*. McGraw-Hill, New York.

Winkler, R. L. (1972): *Introduction to Bayesian Inference and Decision*, Holt, Rinehart and Winston, New York.

ELEVEN

STUDIES IN DECISION MODELING

11.1 THE USE OF INFLUENCE DIAGRAMS IN STRUCTURING COMPLEX DECISION PROBLEMS

The following is reproduced with permission from the paper of the above title by Daniel Owen of Strategic Decisions Group, Menlo Park, and formerly of Stanford Research Institute International, which was published in the *Proceedings of the Second Lawrence Symposium on Systems and Decision Sciences*, 1978.

1 INTRODUCTION

The idea of an influence diagram was originally the result of a need to communicate with computers about the structure of decision problems. Under contract to the Defense Advanced Research Projects Agency, researchers in the Decision Analysis Group of SRI International were working to develop automated aids for decision analysis [1]. They hoped that the decision problem structure could be described to a computer that could partially automate the solution of the decision problem.

My experience with influence diagrams has been in two other areas. First, at SRI International our current use of influence diagrams is not for interacting with computers, but rather for communicating among people. One might describe our use of influence diagrams as participative modeling [2] rather than interactive modeling. Second, in my research at Stanford University, I have attempted to extend the notion of an influence diagram so that it can be used by the decision analyst to conceptualize the relationship between the probability distributions on different variables in a decision model.

After a brief review of influence diagram fundamentals in the next section, the remainder of this paper deals with the use of influence diagrams in participative modeling and the extension of the concept of influence.

2 INFLUENCE DIAGRAM FUNDAMENTALS

An influence between two random variables x and y is said to exist when the variables are not probabilistically independent:

> *Definition.* An influence exists between two random variables x and y if and only if $\{y|x, S\} \neq \{y|S\}$, where $\{y|S\}$ denotes the probability distribution for y, conditioned on the state of information S.

The existence of this influence can be shown diagrammatically by placing the names of the variables within circular nodes and connecting those two nodes with an arrow, such as

which may read "x influences y."

Using this definition, some rules for the manipulation of influence diagrams can be derived and are discussed thoroughly in Reference [1]. For example, the influence diagram of Figure 1a represents the expansion $\{x, y, z|S\} = \{z|x, y, S\} \{y|x, S\} \{x|S\}$. An alternative expansion, represented by Figure 1b, is $\{x, y, z|S\} = \{x|y, z, S\} \{z|y, S\} \{y|S\}$ and therefore, Figure 1b is an allowable rearrangement of the influences of Figure 1a. Comparing Figures 1b and 1c shows that the influence between y and z has been removed in the latter case, and $\{x, y, z|S\} = \{x|z, y, S\} \{z|S\}\{y|S\}$. Each influence diagram is an assertion of probabilistic dependence.

Since an influence diagram implies the existence of a joint probability distribution over the variables in the diagram, those variables must be precisely defined. Variables such as "quality," "market conditions," and "attractiveness" do not take on values that are identifiable events. Consequently, probability distributions cannot be defined over these variables, and they should not be included in an influence diagram.

Decision nodes are represented as squares on influence diagrams. An arrow from a decision node to a state variable node indicates that the probability distribution on the state variable depends on the setting of the decision variable. An arrow from a state variable to a decision variable means that the value of the uncertain state variable will be known at the time the decision is made.

a. $(x, y, z | S) = (z | x, y, S)(y | x, S)(x | S)$

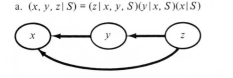

b. $(x, y, z | S) = (x | y, z, S)(z | y, S)(y | S)$

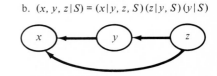

c. $(x, y, z | S) = (x | z, y, S)(z | S)(y | S)$

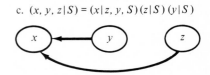

FIGURE 1 The correspondence between influence diagrams and assertions of probabilistic independence

3 USING INFLUENCE DIAGRAMS FOR PARTICIPATIVE MODELING

Three important difficulties arise in structuring a decision problem: unfamiliarity, complexity, and numerous participants. First, unfamiliarity means the analyst's initial unfamiliarity with the political, technical, and economic factors in a particular decision problem. The generality of the decision analysis methodology permits its application to decision problems regardless of the particular discipline or setting in which the problem occurs. Consequently, the decision analyst may be unfamiliar with the relationships of the problem variables. Secondly, complexity refers to the fact that decision models often involve a large number of random variables. Finally, if the problem is complex, there are likely to be many participants in structuring the problem. Even when there is a single decision maker, many experts may be consulted regarding the relationships of the variables. Moreover, several decision analysts may be involved.

An important property of the definition of the existence of influence given above is that it appears to coincide with the decision maker's intuitive use of the word influence. In our several experiences with influence diagrams at SRI International, we found that when a decision maker identified the existence of an influence, the variables later turned out to be probabilistically dependent. Furthermore, influences that were identified as being "strong" represented, roughly speaking, more probabilistic dependence than influences that were identified as "weak." Thus, influence diagrams provide a language through which those untrained in the modeling of complex probabilistic systems can describe their perception of the problem.

An influence diagram is constructed jointly with the decision maker by beginning with the value attributes and working backwards from there. As an example, suppose we have a client who must decide how much to expand his production facilities. If we seek the amount of additional capacity that maximizes the present value of the business, then the value attributes are the cash flows for each future year n. Since those future cash flows are uncertain, the cash flow for each year n is drawn on an influence diagram as a chance node (circle). We ask the decision maker what variable he would most like to know the value of in order to reduce his uncertainty about the cash flow in year n. If he answers "revenue in year n," he is asserting that {cash flow year $n|S$} $\neq$ {cash flow year $n|$revenue year n, S}.

We then ask him if, given the value of revenue for year n, there is another variable, the knowledge of which would further reduce his uncertainty about cash flow. His answer is that he would like to know his total costs for year n. In that case, he is asserting that {cash flow year $n|$revenue year n, S} $\neq$ {cash flow year $n|$revenue year n, costs year n, S}. These influences are shown in Figure 2a.

Next, we select one of the two influencing variables, say revenue in year n, and ask what information the decision maker would like about revenue in year n in order to reduce his uncertainty about the revenue in year n. He may answer that he would like to know the number of units sold in year n. The price of those units is a decision variable and is displayed in a square node. The influence diagram now appears as in Figure 2b.

Notice that in Figure 2a revenues in year n are undoubtedly influenced by costs in year n. Knowing that costs are low would suggest that revenues are also low. Hence, an arrow could have been drawn from costs to revenue. However, in Figure 2b no arrow needs to be drawn from costs to revenue because, given units sold and price, the revenues are independent of costs, i.e., {revenue|units sold, unit price, S} = {revenue|units sold, unit price, costs, S}.

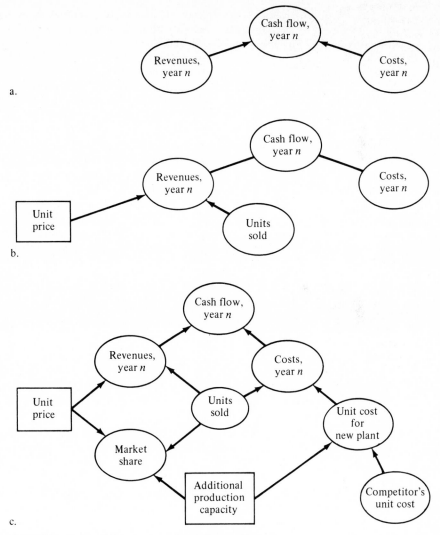

a.

b.

c.

FIGURE 2 Sequential generation of an influence diagram

If this procedure is repeated, an influence diagram such as that in Figure 2c may result. This diagram displays several noteworthy features. First, it is evident from the diagram that the decisions about production capacity and price are closely related. Price must be optimized for each setting of the additional capacity decision variable.

A second feature is the absence of a node called "market size in year *n*," which might influence units sold. If the decision maker is certain about the market size in year *n* because of its predictability, then the revelation of its actual value would do nothing to reduce his uncertainty about units sold. In this case, no node for market size appears on the diagram, as it would in a flow or block diagram. Similarly, unit cost for existing production capacity is well known and not shown as influencing cost in year *n*.

A final noteworthy feature of the diagram is the noncausal influence of the competitor's unit cost on the decision maker's unit cost for the new plant. The decision maker may be uncertain about the performance of the additional production facilities and therefore about the unit cost. If a competitor has a plant of a design similar to the decision maker's new capacity, knowing the competitor's unit cost might considerably reduce the decision maker's uncertainty about his own unit cost. Notice that the relationship between the competitor's unit cost and the unit cost for the new plant is stochastic rather than deterministic. Such stochastic and noncausal relationships are difficult to represent with conventional flow or block diagrams.

Since the influence diagram contains the important probabilistic relationships and decisions as perceived by the decision maker, a consistent decision tree can be constructed directly from this diagram and the necessary conditional probability distributions can be assessed. Because the diagram is generated backwards from the value attributes, the identified variables tend to fan away from the value attributes uniformly, resulting in a more balanced model. Excessive modeling of detail in one area at the expense of other areas is avoided. Furthermore, the backwards procedure helps the decision maker to identify stochastic and noncausal relationships as well as deterministic and [causal] relationships.

REFERENCES

1. Allen C. Miller et al., *Development of Automated Aids for Decision Analysis*, research report to Defense Advanced Research Projects Agency by SRI International, Menlo Park, California (May 1976).
2. Raymond Fritz, "System Methods in the Public Sector: A Dialogue," *Systems, Man, and Cybernetic Review*, Vol. 7, No. 1 (February 1978).
3. Daniel Owen, "The Concept of Influence and Its Use in Structuring Complex Decision Problems," Ph.D. dissertation, Engineering-Economic Systems Department, Stanford University (October 1978).

11.2 R&D TACTICS, AN APPLICATION OF RPD DECISION ANALYSIS

The following is reprinted with permission from the paper of the above title by D. G. S. Davies of the Fulmer Research Institute, England, which was originally published in *R & D Management*, 1982.

Abstract: The application of RPD[1] decision analysis to R&D tactics is discussed and the role of the technique as an aid to self-consistent decision making is emphasized. RPD decision analysis is used to define limits to its own cost effectiveness.

Two example problems are analysed in detail. Simple priority ratings are defined for two special cases: the sequence of independent tests all of which must succeed, and the sequence of independent problem solving attempts, any of which may succeed. The

[1] RPD is the acronym for Research Planning Diagram.

compromise between project duration and project cost is analysed in terms of time dependence of the value of success.

The *discrimination study* is defined as an investigation which aims to provide information for an improved assessment of project success probability.

It is shown that such a study is never worth more than one quarter of the total expected benefits of the project.

1 INTRODUCTION

Uncertainty is an inherent characteristic of research and development projects. Tactical decisions need to be taken in the face of this uncertainty, both at the planning stage and in response to changes in the state of knowledge as the project proceeds.

These decisions are of two kinds. On the one hand, questions of priorities and the deployment of resources must be settled. On the other hand, several radically different approaches to the situation may be available, one of which needs to be selected.

In this paper the application of decision analysis to tactical R&D problems is explained using one example of each type of decision problem.

A firm theoretical framework exists for rational decision making under uncertainty (see for example Schlaifer 1969 or Lindley 1971). It can be summarized in a single principle: "A rational decision maker should choose the option which maximises his expected utility."

Many decision makers, however, make no explicit use of this theory. Genuine difficulties in dealing with uncertain quantities and with subjective measures such as probability and risk aversion have tended to lead to the view that decision analysis results are either trivially obvious or too shaky to be given any credence. I believe that this view is mistaken and that a presentation and discussion of two examples can show the usefulness and power of the technique.

In presenting the examples, RPD notation has been used (Davies 1970, 1974). This offers considerable advantages over the more common decision tree notation in that the time sequence of activities is preserved, parallel paths can be represented and repetition can be avoided by the use of loops and junctions. The notion is largely self-explanatory but three points may need clarification. Firstly, a small circle enclosing a logic AND symbol is called a GATE. A gate holds up progress until it has been reached along all of its incoming arrows. Secondly, the diamonds are of two kinds. Small diamonds are deliberate decisions. At these points the decision maker must choose one and only one of the exits from the diamond. Large diamonds are events at which the state of nature determines which of the exits will be taken. Finally, the end points of the diagram are called OUTCOMES. When an outcome is reached, work stops on all activities in the diagram.

RPD decision analysis is a generalized form of cost-benefit analysis. Each activity in the diagram has a duration and a cost estimate associated with it. Each outcome has a benefit estimate and each exit from an event diamond has a probability assessment.

In the examples which follow it is assumed that the decisions involve little risk and that the timescales are sufficiently short to make discounting of costs and benefits unnecessary. Under these circumstances the utility of an outcome is directly proportional to the difference between the benefit associated with it and the cost of reaching it. We can therefore simplify the presentation considerably by working entirely in net benefit instead of utility.

We also assume that the decision maker is working within a private sphere of authority so that the social pressures which can complicate decision making (Brunsson 1980) do not operate.

2 DECISION ANALYSIS, EXAMPLE 1: "SCHEDULING INDEPENDENT TESTS"

This first example shows the use of RPD decision analysis to solve a scheduling problem.

2.1 Statement of the Problem

A new ceramic material has been developed and seems to be attractive for a particular high temperature engineering application. However, its selection depends on it having sufficient high temperature strength and sufficient thermal shock resistance.

The investigator has decided to proceed to test each of these properties against established criteria and to recommend the material if and only if it passes both tests.

He has the following options:

Option 1. Measure high temperature strength. If the material passes this test then measure thermal shock resistance.

Option 2. Measure thermal shock resistance. If the material passes this test then measure high temperature strength.

Option 3. Carry out both measurements in parallel.

2.2 RPD Formulation

In analysing this example it is convenient to show the individual options in separate diagrams: Figure 1 for the serial options 1 and 2 and Figure 2 for the parallel option 3.

2.3 Estimates and Assessments

Table 1 shows the duration and cost estimates for the two tests and the probabilities assessed for the corresponding event diamonds.

Table 1 Estimates and assessments for example 1

Activity	Outcome	Duration d, weeks	Cost c, £1000	Probability of success p	Benefit b
Do thermal shock testing	—	6	2	0.8	—
Do high temperature strength testing	—	9	3	0.4	—
—	SUCCESS —		—	—	b (total duration)
—	FAILURE —		—	—	0

The analysis also requires benefit estimates to be associated with the outcomes SUCCESS and FAILURE respectively.

The FAILURE benefits are small and for the time being will be taken as zero. SUCCESS benefits will be discussed later; for the moment we shall simply assume that they are some function of the time taken to reach the outcome.

2.4 Analysis

The method of analysis is straightforward. We simply take each option in turn and consider the various possible routes it may take, depending on the contingencies that may arise at the event diamonds.

We consider first the serial options.

2.4.1 The serial options Figure 1 shows in three small diagrams the three routes that may result if we choose a serial option. Also shown in each case are the duration, cost· probability and benefit.

In route (a), for example, both tests are carried out and they both give satisfactory results. The success outcome is reached after time $d_1 + d_2$ and at cost $c_1 + c_2$, and this results in a benefit of $b(d_1 + d_2)$ where b is an as yet undefined function. Route (a) will be followed if and only if two independent events with probabilities p_1 and p_2 occur; the probability of this route is therefore $p_1 p_2$.

The serial approach of Figure 1 can be looked upon as a gamble with three possible results, summarized in Table 2.

Table 2 Serial options gamble

Route	Probability	Net benefit v
Route (a)	$p_1 p_2$	$b(d_1 + d_2) - (c_1 + c_2)$
Route (b)	$p_1(1 - p_2)$	$- (c_1 + c_2)$
Route (c)	$(1 - p_1)$	$- c_1$

When the risk is small, which we assume to be the case in this example, a gamble such as this is evaluated by finding the expected net benefit ($\bar{v}$). This is the sum of the net benefits for the three routes, weighted by their respective probabilities.

In this case the expected net benefit from carrying out test 1 first then test 2 if successful is as follows:

$$\bar{v}_{1 \text{ then } 2} = p_1 p_2 b\{d_1 + d_2\} - p_1 p_2(c_1 + c_2) - p_1(1 - p_2)(c_1 + c_2) - c_1(1 - p_1)$$

$$= p_1 p_2 b\{d_1 + d_2\} - c_1 - c_2 p_1 \tag{1}$$

Reversing the order of the tests in the plan gives:

$$\bar{v}_{2 \text{ then } 1} = p_2 p_1 b\{d_2 + d_1\} - c_2 - c_1 p_2 \tag{2}$$

We can therefore compare the serial options 1 and 2 directly by subtracting equation (2) from equation (1):

$$\bar{v}_{1 \text{ then } 2} - \bar{v}_{2 \text{ then } 1} = c_2(1 - p_1) - c_1(1 - p_2)$$

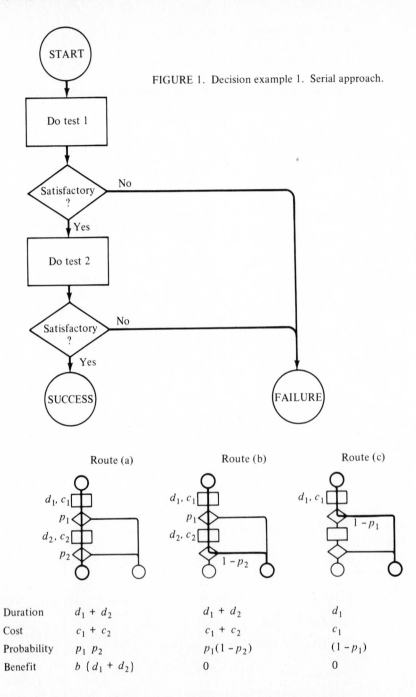

FIGURE 1. Decision example 1. Serial approach.

We are now in a position to substitute the values from Table 1:

$$\bar{v}_{\text{thermal shock first}} - \bar{v}_{\text{HT strength first}} = 3(1 - 0.8) - 2(1 - 0.4)$$

$$= -0.6 \tag{4}$$

Option 1 is therefore £600 less valuable than option 2 and it is clear that, if the serial approach is to be adopted, the high temperature strength testing should be carried out first.

2.4.2 The parallel option Figure 2 shows the parallel option. It is easily interpreted the same way as Figure 1.

In identifying the three possible routes through the diagram we have arbitrarily taken activity 1 to have the shorter duration. In route (a) therefore, the duration is d_2, the larger of d_1 and d_2. In route (b), a satisfactory result of activity 1 occurs before the failure of activity 2. In route (c), however, activity 2 is still in progress when activity 1 fails and arrival at a failure outcome kills the plan. The total cost incurred in route (c) includes a proportionate part of the cost of activity 2 depending on the durations d_1 and d_2.

As before, the results can be regarded as a three-way gamble, summarized in Table 3.

Table 3 Parallel option gamble

Route	Probability	Net benefit v
Route (a)	$p_1 p_2$	$b(d_2) - (c_1 + c_2)$
Route (b)	$p_1(1 - p_2)$	$- (c_1 + c_2)$
Route (c)	$(1 - p_1)$	$- c_1 + c_2 \dfrac{d_1}{d_2}$

The expected net benefit is given by:

$$\bar{v}_{\text{parallel}} = p_1 p_2 b\{d_2\} - p_1 p_2(c_1 + c_2) - p_1(1 - p_2)(c_1 + c_2) - (1 - p_1)\left(c_1 + c_2 \frac{d_1}{d_2}\right)$$

$$= p_1 p_2 b\{d_2\} - c_1 - c_2\left[p_1 + \frac{d_1}{d_2(1 - p_1)}\right] \tag{5}$$

Option 3 can be compared with option 2 by comparing $\bar{v}_{\text{parallel}}$ from equation (5) with $\bar{v}_{2\text{ then }1}$ from equation (2).

$$\bar{v}_{\text{parallel}} - \bar{v}_{2\text{ then }1} = p_1 p_2[b\{d_2\} - b\{d_1 + d_2\}] - c_1(1 - p_2) + c_2(1 - p_1)\left(1 - \frac{d_1}{d_2}\right) \tag{6}$$

Substituting values from Table 1 gives:

$$\bar{v}_{\text{parallel}} - \bar{v}_{2\text{ then }1} = 0.32[b\{9\} - b\{15\}] - 1 \tag{7}$$

This difference will be positive provided that

$$b\{9\} - b\{15\} > £3000 \tag{8}$$

In other words, provided that the achievement of success in nine weeks would be worth at least £3000 more than the achievement of success in fifteen weeks, the parallel option is favoured.

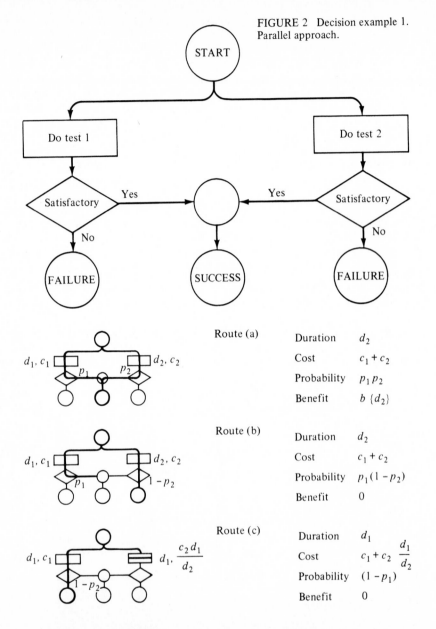

FIGURE 2 Decision example 1. Parallel approach.

Route (a)

Duration	d_2
Cost	$c_1 + c_2$
Probability	$p_1 p_2$
Benefit	$b\{d_2\}$

Route (b)

Duration	d_2
Cost	$c_1 + c_2$
Probability	$p_1(1 - p_2)$
Benefit	0

Route (c)

Duration	d_1
Cost	$c_1 + c_2 \dfrac{d_1}{d_2}$
Probability	$(1 - p_1)$
Benefit	0

2.4.3 Discussion of example 1 We begin by considering the analysis of the two serial options.

The first point to notice is that, with a deterministic approach to planning, the question of which experiment to do first simply would not arise. Doing the experiments in a different order has no effect on the probability of success, or on the time or cost to successful completion. This may explain why little attention seems to be given to this aspect of scheduling, the aim of which is to minimise the expected cost of failure.

Looking again at equation (3) it is clear that experiment 1 has higher priority if and only if:

$$c_2(1 - p_1) > c_1(1 - p_2) \tag{9}$$

Dividing both sides of this inequality by the positive quantity $(1 - p_1)(1 - p_2)$, we get:

$$\frac{c_2}{1 - p_2} > \frac{c_1}{1 - p_1}$$

as the condition for doing experiment 1 first.

In fact it is straightforward to generalize this example to the case when we have an arbitrary number of tests, all of which must be passed as a condition of success and which are to be carried out serially.

The quantity

$$Q = \frac{\text{cost of test}}{1 - \text{probability of success of test}} \tag{11}$$

which we can call the **PRIORITY RATING** of the test, determines the optimum sequence of testing. The experiments should be carried out in increasing order of Q.

We now widen the discussion to include the parallel option.

Carrying out the tests in parallel will always have a higher expected cost than carrying them out in the correct serial sequence. Comparing equations (2) and (5) shows that there is always at least one serial option which has a lower expected cost than the parallel option; in fact, in the specific example discussed here, both serial options are cheaper. The parallel option is more expensive because, with hindsight, the work done on test 2 in route (c) is seen to have been abortive.

The parallel option is justified, when the benefit associated with the outcome is sufficiently time-dependent to offset the cost disadvantage. It is sometimes said that, in research, time is more important than money. On the basis of the current example we can see that this is a rather misleading way of saying that benefits are often extremely time dependent. Notice that in this example it was not necessary to estimate the overall benefits of the test program. The quantity needed was the increase in benefits that would result from arriving at the success outcome six weeks earlier.

3 DECISION ANALYSIS, EXAMPLE 2: "DISCRIMINATION STUDY VERSUS DIRECT TRIAL"

The second example differs from example 1 in that the decision maker has to choose between radically different approaches to the problem.

3.1 Statement of the Problem

In an investigation of the continuous casting of an aluminium alloy, an investigator suggests a modified die design which could obviate the need for expensive and cumbersome ancillary equipment. A mathematical model of the casting process is available which would enable the proposed die design change to be simulated.

The decision maker has three options:

Option 1.   NO ACTION: Reject the proposed die change and proceed with the ancillary equipment.
Option 2.   DIRECT TRIAL: Make a modified die and try it.
Option 3.   DISCRIMINATION STUDY: Carry out a mathematical simulation and, if it is successful, make the modified die and try it. Otherwise proceed with the ancillary equipment.

The computer simulation is rather similar to a feasibility study in that it seeks to determine whether or not the proposed trial is likely to succeed. The term "feasibility study," however, covers a rather broader class of investigations which can sometimes yield information to improve the subsequent trial through reduced cost, increased quality of outcome or increased probability of success. I use the term "discrimination study" for the restricted class of feasibility studies which have no function except to improve the state of knowledge as to whether the trial is likely to succeed.

3.2 RPD Formulation

The three options are shown in a single diagram in Figure 3.

3.3 Estimates and Assessments

The cost of the trial, T, is estimated as £2000 and that of the computer simulation, C, as £200.

We assume that the trial cannot be scheduled immediately but can be phased into the future programme in such a way that it does not affect the overall duration of the project. Under this simplifying assumption, we need not take account of the time-dependence of the benefits, nor of the durations of the activities. The benefit associated with a successful trial, B, is estimated to be £4000 relative to NO ACTION, which is given zero value. B takes account of the cost advantage and operational convenience of dispensing with the ancillary equipment.

The probability of success of the trial, p, is assessed as 0.6. Conditional on the simulation, the following likelihoods are assessed. If the simulation gives satisfactory results the probability of a successful trial, q_1, is judged to be 0.9. If it gives unsatisfactory results, the probability of a successful trial, q_2, is judged to be 0.3. In this case, the mathematical model is a pessimistic one; it is more likely to say "no" when it should say "yes," than to say "yes" when it should say "no."

The analysis also requires the value of r, the probability of a promising result from the simulation. It is important to realise that this value is implicit in the probabilities already assessed. Given p, the probability of a successful trial, and q_1 and q_2, the probability of a successful trial conditional on the two possible results of the simulation, then r is determined by Bayes' theorem (see for example Schlaifer 1969, already referred to). According to Bayes' theorem:

$$
\begin{pmatrix} \text{probability of good trial} \\ \text{given good discr. result} \end{pmatrix} = \frac{\begin{pmatrix} \text{prior probability} \\ \text{of good trial} \end{pmatrix} \times \begin{pmatrix} \text{probability of good} \\ \text{disc. results given} \\ \text{good trial} \end{pmatrix}}{(\text{probability of good discr. results})} \tag{12}
$$

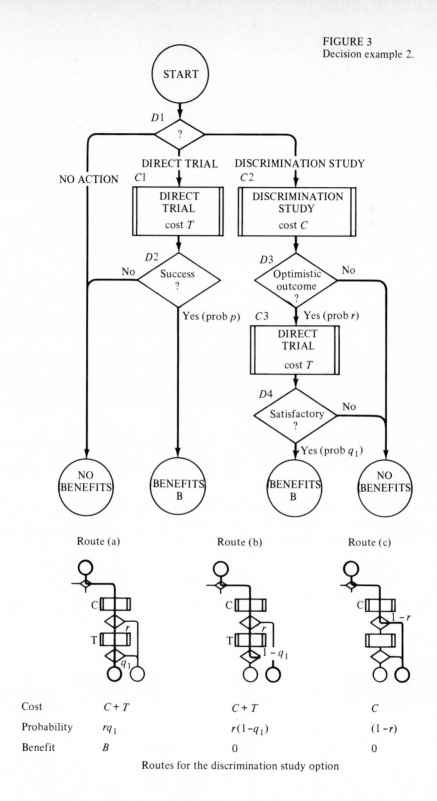

FIGURE 3
Decision example 2.

START

D1

?

NO ACTION   DIRECT TRIAL   DISCRIMINATION STUDY
             C1   C2

DIRECT
TRIAL
cost T

DISCRIMINATION
STUDY
cost C

D2   D3
No   Success   Optimistic   No
      ?   outcome
                   ?

Yes (prob p)   C3   Yes (prob r)

DIRECT
TRIAL
cost T

D4

Satisfactory   No
?

Yes (prob q_1)

NO   BENEFITS   BENEFITS   NO
BENEFITS   B   B   BENEFITS

Route (a)   Route (b)   Route (c)

	Route (a)	Route (b)	Route (c)
Cost	$C + T$	$C + T$	C
Probability	rq_1	$r(1-q_1)$	$(1-r)$
Benefit	B	0	0

Routes for the discrimination study option

also

$$\begin{pmatrix} \text{probability of good trial} \\ \text{given bad discr. result} \end{pmatrix} = \frac{\begin{pmatrix} \text{prior probability} \\ \text{of good trial} \end{pmatrix} \times \begin{pmatrix} \text{probability of bad} \\ \text{disc. results given} \\ \text{good trial} \end{pmatrix}}{(\text{probability of bad discr. results})} \qquad (13)$$

If x is the probability of an encouraging discrimination study result under circumstances which would lead to a good trial, these reduce to:

$$q_1 = \frac{px}{r} \qquad (12)$$

$$q_2 = \frac{p(1 - x)}{1 - r} \qquad (13)$$

Eliminating x gives

$$q_1 r + q_2(1 - r) = p$$

$$\therefore \qquad r = (p - q_2)(q_1 - q_2) \qquad (14)$$

In the present case $p = 0.6$, $q_1 = 0.9$, $q_2 = 0.3$. r is therefore 0.5, i.e., there is a 50 percent chance of getting an encouraging result from the simulation.

3.4 Analysis

3.4.1 The NO ACTION option The NO ACTION option is trivial. Clearly the expected net benefit is zero:

$$\bar{v}_{\text{NO ACTION}} = 0 \qquad (15)$$

3.4.2 The DIRECT TRIAL option The DIRECT TRIAL option is a two-way gamble. The successful route gives a net benefit $V = B - T$ with probability p. The unsuccessful route gives net benefit $V = -T$ with probability $(1 - p)$.

Table 4 Estimates and assessments for example 2

Activity: Direct trial	
Cost	$T = £2000$
Probability of success	$p = 0.6$
Probability of success conditional on promising simulation	$q_1 = 0.9$
Probability of success conditional on unpromising simulation	$q_2 = 0.3$
Activity: Simulation	
Cost	$C = £200$
Probability of promising result	$r = 0.5$
	(calculated from p, q_1, q_2)
Outcome: Benefits	
Benefit	$B = 4000$
Outcome: No benefits	
Benefit	0

The expected net benefit is therefore:

$$\bar{v}_{\text{DIRECT TRIAL}} = pB - T \tag{16}$$

and, using the values in Table 4:

$$\bar{v}_{\text{DIRECT TRIAL}} = £400 \tag{17}$$

This option is therefore superior to NO ACTION.

3.4.3 The DISCRIMINATION STUDY option The three possible routes for this action are shown in Figure 3 and the resulting three-way gamble is summarized in Table 5.

Table 5 Discrimination study gamble

Route	Probability	Net benefit v
Route (a)	rq_1	$B - (C + T)$
Route (b)	$r(1 - q_1)$	$- (C + T)$
Route (c)	$1 - r$	$- T$

The expected net benefit is given by:

$$\bar{v}_{\text{DISCR. STUDY}} = rq_1B - C - rT \tag{18}$$

and, using equation (14) this gives:

$$\bar{v}_{\text{DISC. STUDY}} = \frac{p - q_2}{q_1 - q_2} \cdot q_1B - C - \frac{(p - q_2)T}{q_1 - q_2} \tag{19}$$

Using the values from Table 4:

$$\bar{v}_{\text{DISCR. STUDY}} = £600 \tag{20}$$

Comparing this with equation (17) shows that the best option in this example is DISCRIMINATION STUDY.

3.5 Discussion of Example 2

This example has extremely wide applicability. In many cases, feasibility studies, market surveys and consultancy commissions are discrimination studies in the sense of this example, as are certain research projects.

The key to a discrimination study is that it changes the state of knowledge about the prospects of the trial from probability p to conditional probabilities q_1 and q_2 where

$$0 \leq q_2 \leq p \leq q_1 \leq 1 \tag{21}$$

It is useful to define the value of the study as equal to the maximum cost which would still leave DISCRIMINATION STUDY as the preferred option.

In the present example C must be less than £400 if DISCRIMINATION STUDY is to be preferred to DIRECT TRIAL.

In general, from equations (16) and (19) the value D of the DISCRIMINATION STUDY is given by:

$$pB - T = \frac{p - q_2}{q_1 - q_2} \cdot q_1 B - D - \frac{p - q_2}{q_1 - q_2} \cdot T \tag{22}$$

which simplifies to:

$$D = (T - q_2 B) \frac{q_1 - p}{q_1 - q_2} \tag{23}$$

To avoid those situations where NO ACTION is the preferred option we require that:

$$pB \geq T \tag{24}$$

A discrimination study in which $q_1 = q_2 = p$ has a zero or negative value. The maximum value of D occurs when $q_1 = 1$ and $q_2 = 0$. This is perfect discrimination and gives:

$$D_{\text{perfect}} = T(1 - p) \tag{25}$$

D_{perfect} is sometimes called the value of perfect knowledge (Lindley 1971). From equations (24) and (25), the maximum value that D_{perfect} can take is:

$$D_{\text{perfect, max}} = Bp(1 - p) \tag{26}$$

Under no circumstances can this exceed $0.25B$. We can therefore draw the interesting conclusion that a pure discrimination study is never worth more than one quarter of the anticipated benefits of the trial.

4 GENERAL DISCUSSION

Each of the two examples presented in this paper is simple and yet neither is trivial. In the case of the scheduling example, the discussion leads to a priority rating which can be used to schedule serial testing programs and it also leads to an understanding of the trade-off between project duration and cost.

In discussing this example we have effectively covered a different problem which is, in a sense, dual to it. Suppose that a number of different approaches to a technical problem are suggested and that the problem is considered solved whenever any of the rival schemes succeed, then the analysis of example 1 can be made to apply, simply by interchanging success and failure in Figures 1 and 2.

The priority rating for scheduling the alternative approaches in this related example is:

$$Q' = \text{cost/probability of success} \tag{27}$$

Example 2 illustrates a broad class of decision problems in which the investigator has to select one of several possible different approaches known as modes of investigation. Depending on the conceptual models available to him, the investigator may decide on exploration, model refinement or, as in this case, trial or discrimination. RPD analysis provides a unified approach for the comparative evaluation of these tactics.

However, anyone advocating decision analysis, and putting forward the discrimination study example discussed in this paper, must be prepared to be subjected to his own methods! The question is: "When is decision analysis cost effective?" For a two-way decision, the RPD formulation of this problem is shown in Figure 4. Clearly, decision analysis itself is a close relative of the discrimination study. B is the size of the decision. It is the expected benefit resulting from making the right decision rather than the wrong one. p is the probability of making the right decision without analysis; it measures the confidence of the decision maker. C is the cost of the analysis. q is the probability of making the right decision after analysis; it measures the effectiveness of the analysis. The decision maker usually finds it difficult to assess p and B, especially since, by the terms of the problem, they must be guessed without detailed analysis.

For a rational decision maker:

$$0.5 \leq p \leq q \leq 1 \tag{28}$$

Arguments similar to those of example 2 show that DECISION ANALYSIS is the preferred option if and only if

$$C \leq B(q - p) \tag{29}$$

The value of a decision analysis therefore increases with its effectiveness and with the size of the decision and it decreases with the prior confidence of the decision maker. From equations (28) and (29) it is clear that a decision analysis is never worth more than half of the size of the decision.

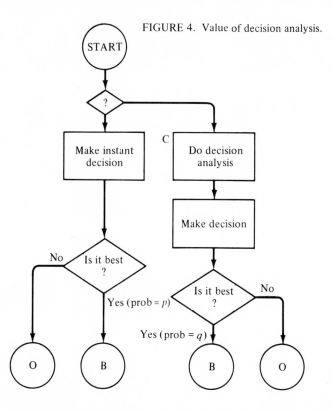

FIGURE 4. Value of decision analysis.

Deeper concern about the value of decision analysis is sometimes caused by the vague nature of the quantities which it uses. Duration and cost estimates are uncertain quantities as are benefit estimates, which often contain the additional problem of subjectivity. Probability assessments are inherently subjective.

It is important to realize, however, that all decisions are inherently subjective and that decision analysis only seeks to render explicit those considerations which are usually implicit in the decision making process.

The modest aim of decision analysis is to ensure that the decision maker's estimates and assessments are mutually consistent and that his decision is rationally based on them. It cannot improve the accuracy of his data, but it can ensure that they are consistently applied.

A good example of the consistency requirement is provided by the calculation of the value of r in example 2. In most applications of Bayes' theorem prior probability assessments are combined with likelihood estimates to produce posterior probabilities.

In this case however the prior and the posterior probabilities are used to estimate the likelihoods. Consistency is all that is demanded. It makes no difference which probabilities the decision maker assesses directly, and which he calculates from them, as long as he ends with a consistent set which he judges to be a true expression of his belief.

RPD analysis provides a basis for the resolution of much more complicated problems than those discussed here. With computer assistance it is feasible to analyse situations with numerous decisions embedded in a rich logical structure of alternative futures and parallel lines of activity. Allowance can be made for the decision maker's attitude to risk and for discounting. Estimates can be included in the form of probability distributions. Sensitivity analysis can be used to determine the robustness of decisions in the face of uncertainties in the estimates. However, the basic ideas remain those described in this paper and despite the availability of sophisticated tools, all decision problems should be approached with a ruthless desire to simplify.

The R&D investigator, like any other decision maker, can expect great help from decision analysis provided that he remains in control of it and ensures that the analysis itself is cost effective.

REFERENCES

Brunsson, N. (1980) "The functions of project evaluation", *R & D Management*, Vol. 10, p. 61.

Davies, D. G. S. (1970) "Research Planning Diagrams", *R & D Management*, Vol. 1, p. 22.

Davies, D. G. S. (1974) "The RPD System for Project Planning under Uncertainty". Fourth Internat. Congress. Project Management in the Seventies. Paris: AFCET Vol. II, p. 175.

Lindley, D. V. (1971) *Making Decisions*, London: Wiley.

Schlaifer, R. (1969) "Analysis of Decisions under Uncertainty", New York: McGraw-Hill.

TWELVE

SUMMARY AND CRITIQUE

12.1 SUMMARY

Decision analysis in practice is a set of formal procedures that seek to aid a decision maker in facing problems that are too complex for a purely intuitive choice. Decision analysts seek to provide insight on a decision problem and the decision maker's relationship to it through explicit tests of coherence. In so far as it is an applied subject, its realm of definition is largely determined by what self-styled *decision analysts* are doing. There are many of these around, earning a living as management consultants, and the methodological style varies by both technique and contextual preoccupations. There are several consulting groups whose expertise is mainly in dealing with the complexity of multiple-attribute decisions, others who focus upon hierarchical models, of both inference and objectives, and also others whose expertise is mainly in the construction of large-scale decision trees. Despite this, we can identify two characteristics that pervade the approaches of applied decision analysts. They are (1) analytical decomposition and (2) personal nature of the decision model.

Fundamental to most of the current philosophy of decision analysis is the belief in the value of the "divide and conquer" approach to complexity. Problems which are seen to be too complex because of multiple uncertainties, objectives, options, risk, timings, and individual actors can, decision analysts would argue, be analyzed effectively by decomposing the structure of the problem into a model that allows the separate focus of attention upon constituent elements. The personal nature of the decision model is a recognition by decision analysts that all they can do is to subject a decision maker's opinions and preferences to tests of coherence through the model: they do not tell a decision maker what he or she *should* believe, or what his or her objectives *should* be. Thus, the encoding of subjective preferences is a salient characteristic, undertaken both for input to the decision model and to facilitate coherence on the part of the decision maker.

From this perspective of analysis for personal coherence, we have looked at several aspects of application. We looked first at the nature of decision criteria.

Upon what basis can a decision maker choose between even simple options in the face of uncertainty? Several criteria were examined, all of which were useful to some extent, but had various shortcomings. The only criterion which theoretically took account of the decision maker's attitude to risk was that of expected utility. This criterion requires a utility function to be assessed upon the basis of the decision maker's responses to several contrived but simple choice situations. This utility function can then transform the payoffs in a more complicated problem in such a way that choosing the action which maximizes the expected value of utility would be consistent with the decision maker's responses to the simpler choices. Hence we see the application of both the decomposition and the personalist themes in decision analysis. The theory of expected utility does impose some assumptions upon the consistency of the decision maker's behavior, which may or may not be valid in particular circumstances, and does require the assessment of the utility function. This assessment task is sometimes seen as tedious and will, to a greater or lesser extent, introduce some forms of bias through the actual way in which the procedure works. Thus, analysis by dominance is attractive whenever possible in that it allows a ranking of options purely upon the basis of identifying a risk characteristic (for example, risk aversion). We looked at several forms of dominance analysis. We also looked at the application of utility theory to situations with multiple conflicting objectives and saw how the expected utility criterion could be generalized from the single payoff dimension to the multiple case. Some decision problems involve attributes that are unpalatable to think of, and this poses special problems for the decision analysis approach of explication. In this respect we looked at the nature of decision making where risks to human life were involved. We then turned our attention from the value side to the uncertainty complications. We discussed the nature of subjective probabilities, encoding belief as a probability measure and the bayesian model for incorporating this with empirical data. We looked at the way assessments could be evaluated and improved, through both feedback and causal decomposition. Finally, we looked at decision tree models, plus variations, for analyzing multiple-stage decision problems and the impact of information.

We have been rather preoccupied with the individual and formal aspects of decision analysis. We have not considered multiple decision makers to any great extent; problems associated with consensus formation and conflict resolution, for example. Decision analysts do cope with these problems, but a substantial treatment should be founded in the theories of group and social decision making, which are large in scope and should really be covered separately. Likewise, in our concentration upon the formal coherence testing of an individual, we have not discussed the interventionist impact of the decision analyst within an organization. Again, this omission is not to be interpreted as denigrating the importance of this issue, but just a reflection that it involves wider issues of organizational behavior outside our focus.

The basic framework of decompositions of uncertainty and value and the personal interaction of the decision maker can provide a basis for the inclusion of many more elaborate quantitive techniques than have been considered here.

In fact, decision analysis should not be seen so much as a branch of the study of management science, but as an overall approach to its application. Thus, the techniques of mathematical programming and queuing, for example, are increasingly being applied as part of a decision analysis model rather than as an end in themselves. Modelling for decision analysis, as we have noted repeatedly in this text, exists primarily to provide a basis for greater insight on the part of the decision maker, to be pursued only so far as its usefulness remains apparent and not at all necessarily for increased scientific accuracy.

12.2 CRITIQUE

The usefulness of decision analysis is usually advocated to depend upon its ability to provide greater insight to the decision maker, to provide a basis for communicating and justifying an analysis, and as a means of opening up a problem for discussion and conflict resolution. Much research still needs to be done on technical aspects of the method, such as the mathematical analysis of more complicated structures, personal assessment biases, and the interactive role of the decision analyst in an organization. We will not criticize the method for technicalities.

The overall *approach* of analytic decomposition is criticized on a number of fronts. It may be that too much reliance upon the construction of a disciplined structure for the decision model may divert attention from the *creative* need in problem solving. The most original and worthwhile solutions often come from seeing a problem in unconventional terms, and there is clearly a danger that too much attention given to analyzing a particular decision model could be myopic in this wider requirement. Decision analysts would say that by focusing attention explicitly upon the elements of structure, conventional wisdom is questioned, and with nothing being taken for granted, this can stimulate original thought on the problem. Clearly, the use of influence diagrams, being a less constrained structuring device, is motivated by the need for creative engineering of alternative decision models. Nevertheless, concern is sometimes expressed by cognitive psychologists that decision analysts do impose an *analytical* pattern of thinking upon their clients, who may be more adept at other styles of though ("lateral," "synthetic," "imaginitive," "divergent," "intuitive"), the validity of which should not be ignored.

A related criticism of the decomposition principle is that it may oversimplify the context of the problem such that it loses more than it gains. The decision maker, particularly in utility function assessment, is asked very simple, contrived questions, which may put the decision maker in a less serious frame of mind than that with which he or she would like to face the real problem. Decision analysts are certainly exhorted to beware of such spurious "frivolity" in practice, along with other aspects of assessment bias, but despite advances in practical research, this does remain a criticism in principle of the analytical approach.

In the wider context of management science, the analytical approach has come under similar fundamental criticism. Howard (1980) observes the cultural aspect of analysis as being a Western process of thought and that other cultures, particularly in the East, prefer to face problems in a holistic, more intuitive way. Complex problems do not require the replacement of intuition by analysis, but rather more time for intuition to arrive at a solution. Leavitt (1975), more relevantly to management science, discusses the spurious credibility and power of *analysts* in an organizational setting, which he suggests is disproportionate to the real contextual experience of these people. Notwithstanding the abilities of decision analysts, concern about the role that such people, who have little or no knowledge of a particular business or industry, play in the formulation of important decisions is understandable. Many people are wary of bringing in expert consultants who know a lot about a particular situation on account of their lack of permanent commitment to the results of their advice. To bring in, at a high level, individuals who know nothing about the business may seem doubly worrying. Decision analysts respond that they do not seek to bring any substantial expertise to a problem, only an ability to test the coherence of their clients. It is toward this that responsible analysts must aspire, but it is inevitable that being agents of intervention in an organization, they can be misused for political reasons.

This concern with the political and ethical implications of decision analysis was evident in several questions to Rex Brown of Decision Science Consortium when he appeared as a guest on a radio broadcast hosted by Fred Fiske (WAMU, January 8, 1980). Here are three examples:

Listener: If decision analysis is used by politicians who are rather naive about computers and are anxious to get decisions, it might lead them to favor those people who will give them percentile data over those people giving general unquantified data. Mr. McNamara was said to come to people and say, "Well, I'd like a figure on that," and they'd say, "This thing shouldn't be quantified because the source of information is just poor." And he'll say "Well, if you won't give me a number, I'll go to somebody who will." Those people would be left out of the process.

Brown: There is a danger that imposing a certain process may screen out and discriminate against certain types of valuable input. On the other hand, the decision maker can always quantify implications (like probabilities) from the more qualitive inputs he receives. It may be that those of his experts who are adept in formulating their input in quantitative terms may have an edge in getting his ear; but then that's no worse than the masters of impassioned rhetoric getting his ear, as they seem to now.

Fiske: We're opening up all kinds of new areas for malfeasance and immorality. For example, does the competition buy off the decision analyst to lead his competition to a wrong decision? What an enormous bribe that would be worth!

Brown: Well, it's an intriguing idea to think that we have a power that is worth buying. I think that we have much less power and *should* have much less power than the question suggests.

Fiske: Now, what you do is to come into an organization where the people, the executives, presumably know much more about the subject matter involved and the decision to be made, and to advise them on making the proper decision. Is that a fair summary of your activities?

Brown: It's literally fair; but it may be misleading. It might carry the suggestion that we have in our heads a grain of divine inspirational knowledge which somehow exceeds theirs; and that would be ridiculous. What we have is something much more modest. It's an occasionally helpful illuminating device, a way of amplifying the intelligence and experience of the man who's been doing fine up until now.

Evidently the role of the decision analyst in practice should be a modest and sensitive one. A fair amount of criticism is leveled at decision analysis, but for the most part it is constructive. New ways of altering the way that decision making in our society has evolved must necessarily be subjected to high standards of scrutiny. Yet, so long as people wish to act responsibly, and demonstrate that fact, decision analysis as a field of study and practice is here to stay. It will undoubtedly change its character as research insights develop, but the rapid growth in published studies of applications during the past 15 years is now testimony to the fact that this current stage of evolution has achieved the benchmarks of practical relevance and usefulness.

REFERENCES

Howard, R. A. (1980): "An Assessment of Decision Analysis," *Operations Research*, vol. 28, no. 1, pp. 4–27.

Keeney, R. (1982): "Decision Analysis: State of the Field," Decision Analysis Technical Report 82.2, Woodward-Clyde Consultants, San Francisco.

Leavitt, H. J. (1975): "Beyond the Analytic Manager," *California Management Review*, vol. 17, no. 3, pp. 5–12.

Ulvila, J. W., and Rex V. Brown (1981): "Decision Analysis Comes of Age," Decision Science Consortium, Falls Church, Va.

APPENDIX

STATISTICAL TABLES

Table 1 The binomial distribution function

$$F(x) = \sum_{k=0}^{x} \binom{n}{k} p^k (1 - p)^{n-k}$$

n	x	0.05	0.10	0.15	0.20	0.25	p 0.30	0.35	0.40	0.45	0.50
2	0	0.9025	0.8100	0.7225	0.6400	0.5625	0.4900	0.4225	0.3600	0.3025	0.2500
	1	0.9975	0.9900	0.9775	0.9600	0.9375	0.9100	0.8775	0.8400	0.7975	0.7500
3	0	0.8574	0.7290	0.6141	0.5120	0.4219	0.3430	0.2746	0.2160	0.1664	0.1250
	1	0.9928	0.9720	0.9392	0.8960	0.8438	0.7840	0.7182	0.6480	0.5748	0.5000
	2	0.9999	0.9990	0.9966	0.9920	0.9844	0.9730	0.9571	0.9360	0.9089	0.8750
4	0	0.8145	0.6561	0.5220	0.4096	0.3164	0.2401	0.1785	0.1296	0.0915	0.0625
	1	0.9860	0.9477	0.8905	0.8192	0.7383	0.6517	0.5630	0.4752	0.3910	0.3125
	2	0.9995	0.9963	0.9880	0.9728	0.9492	0.9163	0.8735	0.8208	0.7585	0.6875
	3	1.0000	0.9999	0.9995	0.9984	0.9961	0.9919	0.9850	0.9744	0.9590	0.9375
5	0	0.7738	0.5905	0.4437	0.3277	0.2373	0.1681	0.1160	0.0778	0.0503	0.0312
	1	0.9774	0.9185	0.8352	0.7373	0.6328	0.5282	0.4284	0.3370	0.2562	0.1875
	2	0.9988	0.9914	0.9734	0.9421	0.8965	0.8369	0.7648	0.6826	0.5931	0.5000
	3	1.0000	0.9995	0.9978	0.9933	0.9844	0.9692	0.9460	0.9130	0.8688	0.8125
	4	1.0000	1.0000	0.9999	0.9997	0.9990	0.9976	0.9947	0.9898	0.9815	0.9688
6	0	0.7351	0.5314	0.3771	0.2621	0.1780	0.1176	0.0754	0.0467	0.0277	0.0156
	1	0.9672	0.8857	0.7765	0.6554	0.5339	0.4202	0.3191	0.2333	0.1636	0.1094
	2	0.9978	0.9842	0.9527	0.9011	0.8306	0.7443	0.6471	0.5443	0.4415	0.3438
	3	0.9999	0.9987	0.9941	0.9830	0.9624	0.9295	0.8826	0.8208	0.7447	0.6562
	4	1.0000	0.9999	0.9996	0.9984	0.9954	0.9891	0.9777	0.9590	0.9308	0.8906
	5	1.0000	1.0000	1.0000	0.9999	0.9998	0.9993	0.9982	0.9959	0.9917	0.9844
7	0	0.6983	0.4783	0.3206	0.2097	0.1335	0.0824	0.0490	0.0280	0.0152	0.0078
	1	0.9556	0.8503	0.7166	0.5767	0.4449	0.3294	0.2338	0.1586	0.1024	0.0625
	2	0.9962	0.9743	0.9262	0.8520	0.7564	0.6471	0.5323	0.4199	0.3164	0.2266
	3	0.9998	0.9973	0.9879	0.9667	0.9294	0.8740	0.8002	0.7102	0.6083	0.5000
	4	1.0000	0.9998	0.9988	0.9953	0.9871	0.9712	0.9444	0.9037	0.8471	0.7734
	5	1.0000	1.0000	0.9999	0.9996	0.9987	0.9962	0.9910	0.9812	0.9643	0.9375
	6	1.0000	1.0000	1.0000	1.0000	0.9999	0.9998	0.9994	0.9984	0.9963	0.9922
8	0	0.6634	0.4305	0.2725	0.1678	0.1001	0.0576	0.0319	0.0168	0.0084	0.0039
	1	0.9428	0.8131	0.6572	0.5033	0.3671	0.2553	0.1691	0.1064	0.0632	0.0352
	2	0.9942	0.9619	0.8948	0.7969	0.6785	0.5518	0.4278	0.3154	0.2201	0.1445
	3	0.9996	0.9950	0.9786	0.9437	0.8862	0.8059	0.7064	0.5941	0.4770	0.3633
	4	1.0000	0.9996	0.9971	0.9896	0.9727	0.9420	0.8939	0.8263	0.7396	0.6367
	5	1.0000	1.0000	0.9998	0.9988	0.9958	0.9887	0.9747	0.9502	0.9115	0.8555
	6	1.0000	1.0000	1.0000	0.9999	0.9996	0.9987	0.9964	0.9915	0.9819	0.9648
	7	1.0000	1.0000	1.0000	1.0000	1.0000	0.9999	0.9998	0.9993	0.9983	0.9961

Source: Reprinted from *Tables of the Binomial Probability Distribution,* National Bureau of Standards, Applied Mathematics Series, No. 6, U.S. Department of Commerce, Washington, D.C., 1952.

Table 1 (Continued)

n	x	0.05	0.10	0.15	0.20	0.25	0.30	0.35	0.40	0.45	0.50
9	0	0.6302	0.3874	0.2316	0.1342	0.0751	0.0404	0.0207	0.0101	0.0046	0.0020
	1	0.9288	0.7748	0.5995	0.4362	0.3003	0.1960	0.1211	0.0705	0.0385	0.0195
	2	0.9916	0.9470	0.8591	0.7382	0.6007	0.4628	0.3373	0.2318	0.1495	0.0898
	3	0.9994	0.9917	0.9661	0.9144	0.8343	0.7297	0.6089	0.4826	0.3614	0.2539
	4	1.0000	0.9991	0.9944	0.9804	0.9511	0.9012	0.8283	0.7334	0.6214	0.5000
	5	1.0000	0.9999	0.9994	0.9969	0.9900	0.9747	0.9464	0.9006	0.8342	0.7461
	6	1.0000	1.0000	1.0000	0.9997	0.9987	0.9957	0.9888	0.9750	0.9502	0.9102
	7	1.0000	1.0000	1.0000	1.0000	0.9999	0.9996	0.9986	0.9962	0.9909	0.9805
	8	1.0000	1.0000	1.0000	1.0000	1.0000	1.0000	0.9999	0.9997	0.9992	0.9980
10	0	0.5987	0.3487	0.1969	0.1074	0.0563	0.0282	0.0135	0.0060	0.0025	0.0010
	1	0.9139	0.7361	0.5443	0.3758	0.2440	0.1493	0.0860	0.0464	0.0232	0.0107
	2	0.9885	0.9298	0.8202	0.6778	0.5256	0.3828	0.2616	0.1673	0.0996	0.0547
	3	0.9990	0.9872	0.9500	0.8791	0.7759	0.6496	0.5138	0.3823	0.2660	0.1719
	4	0.9999	0.9984	0.9901	0.9672	0.9219	0.8497	0.7515	0.6331	0.5044	0.3770
	5	1.0000	0.9999	0.9986	0.9936	0.9803	0.9527	0.9051	0.8338	0.7384	0.6230
	6	1.0000	1.0000	0.9999	0.9991	0.9965	0.9894	0.9740	0.9452	0.8980	0.8281
	7	1.0000	1.0000	1.0000	0.9999	0.9996	0.9984	0.9952	0.9877	0.9726	0.9453
	8	1.0000	1.0000	1.0000	1.0000	1.0000	0.9999	0.9995	0.9983	0.9955	0.9893
	9	1.0000	1.0000	1.0000	1.0000	1.0000	1.0000	1.0000	0.9999	0.9997	0.9990
11	0	0.5688	0.3138	0.1673	0.0859	0.0422	0.0198	0.0088	0.0036	0.0014	0.0005
	1	0.8981	0.6974	0.4922	0.3221	0.1971	0.1130	0.0606	0.0302	0.0139	0.0059
	2	0.9848	0.9104	0.7788	0.6174	0.4552	0.3127	0.2001	0.1189	0.0652	0.0327
	3	0.9984	0.9815	0.9306	0.8389	0.7133	0.5696	0.4256	0.2963	0.1911	0.1133
	4	0.9999	0.9972	0.9841	0.9496	0.8854	0.7897	0.6683	0.5328	0.3971	0.2744
	5	1.0000	0.9997	0.9973	0.9883	0.9657	0.9218	0.8513	0.7535	0.6331	0.5000
	6	1.0000	1.0000	0.9997	0.9980	0.9924	0.9784	0.9499	0.9006	0.8262	0.7256
	7	1.0000	1.0000	1.0000	0.9998	0.9988	0.9957	0.9878	0.9707	0.9390	0.8867
	8	1.0000	1.0000	1.0000	1.0000	0.9999	0.9994	0.9980	0.9941	0.9852	0.9673
	9	1.0000	1.0000	1.0000	1.0000	1.0000	1.0000	0.9998	0.9993	0.9978	0.9941
	10	1.0000	1.0000	1.0000	1.0000	1.0000	1.0000	1.0000	1.0000	0.9998	0.9995
12	0	0.5404	0.2824	0.1422	0.0687	0.0317	0.0138	0.0057	0.0022	0.0008	0.0002
	1	0.8816	0.6590	0.4435	0.2749	0.1584	0.0850	0.0424	0.0196	0.0083	0.0032
	2	0.9804	0.8891	0.7358	0.5583	0.3907	0.2528	0.1513	0.0834	0.0421	0.0193
	3	0.9978	0.9744	0.9078	0.7946	0.6488	0.4925	0.3467	0.2253	0.1345	0.0730
	4	0.9998	0.9957	0.9761	0.9274	0.8424	0.7237	0.5833	0.4382	0.3044	0.1938
	5	1.0000	0.9995	0.9954	0.9806	0.9456	0.8822	0.7873	0.6652	0.5269	0.3872
	6	1.0000	0.9999	0.9993	0.9961	0.9857	0.9614	0.9154	0.8418	0.7393	0.6128
	7	1.0000	1.0000	0.9999	0.9994	0.9972	0.9905	0.9745	0.9427	0.8883	0.8062
	8	1.0000	1.0000	1.0000	0.9999	0.9996	0.9983	0.9944	0.9847	0.9644	0.9270
	9	1.0000	1.0000	1.0000	1.0000	1.0000	0.9998	0.9992	0.9972	0.9921	0.9807
	10	1.0000	1.0000	1.0000	1.0000	1.0000	1.0000	0.9999	0.9997	0.9989	0.9968
	11	1.0000	1.0000	1.0000	1.0000	1.0000	1.0000	1.0000	1.0000	0.9999	0.9998

Table 1 (Continued)

n	x	0.05	0.10	0.15	0.20	0.25	p 0.30	0.35	0.40	0.45	0.50
13	0	0.5133	0.2542	0.1209	0.0550	0.0238	0.0097	0.0037	0.0013	0.0004	0.0001
	1	0.8646	0.6213	0.3983	0.2336	0.1267	0.0637	0.0296	0.0126	0.0049	0.0017
	2	0.9755	0.8661	0.6920	0.5017	0.3326	0.2025	0.1132	0.0579	0.0269	0.0112
	3	0.9969	0.9658	0.8820	0.7473	0.5843	0.4206	0.2783	0.1686	0.0929	0.0461
	4	0.9997	0.9935	0.9658	0.9009	0.7940	0.6543	0.5005	0.3530	0.2279	0.1334
	5	1.0000	0.9991	0.9925	0.9700	0.9198	0.8346	0.7159	0.5744	0.4268	0.2905
	6	1.0000	0.9999	0.9987	0.9930	0.9757	0.9376	0.8705	0.7712	0.6437	0.5000
	7	1.0000	1.0000	0.9998	0.9988	0.9944	0.9818	0.9538	0.9023	0.8212	0.7095
	8	1.0000	1.0000	1.0000	0.9998	0.9990	0.9960	0.9874	0.9679	0.9302	0.8666
	9	1.0000	1.0000	1.0000	1.0000	0.9999	0.9993	0.9975	0.9922	0.9797	0.9539
	10	1.0000	1.0000	1.0000	1.0000	1.0000	0.9999	0.9997	0.9987	0.9959	0.9888
	11	1.0000	1.0000	1.0000	1.0000	1.0000	1.0000	1.0000	0.9999	0.9995	0.9983
	12	1.0000	1.0000	1.0000	1.0000	1.0000	1.0000	1.0000	1.0000	1.0000	0.9999
14	0	0.4877	0.2288	0.1028	0.0440	0.0178	0.0068	0.0024	0.0008	0.0002	0.0001
	1	0.8470	0.5846	0.3567	0.1979	0.1010	0.0475	0.0205	0.0081	0.0029	0.0009
	2	0.9699	0.8416	0.6479	0.4481	0.2811	0.1608	0.0839	0.0398	0.0170	0.0065
	3	0.9958	0.9559	0.8535	0.6982	0.5213	0.3552	0.2205	0.1243	0.0632	0.0287
	4	0.9996	0.9908	0.9533	0.8702	0.7415	0.5842	0.4227	0.2793	0.1672	0.0898
	5	1.0000	0.9985	0.9885	0.9561	0.8883	0.7805	0.6405	0.4859	0.3373	0.2120
	6	1.0000	0.9998	0.9978	0.9884	0.9617	0.9067	0.8164	0.6925	0.5461	0.3953
	7	1.0000	1.0000	0.9997	0.9976	0.9897	0.9685	0.9247	0.8499	0.7414	0.6047
	8	1.0000	1.0000	1.0000	0.9996	0.9978	0.9917	0.9757	0.9417	0.8811	0.7880
	9	1.0000	1.0000	1.0000	1.0000	0.9997	0.9983	0.9940	0.9825	0.9574	0.9102
	10	1.0000	1.0000	1.0000	1.0000	1.0000	0.9998	0.9989	0.9961	0.9886	0.9713
	11	1.0000	1.0000	1.0000	1.0000	1.0000	1.0000	0.9999	0.9994	0.9978	0.9935
	12	1.0000	1.0000	1.0000	1.0000	1.0000	1.0000	1.0000	0.9999	0.9997	0.9991
	13	1.0000	1.0000	1.0000	1.0000	1.0000	1.0000	1.0000	1.0000	1.0000	0.9999
15	0	0.4633	0.2059	0.0874	0.0352	0.0134	0.0047	0.0016	0.0005	0.0001	0.0000
	1	0.8290	0.5490	0.3186	0.1671	0.0802	0.0353	0.0142	0.0052	0.0017	0.0005
	2	0.9638	0.8159	0.6042	0.3980	0.2361	0.1268	0.0617	0.0271	0.0107	0.0037
	3	0.9945	0.9444	0.8227	0.6482	0.4613	0.2969	0.1727	0.0905	0.0424	0.0176
	4	0.9994	0.9873	0.9383	0.8358	0.6865	0.5155	0.3519	0.2173	0.1204	0.0592
	5	0.9999	0.9978	0.9832	0.9389	0.8516	0.7216	0.5643	0.4032	0.2608	0.1509
	6	1.0000	0.9997	0.9964	0.9819	0.9434	0.8689	0.7548	0.6098	0.4522	0.3036
	7	1.0000	1.0000	0.9996	0.9958	0.9827	0.9500	0.8868	0.7869	0.6535	0.5000
	8	1.0000	1.0000	0.9999	0.9992	0.9958	0.9849	0.9578	0.9050	0.8182	0.6964
	9	1.0000	1.0000	1.0000	0.9999	0.9992	0.9963	0.9876	0.9662	0.9231	0.8491
	10	1.0000	1.0000	1.0000	1.0000	0.9999	0.9993	0.9972	0.9907	0.9745	0.9408
	11	1.0000	1.0000	1.0000	1.0000	1.0000	0.9999	0.9995	0.9981	0.9937	0.9824
	12	1.0000	1.0000	1.0000	1.0000	1.0000	1.0000	0.9999	0.9997	0.9989	0.9963
	13	1.0000	1.0000	1.0000	1.0000	1.0000	1.0000	1.0000	1.0000	0.9999	0.9995
	14	1.0000	1.0000	1.0000	1.0000	1.0000	1.0000	1.0000	1.0000	1.0000	1.0000

Table 1 (Continued)

n	x	0.05	0.10	0.15	0.20	0.25	p 0.30	0.35	0.40	0.45	0.50
16	0	0.4401	0.1853	0.0743	0.0281	0.0100	0.0033	0.0010	0.0003	0.0001	0.0000
	1	0.8108	0.5147	0.2839	0.1407	0.0635	0.0261	0.0098	0.0033	0.0010	0.0003
	2	0.9571	0.7892	0.5614	0.3518	0.1971	0.0994	0.0451	0.0183	0.0066	0.0021
	3	0.9930	0.9316	0.7899	0.5981	0.4050	0.2459	0.1339	0.0651	0.0281	0.0106
	4	0.9991	0.9830	0.9209	0.7982	0.6302	0.4499	0.2892	0.1666	0.0853	0.0384
	5	0.9999	0.9967	0.9765	0.9183	0.8103	0.6598	0.4900	0.3288	0.1976	0.1051
	6	1.0000	0.9995	0.9944	0.9733	0.9204	0.8247	0.6881	0.5272	0.3660	0.2272
	7	1.0000	0.9999	0.9989	0.9930	0.9729	0.9256	0.8406	0.7161	0.5629	0.4018
	8	1.0000	1.0000	0.9998	0.9985	0.9925	0.9743	0.9329	0.8577	0.7441	0.5982
	9	1.0000	1.0000	1.0000	0.9998	0.9984	0.9929	0.9771	0.9417	0.8759	0.7728
	10	1.0000	1.0000	1.0000	1.0000	0.9997	0.9984	0.9938	0.9809	0.9514	0.8949
	11	1.0000	1.0000	1.0000	1.0000	1.0000	0.9997	0.9987	0.9951	0.9851	0.9616
	12	1.0000	1.0000	1.0000	1.0000	1.0000	1.0000	0.9998	0.9991	0.9965	0.9894
	13	1.0000	1.0000	1.0000	1.0000	1.0000	1.0000	1.0000	0.9999	0.9994	0.9979
	14	1.0000	1.0000	1.0000	1.0000	1.0000	1.0000	1.0000	1.0000	1.0000	0.9997
	15	1.0000	1.0000	1.0000	1.0000	1.0000	1.0000	1.0000	1.0000	1.0000	1.0000
17	0	0.4181	0.1668	0.0631	0.0225	0.0075	0.0023	0.0007	0.0002	0.0000	0.0000
	1	0.7922	0.4818	0.2525	0.1182	0.0501	0.0193	0.0067	0.0021	0.0006	0.0001
	2	0.9497	0.7618	0.5198	0.3096	0.1637	0.0774	0.0327	0.0123	0.0041	0.0012
	3	0.9912	0.9174	0.7556	0.5489	0.3530	0.2019	0.1028	0.0464	0.0184	0.0064
	4	0.9988	0.9779	0.9013	0.7582	0.5739	0.3887	0.2348	0.1260	0.0596	0.0245
	5	0.9999	0.9953	0.9681	0.8943	0.7653	0.5968	0.4197	0.2639	0.1471	0.0717
	6	1.0000	0.9992	0.9917	0.9623	0.8929	0.7752	0.6188	0.4478	0.2902	0.1662
	7	1.0000	0.9999	0.9983	0.9891	0.9598	0.8954	0.7872	0.6405	0.4743	0.3145
	8	1.0000	1.0000	0.9997	0.9974	0.9876	0.9597	0.9006	0.8011	0.6626	0.5000
	9	1.0000	1.0000	1.0000	0.9995	0.9969	0.9873	0.9617	0.9081	0.8166	0.6855
	10	1.0000	1.0000	1.0000	0.9999	0.9994	0.9968	0.9880	0.9652	0.9174	0.8338
	11	1.0000	1.0000	1.0000	1.0000	0.9999	0.9993	0.9970	0.9894	0.9699	0.9283
	12	1.0000	1.0000	1.0000	1.0000	1.0000	0.9999	0.9994	0.9975	0.9914	0.9755
	13	1.0000	1.0000	1.0000	1.0000	1.0000	1.0000	0.9999	0.9995	0.9981	0.9936
	14	1.0000	1.0000	1.0000	1.0000	1.0000	1.0000	1.0000	0.9999	0.9997	0.9988
	15	1.0000	1.0000	1.0000	1.0000	1.0000	1.0000	1.0000	1.0000	1.0000	0.9999
	16	1.0000	1.0000	1.0000	1.0000	1.0000	1.0000	1.0000	1.0000	1.0000	1.0000
18	0	0.3972	0.1501	0.0536	0.0180	0.0056	0.0016	0.0004	0.0001	0.0000	0.0000
	1	0.7735	0.4503	0.2241	0.0991	0.0395	0.0142	0.0046	0.0013	0.0003	0.0001
	2	0.9419	0.7338	0.4797	0.2713	0.1353	0.0600	0.0236	0.0082	0.0025	0.0007
	3	0.9891	0.9018	0.7202	0.5010	0.3057	0.1646	0.0783	0.0328	0.0120	0.0038
	4	0.9985	0.9718	0.8794	0.7164	0.5187	0.3327	0.1886	0.0942	0.0411	0.0154
	5	0.9998	0.9936	0.9581	0.8671	0.7175	0.5344	0.3550	0.2088	0.1077	0.0481
	6	1.0000	0.9988	0.9882	0.9487	0.8610	0.7217	0.5491	0.3743	0.2258	0.1189
	7	1.0000	0.9998	0.9973	0.9837	0.9431	0.8593	0.7283	0.5634	0.3915	0.2403
	8	1.0000	1.0000	0.9995	0.9957	0.9807	0.9404	0.8609	0.7368	0.5778	0.4073
	9	1.0000	1.0000	0.9999	0.9991	0.9946	0.9790	0.9403	0.8653	0.7473	0.5927

Table 1 (Continued)

n	x	0.05	0.10	0.15	0.20	0.25	0.30	0.35	0.40	0.45	0.50
18	10	1.0000	1.0000	1.0000	0.9998	0.9988	0.9939	0.9788	0.9424	0.8720	0.7597
	11	1.0000	1.0000	1.0000	1.0000	0.9998	0.9986	0.9938	0.9797	0.9463	0.8811
	12	1.0000	1.0000	1.0000	1.0000	1.0000	0.9997	0.9986	0.9942	0.9817	0.9519
	13	1.0000	1.0000	1.0000	1.0000	1.0000	1.0000	0.9997	0.9987	0.9951	0.9846
	14	1.0000	1.0000	1.0000	1.0000	1.0000	1.0000	1.0000	0.9998	0.9990	0.9962
	15	1.0000	1.0000	1.0000	1.0000	1.0000	1.0000	1.0000	1.0000	0.9999	0.9993
	16	1.0000	1.0000	1.0000	1.0000	1.0000	1.0000	1.0000	1.0000	1.0000	0.9999
19	0	0.3774	0.1351	0.0456	0.0144	0.0042	0.0011	0.0003	0.0001	0.0000	0.0000
	1	0.7547	0.4203	0.1985	0.0829	0.0310	0.0104	0.0031	0.0008	0.0002	0.0000
	2	0.9335	0.7054	0.4413	0.2369	0.1113	0.0462	0.0170	0.0055	0.0015	0.0004
	3	0.9868	0.8850	0.6841	0.4551	0.2630	0.1332	0.0591	0.0230	0.0077	0.0022
	4	0.9980	0.9648	0.8556	0.6733	0.4654	0.2822	0.1500	0.0696	0.0280	0.0096
	5	0.9998	0.9914	0.9463	0.8369	0.6678	0.4739	0.2968	0.1629	0.0777	0.0318
	6	1.0000	0.9983	0.9837	0.9324	0.8251	0.6655	0.4812	0.3081	0.1727	0.0835
	7	1.0000	0.9997	0.9959	0.9767	0.9225	0.8180	0.6656	0.4878	0.3169	0.1796
	8	1.0000	1.0000	0.9992	0.9933	0.9713	0.9161	0.8145	0.6675	0.4940	0.3238
	9	1.0000	1.0000	0.9999	0.9984	0.9911	0.9674	0.9125	0.8139	0.6710	0.5000
	10	1.0000	1.0000	1.0000	0.9997	0.9977	0.9895	0.9653	0.9115	0.8159	0.6762
	11	1.0000	1.0000	1.0000	1.0000	0.9995	0.9972	0.9886	0.9648	0.9129	0.8204
	12	1.0000	1.0000	1.0000	1.0000	0.9999	0.9994	0.9969	0.9884	0.9658	0.9165
	13	1.0000	1.0000	1.0000	1.0000	1.0000	0.9999	0.9993	0.9969	0.9891	0.9682
	14	1.0000	1.0000	1.0000	1.0000	1.0000	1.0000	0.9999	0.9994	0.9972	0.9904
	15	1.0000	1.0000	1.0000	1.0000	1.0000	1.0000	1.0000	0.9999	0.9995	0.9978
	16	1.0000	1.0000	1.0000	1.0000	1.0000	1.0000	1.0000	1.0000	0.9999	0.9996
	17	1.0000	1.0000	1.0000	1.0000	1.0000	1.0000	1.0000	1.0000	1.0000	1.0000
20	0	0.3585	0.1216	0.0388	0.0115	0.0032	0.0008	0.0002	0.0000	0.0000	0.0000
	1	0.7358	0.3917	0.1756	0.0692	0.0243	0.0076	0.0021	0.0005	0.0001	0.0000
	2	0.9245	0.6769	0.4049	0.2061	0.0913	0.0355	0.0121	0.0036	0.0009	0.0002
	3	0.9841	0.8670	0.6477	0.4114	0.2252	0.1071	0.0444	0.0160	0.0049	0.0013
	4	0.9974	0.9568	0.8298	0.6296	0.4148	0.2375	0.1182	0.0510	0.0189	0.0059
	5	0.9997	0.9887	0.9327	0.8042	0.6172	0.4164	0.2454	0.1256	0.0553	0.0207
	6	1.0000	0.9976	0.9781	0.9133	0.7858	0.6080	0.4166	0.2500	0.1299	0.0577
	7	1.0000	0.9996	0.9941	0.9679	0.8982	0.7723	0.6010	0.4159	0.2520	0.1316
	8	1.0000	0.9999	0.9987	0.9900	0.9591	0.8867	0.7624	0.5956	0.4143	0.2517
	9	1.0000	1.0000	0.9998	0.9974	0.9861	0.9520	0.8782	0.7553	0.5914	0.4119
	10	1.0000	1.0000	1.0000	0.9994	0.9961	0.9829	0.9468	0.8725	0.7507	0.5881
	11	1.0000	1.0000	1.0000	0.9999	0.9991	0.9949	0.9804	0.9435	0.8692	0.7483
	12	1.0000	1.0000	1.0000	1.0000	0.9998	0.9987	0.9940	0.9790	0.9420	0.8684
	13	1.0000	1.0000	1.0000	1.0000	1.0000	0.9997	0.9985	0.9935	0.9786	0.9423
	14	1.0000	1.0000	1.0000	1.0000	1.0000	1.0000	0.9997	0.9984	0.9936	0.9793
	15	1.0000	1.0000	1.0000	1.0000	1.0000	1.0000	1.0000	0.9997	0.9985	0.9941
	16	1.0000	1.0000	1.0000	1.0000	1.0000	1.0000	1.0000	1.0000	0.9997	0.9987
	17	1.0000	1.0000	1.0000	1.0000	1.0000	1.0000	1.0000	1.0000	1.0000	0.9998
	18	1.0000	1.0000	1.0000	1.0000	1.0000	1.0000	1.0000	1.0000	1.0000	1.0000

Table 2 The normal density function

$\pm z$	0.00	0.01	0.02	0.03	0.04	0.05	0.06	0.07	0.08	0.09
0.0	0.3989	0.3989	0.3989	0.3988	0.3986	0.3984	0.3982	0.3980	0.3977	0.3973
0.1	0.3970	0.3965	0.3961	0.3956	0.3951	0.3945	0.3939	0.3932	0.3925	0.3918
0.2	0.3910	0.3902	0.3894	0.3885	0.3876	0.3867	0.3857	0.3847	0.3836	0.3825
0.3	0.3814	0.3802	0.3790	0.3778	0.3765	0.3752	0.3739	0.3725	0.3712	0.3697
0.4	0.3683	0.3668	0.3653	0.3637	0.3621	0.3605	0.3589	0.3572	0.3555	0.3538
0.5	0.3521	0.3503	0.3485	0.3467	0.3448	0.3429	0.3410	0.3391	0.3372	0.3352
0.6	0.3332	0.3312	0.3292	0.3271	0.3251	0.3230	0.3209	0.3187	0.3166	0.3144
0.7	0.3123	0.3101	0.3079	0.3056	0.3034	0.3011	0.2989	0.2966	0.2943	0.2920
0.8	0.2897	0.2874	0.2850	0.2827	0.2803	0.2780	0.2756	0.2732	0.2709	0.2685
0.9	0.2661	0.2637	0.2613	0.2589	0.2565	0.2541	0.2516	0.2492	0.2468	0.2444
1.0	0.2420	0.2396	0.2371	0.2347	0.2323	0.2299	0.2275	0.2251	0.2227	0.2203
1.1	0.2179	0.2155	0.2131	0.2107	0.2083	0.2059	0.2036	0.2012	0.1989	0.1965
1.2	0.1942	0.1919	0.1895	0.1872	0.1849	0.1826	0.1804	0.1781	0.1758	0.1736
1.3	0.1714	0.1691	0.1669	0.1647	0.1626	0.1604	0.1582	0.1561	0.1539	0.1518
1.4	0.1497	0.1478	0.1456	0.1435	0.1415	0.1394	0.1374	0.1354	0.1334	0.1315
1.5	0.1295	0.1276	0.1257	0.1238	0.1219	0.1200	0.1182	0.1163	0.1145	0.1127
1.6	0.1109	0.1092	0.1074	0.1057	0.1040	0.1023	0.1006	0.0989	0.0973	0.0957
1.7	0.0940	0.0925	0.0909	0.0893	0.0878	0.0863	0.0848	0.0833	0.0818	0.0804
1.8	0.0790	0.0775	0.0761	0.0748	0.0734	0.0721	0.0707	0.0694	0.0681	0.0669
1.9	0.0656	0.0644	0.0632	0.0620	0.0608	0.0596	0.0584	0.0573	0.0562	0.0551
2.0	0.0540	0.0529	0.0519	0.0508	0.0498	0.0488	0.0478	0.0468	0.0459	0.0449
2.1	0.0440	0.0431	0.0422	0.0413	0.0404	0.0396	0.0387	0.0379	0.0371	0.0363
2.2	0.0355	0.0347	0.0339	0.0332	0.0325	0.0317	0.0310	0.0303	0.0297	0.0290
2.3	0.0283	0.0277	0.0270	0.0264	0.0258	0.0252	0.0246	0.0241	0.0235	0.0229
2.4	0.0224	0.0219	0.0213	0.0208	0.0203	0.0198	0.0194	0.0189	0.0184	0.0180
2.5	0.0175	0.0171	0.0167	0.0163	0.0158	0.0154	0.0151	0.0147	0.0143	0.0139
2.6	0.0136	0.0132	0.0129	0.0126	0.0122	0.0119	0.0116	0.0113	0.0110	0.0107
2.7	0.0104	0.0101	0.0099	0.0096	0.0093	0.0091	0.0088	0.0086	0.0084	0.0081
2.8	0.0079	0.0077	0.0075	0.0073	0.0071	0.0069	0.0067	0.0065	0.0063	0.0061
2.9	0.0060	0.0058	0.0056	0.0055	0.0053	0.0051	0.0050	0.0048	0.0047	0.0046
3.0	0.0044	0.0043	0.0042	0.0040	0.0039	0.0038	0.0037	0.0036	0.0035	0.0034
3.1	0.0033	0.0032	0.0031	0.0030	0.0029	0.0028	0.0027	0.0026	0.0025	0.0025
3.2	0.0024	0.0023	0.0022	0.0022	0.0021	0.0020	0.0020	0.0019	0.0018	0.0018
3.3	0.0017	0.0017	0.0016	0.0016	0.0015	0.0015	0.0014	0.0014	0.0013	0.0013
3.4	0.0012	0.0012	0.0012	0.0011	0.0011	0.0100	0.0010	0.0010	0.0009	0.0009

Source: Reprinted from Mood and Graybill, *Introduction to the Theory of Statistics*, 3d ed., McGraw-Hill, New York, 1973.

Table 3 Cumulative normal distribution

z	0.00	0.01	0.02	0.03	0.04	0.05	0.06	0.07	0.08	0.09
0.0	0.5000	0.5040	0.5080	0.5120	0.5160	0.5199	0.5199	0.5279	0.5319	0.5359
0.1	0.5398	0.5438	0.5478	0.5517	0.5557	0.5596	0.5636	0.5675	0.5714	0.5753
0.2	0.5793	0.5832	0.5871	0.5910	0.5948	0.5987	0.6026	0.6064	0.6103	0.6141
0.3	0.6179	0.6217	0.6255	0.6293	0.6331	0.6368	0.6406	0.6443	0.6480	0.6517
0.4	0.6554	0.6591	0.6628	0.6664	0.6700	0.6736	0.6772	0.6808	0.6844	0.6879
0.5	0.6915	0.6950	0.6985	0.7019	0.7054	0.7088	0.7123	0.7157	0.7190	0.7224
0.6	0.7257	0.7291	0.7324	0.7357	0.7389	0.7422	0.7454	0.7486	0.7517	0.7549
0.7	0.7580	0.7611	0.7642	0.7673	0.7704	0.7734	0.7764	0.7794	0.7823	0.7852
0.8	0.7881	0.7910	0.7939	0.7967	0.7995	0.8023	0.8051	0.8078	0.8106	0.8133
0.9	0.8159	0.8186	0.8212	0.8238	0.8264	0.8289	0.8315	0.8340	0.8365	0.8389
1.0	0.8413	0.8438	0.8461	0.8485	0.8508	0.8531	0.8554	0.8577	0.8599	0.8621
1.1	0.8643	0.8665	0.8686	0.8708	0.8729	0.8749	0.8770	0.8790	0.8810	0.8830
1.2	0.8849	0.8869	0.8888	0.8907	0.8925	0.8944	0.8962	0.8980	0.8997	0.9015
1.3	0.9032	0.9049	0.9066	0.9082	0.9099	0.9115	0.9131	0.9147	0.9162	0.9177
1.4	0.9192	0.9207	0.9222	0.9236	0.9251	0.9265	0.9279	0.9292	0.9306	0.9319
1.5	0.9332	0.9345	0.9357	0.9370	0.9382	0.9394	0.9406	0.9418	0.9429	0.9441
1.6	0.9452	0.9463	0.9474	0.9484	0.9495	0.9505	0.9515	0.9525	0.9535	0.9545
1.7	0.9554	0.9564	0.9573	0.9582	0.9591	0.9599	0.9608	0.9616	0.9625	0.9633
1.8	0.9641	0.9649	0.9656	0.9664	0.9671	0.9678	0.9686	0.9693	0.9699	0.9706
1.9	0.9713	0.9719	0.9726	0.9732	0.9738	0.9744	0.9750	0.9756	0.9761	0.9767
2.0	0.9772	0.9778	0.9783	0.9788	0.9793	0.9798	0.9803	0.9808	0.9812	0.9817
2.1	0.9821	0.9826	0.9830	0.9834	0.9838	0.9842	0.9846	0.9850	0.9854	0.9857
2.2	0.9861	0.9864	0.9868	0.9871	0.9875	0.9878	0.9881	0.9884	0.9887	0.9890
2.3	0.9893	0.9896	0.9898	0.9901	0.9904	0.9906	0.9909	0.9911	0.9913	0.9916
2.4	0.9918	0.9920	0.9922	0.9925	0.9927	0.9929	0.9931	0.9932	0.9934	0.9936
2.5	0.9938	0.9940	0.9941	0.9943	0.9945	0.9946	0.9948	0.9949	0.9951	0.9952
2.6	0.9953	0.9955	0.9956	0.9957	0.9959	0.9960	0.9961	0.9962	0.9963	0.9964
2.7	0.9965	0.9966	0.9967	0.9968	0.9969	0.9970	0.9971	0.9972	0.9973	0.9974
2.8	0.9974	0.9975	0.9976	0.9977	0.9977	0.9978	0.9979	0.9979	0.9980	0.9981
2.9	0.9981	0.9982	0.9982	0.9983	0.9984	0.9984	0.9985	0.9985	0.9986	0.9986
3.0	0.9987	0.9987	0.9987	0.9988	0.9988	0.9989	0.9989	0.9989	0.9990	0.9990
3.1	0.9990	0.9991	0.9991	0.9991	0.9992	0.9992	0.9992	0.9992	0.9993	0.9993
3.2	0.9993	0.9993	0.9994	0.9994	0.9994	0.9994	0.9994	0.9995	0.9995	0.9995
3.3	0.9995	0.9995	0.9995	0.9996	0.9996	0.9996	0.9996	0.9996	0.9996	0.9997
3.4	0.9997	0.9997	0.9997	0.9997	0.9997	0.9997	0.9997	0.9777	0.9777	0.9998

Source: Reprinted from Mood and Graybill, *Introduction to the Theory of Statistics*, 3d ed., McGraw-Hill, New York, 1973.

Table 4 Random digits

2271	2572	8665	3272	9033	8256	2822	3646	7599	0270
3025	0788	5311	7792	1837	4739	4552	3234	5572	9885
3382	6151	1011	3776	9951	7709	8060	2258	8536	2290
7870	5799	6032	9043	4526	8100	1957	9539	5370	0046
1697	0002	2340	6959	1915	1626	1297	1533	6572	3835
3395	3381	1862	3250	8614	5683	6757	5628	2551	6971
6081	6526	3028	2338	5702	8819	3679	4829	9909	4712
3470	9879	2935	1141	6398	6387	5634	9589	3212	7963
0432	8641	5020	6612	1038	1547	0948	4278	0020	6509
4995	5596	8286	8377	8567	8237	3520	8244	5694	3326
8246	6718	3851	5870	1216	2107	1387	1621	5509	5772
7825	8727	2849	3501	3551	1001	0123	7873	5926	6078
6258	2450	2962	1183	3666	4156	4454	8239	4551	2920
3235	5783	2701	2378	7460	3398	1223	4688	3674	7872
2525	9008	5997	0885	1053	2340	7066	5328	6412	5054
5852	9739	1457	8999	2789	9068	9829	1336	3148	7875
0440	3769	7864	4029	4494	9829	1339	4910	1303	9161
0820	4641	2375	2542	4093	5364	1145	2848	2792	0431
7114	2842	8554	6881	6377	9427	8216	1193	8042	8449
6558	9301	9096	0577	8520	5923	4717	0188	8545	8745
0345	9937	5569	0279	8951	6183	7787	7808	5149	2185
7430	2074	9427	8422	4082	5629	2971	9456	0649	7981
8030	7345	3389	4739	5911	1022	9189	2565	1982	8577
6272	6718	3849	4715	3156	2823	4174	7833	5600	7702
4894	9847	5611	4763	8755	3388	5114	3274	6681	3657
2676	5984	6806	2692	4012	0934	2436	0869	9557	2490
9305	2074	9378	7670	8284	7431	7361	2912	2251	7395
5138	2461	7213	1905	7775	9881	8782	6272	0632	4418
2452	4200	8674	9202	0812	3986	1143	7343	2264	9072
8882	3033	8746	7390	8609	1144	2531	6944	8869	1570
1087	9336	8020	9166	4472	8293	2904	7949	3165	7400
5666	2841	8134	9588	2915	4116	2802	6917	3993	8764
9790	2228	9702	1690	7170	7511	1937	0723	4505	7155
3250	8860	3294	2684	6572	3415	5750	8726	2647	6596
5450	3922	0951	0890	6434	2306	2781	1066	3681	2404
5765	0765	7311	5270	5910	7009	0240	7435	4568	6484
8408	1939	0599	5347	2160	7376	4696	6969	0787	3838
8460	7658	6906	9177	1492	4680	3719	3456	8681	6736
4198	7244	3849	4819	1008	6781	3388	5253	7041	6712
9872	4441	6712	9614	2736	5533	9062	2534	0855	7946
6485	0487	0004	5563	1481	1546	8245	6116	6920	0990
2064	0512	9509	0341	8131	7778	8609	9417	1216	4189
9927	8987	5321	3125	9992	9449	5951	5872	2057	5731
4918	9690	6121	8770	6053	6931	7252	5409	1869	4229
8099	5821	3899	2685	6781	3178	0096	2986	8878	8991
1901	4974	1262	6810	4673	8772	6616	2632	7891	9970
8273	6675	4925	3924	2274	3860	1662	7480	8674	4503
2878	8213	3170	5126	0434	9481	7029	8688	4027	3340
6088	1182	3242	0835	1765	8819	3462	9820	5759	4189
5773	6600	5306	0354	8295	0148	6608	9064	3421	8570

Table 5 Fractiles of the Student's t distribution

$F(t)$ / v	0.60	0.70	0.80	0.90	0.95	0.975	0.99
1	0.325	0.727	1.376	3.078	6.314	12.71	31.82
2	0.289	0.617	1.061	1.886	2.920	4.303	6.965
3	0.277	0.584	0.978	1.638	2.353	3.182	4.541
4	0.271	0.569	0.941	1.533	2.132	2.776	3.747
5	0.267	0.559	0.920	1.476	2.015	2.571	3.365
6	0.265	0.553	0.906	1.440	1.943	2.447	3.143
7	0.263	0.549	0.896	1.415	1.895	2.365	2.998
8	0.262	0.546	0.889	1.397	1.860	2.306	2.896
9	0.261	0.543	0.883	1.383	1.833	2.262	2.821
10	0.260	0.542	0.879	1.372	1.812	2.228	2.764
11	0.260	0.540	0.876	1.363	1.796	2.201	2.718
12	0.259	0.539	0.873	1.356	1.782	2.179	2.681
13	0.259	0.538	0.870	1.350	1.771	2.160	2.650
14	0.258	0.537	0.868	1.345	1.761	2.145	2.624
15	0.258	0.536	0.865	1.341	1.753	2.131	2.602
16	0.258	0.535	0.865	1.337	1.746	2.120	2.583
17	0.257	0.534	0.863	1.333	1.740	2.110	2.567
18	0.257	0.534	0.862	1.330	1.734	2.101	2.552
19	0.257	0.533	0.861	1.328	1.729	2.093	2.539
20	0.257	0.533	0.860	1.325	1.725	2.086	2.528
21	0.257	0.532	0.859	1.323	1.721	2.080	2.518
22	0.256	0.532	0.858	1.321	1.717	2.074	2.508
23	0.256	0.532	0.858	1.319	1.714	2.069	2.500
24	0.256	0.531	0.857	1.318	1.711	2.064	2.492
25	0.256	0.531	0.856	1.316	1.708	2.060	2.485
26	0.256	0.531	0.856	1.315	1.706	2.056	2.479
27	0.256	0.531	0.855	1.314	1.703	2.052	2.473
28	0.256	0.530	0.855	1.313	1.701	2.048	2.467
29	0.256	0.530	0.854	1.311	1.699	2.045	2.462
30	0.256	0.530	0.854	1.310	1.697	2.042	2.457
40	0.255	0.529	0.851	1.303	1.684	2.021	2.423
50	0.255	0.528	0.849	1.298	1.676	2.009	2.403
60	0.254	0.527	0.848	1.296	1.671	2.000	2.390
80	0.254	0.527	0.846	1.292	1.664	1.990	2.374
100	0.254	0.526	0.845	1.290	1.660	1.984	2.365
200	0.254	0.525	0.843	1.286	1.653	1.972	2.345
500	0.253	0.525	0.842	1.283	1.648	1.965	2.334
∞	0.253	0.524	0.842	1.282	1.645	1.960	2.326

Source: Reprinted by permission of the authors and publishers from R. A. Fisher and F. Yates, *Statistical Tables for Biological, Agricultural and Medical Research*, Longman, London, 1974, Table III.

AUTHOR INDEX

SUBJECT INDEX